MW01227163

The Habit Principles

A Framework for Leaders to Re-Engineer Habits for Elite Performance

Rich Bello

AROOTAH

© Copyright 2023 by Rich Bello - All rights reserved.
It is not legal to reproduce, duplicate, or transmit any part of this document in either electronic means or printed format. Recording of this publication is strictly prohibited.

The materials and opinions in this book are for informational and educational purposes only, are not intended to take the place of any expert medical, physical, mental, or psychological health care, nor are they meant to diagnose, treat, prevent, or cure any physical, medical, mental, emotional, or psychological ailment, disease, or condition. The materials and opinions presented herein are not being offered by Arootah or its representatives, coaches, or employees in the capacity of a licensed therapist, health care professional, or mental health expert and should not be used as a substitute, replacement, alternative, or proxy for professional medical, physical, emotional, mental, or psychological health care treatment, counseling, therapy, psychoanalysis, substance abuse treatment, or any other mental or physical health advice, guidance, or counsel. You should maintain a relationship with a physician or other appropriate healthcare provider who is available to provide emergent and urgent care. If you encounter a medical emergency and are not able to obtain care from my primary care physician, contact 911 or report to a hospital emergency department.

About The Author

RICH BELLO
Chairman and Chief Executive Officer, Arootah
Co-Founder, Chief Operating Officer,
Blue Ridge Capital

Rich Bello is the chairman and CEO of Arootah, an organization that specializes in empowering leaders with peak performance strategies that unlock their potential in their personal and professional lives.

Rich has a deep-rooted passion for both personal and professional development. Rich and the Arootah team empower clients to reach their highest potential. He helps clients achieve maximum results by setting clear objectives and designing strategic plans with accountability strategies for execution.

Before Arootah, Rich served as co-founder and chief operating officer of Blue Ridge Capital, a firm with approximately $10 billion in assets under management at its peak. Prior to his 25 years at Blue Ridge, Rich held senior positions at Ernst and Young, Tiger Management, and Morgan Stanley. He studied at The Wharton School of the University of Pennsylvania.

Amongst his various philanthropic endeavors, Rich founded and proudly serves on the iMentor Advisory Board of Directors. This organization has mentored more than 36,000 high school and college students, most of whom are from low-income communities.

Acknowledgments

I extend my heartfelt gratitude to the remarkable coaches who have played an instrumental role in guiding and igniting my inner spirit. Their unwavering patience, profound wisdom, compassionate support, and firm yet loving guidance have propelled me through life's challenges and inspired me to strive for constant personal and professional growth.

I am deeply grateful to my esteemed colleagues and our visionary leader at Blue Ridge Capital for granting me the incredible opportunity to refine the craft I am so passionate about — personal and professional growth and business excellence. Your continual commitment to upholding the highest standards has been a constant source of inspiration to me.

I express my sincere appreciation to the exceptional Arootah team for their tireless dedication and collaborative effort in bringing this book to fruition. Each team member's contributions were invaluable, and I extend my deepest gratitude to Christina, whose boundless passion and dedication infused *every* aspect of this book. Jack, the Chief, your exceptional coordination skills ensured every detail, no matter how small, fell seamlessly into place. Terese, the cover you created is simply stunning, and I am grateful for your artistry. Mary Ann, your meticulous editing and persistent pursuit of excellence challenged and elevated every word until the very end. Alana, your willingness to go above and beyond in any task is truly commendable. Anthony, your vast experience in writing and publishing provided invaluable guidance that shaped this book. Raed, Jeff, and Luther, your incredible work on the accompanying app has truly enhanced the reader experience. Diana, your steadfast support in everything I do is immeasurable and deserving of endless recognition. And to Kim, last but certainly not least, the embodiment of expertise in every endeavor you undertake, your ability to make a significant impact at a moment's notice is awe-inspiring.

Lastly, but most importantly, I want to express my deep gratitude to my family for their unwavering love and support, even as I beta tested The Principles on them. Your enduring patience and belief in me have been the foundation of my journey. I love each and every one of you dearly.

Without the support, guidance, and dedication of all these incredible individuals, this book would not have been possible. Thank you for being part of this transformative endeavor and for enriching my life in countless ways.

Contents

Introduction

"Cultivating the gardens of our minds, we sow seeds of habits.
With care and attention, we decide whether to harvest flowers or weeds."
— Anonymous

Habits play a powerful role in our personal lives, careers, and businesses. In fact, one could easily make the case that the mastery of habits can be deemed the paramount skill, as they hold the utmost influence in determining the quality of our lives. They have the potential to be both a blessing and a curse, shaping our actions and controlling our future outcomes. Some studies show that the majority of our daily behavior is habitual, meaning we are operating on autopilot most of the time. Given our operating system then, it is crucial we install the right programs in our lives in order to align our behavior with our deepest values and goals.

Positive habits provide us with incredible benefits in nearly every aspect of our lives. In our personal lives, good habits such as regular exercise, healthy eating, and mindfulness practices contribute to physical fitness, mental clarity, and emotional balance. These habits provide us with efficiency, consistency, and a sense of well-being.

In our careers, positive habits enable us to prioritize tasks, organize our work, and maintain a proactive mindset. These habits help us foster productivity, effective time management, and continuous professional development.

In our businesses, effective communication, collaboration, and problem-solving habits create a positive work culture and drive teamwork. Strategic planning, market research, and adaptability habits also ensure we remain ahead of the curve while scaling a competitive landscape. Ultimately, our good habits enhance operations, customer service, and overall success.

Our negative habits, however, can result in extremely painful consequences, including an early and painful death. In our personal lives, the relentless grip of bad habits, including chronic procrastination, unhealthy coping mechanisms, and self-limiting beliefs, inflicts excruciating pain by perpetuating self-sabotaging cycles and paving the treacherous path towards physical and emotional deterioration. In our careers, detrimental habits such as disorganization, risk aversion, and resistance to change limit our growth and advancement. In businesses, negative habits such as poor communication, lack of accountability, and resistance to innovation create toxic work environments and hinder progress. Ultimately, our bad habits create roadblocks that prevent us from reaching our fullest potential.

By understanding the mechanisms behind habit formation and transformation, we gain the power to break free from the detrimental patterns and addictive behaviors that do not align with who we are. In this book, we embark on a comprehensive exploration of habits, their profound impact, and the strategies we can use to harness their power. By delving into the depths of the habit realm, we equip ourselves with invaluable insights and practical tools to break free from self-limiting cycles and unlock our true potential.

Throughout our journey together, we will examine the principles and concepts that form the foundation of habit mastery. From deciphering the habit loop and understanding the biology, psychology, and neurology behind habits, to exploring the role of triggers, rewards, and consequences, each step will bring us closer to unleashing the remarkable power within us.

In the chapters ahead, we will dive into the principles that will guide our quest for habit transformation. We will master the art of designing our personalized habit plans, infuse accountability into our journey, and explore the profound connection between our present selves and our future selves. We will delve into the power of rewiring our minds, differentiating habits from addictions, and unraveling the hidden potential of momentum. Finally, we will embrace conscious intervention as a catalyst for lasting change.

By embracing these principles, we will unveil the secrets to breaking free from self-sabotaging patterns and building a life brimming with purpose, fulfillment, and success. Whether you seek personal growth, desire to optimize your career, or aspire to revolutionize your business, the wisdom found within these pages will empower you to create positive and sustainable transformations.

Through thought-provoking discussions, practical exercises, and real-life case studies, you will develop the essential skills you need to master your habits and redefine your life's trajectory. Every concept and strategy is crafted with your best interests in mind, empowering you to shape your habits, rather than be subject to them. By leveraging the principles of habit transformation, we can create positive change, overcome obstacles, and achieve our goals with greater efficiency and effectiveness. The 10 principles outlined here provide practical tools, strategies, and insights we can use to identify, plan, and transform our habits. Each principle serves as a steppingstone towards personal growth, career advancement, and business success. By studying habits and employing *The Habit Principles*, we can break free from the shackles of negative habits and cultivate positive ones. This transformative journey empowers us to align our habits with our values and aspirations, unlocking the potential for personal and professional greatness.

My life's mission has always been centered on attaining peak performance and sharing this pursuit with others. Like many people, I find that I learn much more teaching others than focusing on my own self-improvement. So, this book, crafted with the invaluable input from my dedicated team, is an extension of my commitment to serve those wrestling with their habits, the crucial building blocks of our lives. This is more than just a guide; it's an opportunity to join us in a journey of metamorphosis.

Are you ready to embark on this enlightening expedition into the realm of habits? If so, join us as we unlock the untapped potential that lies dormant within us. The time has come to rewrite the narrative of our lives, and this book will be your trusted guide as we embark on this transformative quest. Get ready to uncover the secrets, embrace change, and unlock the path to habit mastery.

Principle 1:
Master the Art & Science of Habits

Unveiling the Key Elements of Behavior Change

"Knowledge is power. Information is liberating. Education is the premise of progress, in every society, in every family."
- Kofi Annan

In this chapter, we will embark on a journey to understand the fundamental principles of habit transformation. We will explore the power of habits and their profound impact on our lives, careers, and businesses. Through a deeper understanding of habits, we can gain the knowledge and tools necessary to shape our behaviors and achieve lasting change.

Key Question:
What are the core components and processes involved in forming, maintaining, and changing habits?

By delving into the complexities of habits, we will uncover the key elements that drive habit formation and modification. We will learn about the habit loop and how triggers, cravings, behaviors, and rewards shape our daily actions. Understanding this loop will empower us to identify the triggers that lead to both positive and negative habits and take deliberate steps to transform them. Moreover, we will explore the purpose of habits and their role in conserving mental energy, automating routine tasks, and unlocking our potential for creativity and innovation.

Studies show that between 40 – 95% percent of people's daily activities
are performed each day habitually in almost the same situations[1].
Habits emerge through associative learning.
"We find patterns of behavior that allow us to reach goals. We repeat
what works, and when actions are repeated in a stable context, we form
associations between cues and response" – Wendy Woods[2]

Ultimately, our goal in learning these principles is to gain control over our habits and harness their power to drive personal and professional growth. By mastering the fundamentals of habit transformation, we can create positive change in our lives, overcome obstacles, and achieve our goals with greater efficiency and effectiveness. So, let us dive into the world of habits and embark on a transformative journey toward a better and more intentional way of living.

What are Habits?

Habits are sets of repeated behaviors that tend to occur subconsciously. When we regularly repeat these behaviors over time, they can become automatic. It is critical that we choose our actions wisely and intentionally to take ownership over our lives and our destinies.

While habits involve action, however, they are more than just behaviors. We form habits through a complex interplay of psychological, neurological, and biological conditions, and this interplay can have a profound impact on our thoughts, emotions, and behavior. These conditions include our underlying beliefs, values, attitudes, and brain structure.

---

[1] Callaghan, Rory. "Our 3 Brains: Why 95% of Our Behaviors Are Not Conscious." Rory Callaghan, 22 May 2022, https://www.rorycallaghan.com/our-3-brains-why-95-of-our-behaviors-are-not-conscious/.

[2] Society for Personality and Social Psychology. "How we form habits, change existing ones." ScienceDaily.ScienceDaily,8August2014.
<www.sciencedaily.com/releases/2014/08/140808111931.htm>.

Understanding how to build positive habits and break negative ones is literally a *superpower*. The routines we repeat regularly — often daily — form the pathways we use to achieve our goals or become the obstacles on those pathways that keep us from success. Good habits unlock productivity and peak performance and free up mental space, so we can focus on priorities. Bad habits, on the other hand, sap our energy, waste time, and slowly erode any hope we have of success.

The good news is anyone can form and optimize newer and better habits. You have the power to adopt new routines and eliminate old ones from your life. By leveraging research-backed strategies and tools to shape your habits, you can develop a systematic approach to continuous self-improvement and progress. Systematically and intentionally eradicating bad habits clears the ground upon which to grow good ones. Every good habit you implement in your life builds on itself to improve your productivity and effectiveness exponentially. The impact of multiple good habits compounded over time is transformational.

The Habit Loop
A habit loop is the fundamental process that drives all habitual behavior. Understanding how habit loops work provides critical insights into why habits form and how they can be changed.

Habit loops form because your brain seeks to conserve energy by automatically responding to cues based on learned patterns and rewards. Over time, through repetition, habit loops become encoded in your neural pathways so that you act without much awareness or intent. The habit loop consists of four stages which will be explored in greater detail later on in this chapter:

1. **Trigger:** The trigger, also known as the cue, is the initial signal or stimulus that prompts the brain to initiate a habit.

2. **Craving:** The craving stage is where the brain experiences a strong desire or urge to engage in the habit.

3. **Behavior:** The behavior stage involves the actual execution of the habit. It is the behavior or action that is performed in response to the cue and craving.

4. **Reward:** The reward stage is the consequence or outcome that follows the habit's execution. It provides a sense of satisfaction, pleasure, or relief, reinforcing the habit loop.

Let's consider the habit of going for a run every morning.

Trigger: The alarm clock goes off at 6:00 AM.

Craving: You experience a strong desire to feel energized, improve your fitness, and start your day on a positive note.

Behavior: You put on your running shoes, change into workout clothes, and head out for a run in the park.

Reward: After completing your run, you experience a sense of accomplishment, increased energy, and a boost in mood. You also enjoy the fresh air and the peacefulness of the surroundings.

Over time, this habit loop becomes ingrained in your routine. The sound of the alarm clock acts as the trigger, triggering your craving for the positive benefits of running. This prompts you to engage in the behavior of putting on your running gear and heading out for a run. The reward of feeling accomplished and energized reinforces the habit loop, making you more likely to repeat the behavior in the future. This is one of thousands, or more, that we can experience.

Habits vs. Instincts

Understanding the difference between habit and instinct is crucial for self-mastery.

Habits are the product of your choices, environment, and experiences. They are learned and conditioned, molded by nurture rather than fixed nature. Because habits are acquired, you can optimize, change, or replace them at will through intentional practice and persistence. Habits are fundamental to progress and productivity. The ability to hack into your habits and reprogram them serves as a profound competitive advantage.

Instincts, on the other hand, originate in human evolution. They are inborn, intended to equip us with tools for survival and reproduction. While habits leverage higher brain areas such as the prefrontal cortex, instincts are functions of our ancestral "lizard brain" — the basal ganglia, amygdala, etc. Instincts drive innate impulses, gut reactions, and intuitions, which lay outside of our conscious control or intentional design. They cannot be directly broken through habit change techniques alone since they emerge from nature rather than nurture. But can instincts be conquered, or are we forever subject to them? The truth lies somewhere in the middle.

You cannot erase instincts completely, but you can build awareness and habits to avoid being ruled by them. Label and examine your instinctive responses to weaken the authority you give them in your decision making. Pause before reacting to give your mind time for logical reasoning. Question instinctive assumptions and look for contradicting facts. Develop habits such as patience, critical thinking, and skepticism to verify your gut intuitions. Seek out diverse experiences that challenge narrow-minded instincts.

While instincts are an innate and enduring part of human psychology, they lose their grip over you as your mind expands beyond them. You can cultivate choice when confronting your instincts to restrain your reactive impulses. Habits become the vehicle for navigating instincts with intention instead of allowing instincts to drive you.

Let's say you have a habit of practicing deep breathing exercises whenever you encounter a stressful situation. This habit has been developed through intentional practice and repetition. The trigger for this habit is the feeling of stress or anxiety, which serves as a cue. When you experience stress, you instinctively feel the urge to engage in a calming activity to reduce tension. In this case, the instinctual response is the innate need for relaxation and self-preservation. By practicing deep breathing as a habit, you have harnessed your instinctual response to stress and channeled it into a constructive and beneficial behavior.

In this example, the habit of deep breathing is a conscious choice that you have learned and developed. It is directly related to your instinctual response to stress, which is an innate impulse for relaxation and self-preservation. By recognizing the connection between your instinctual response and the habit you have cultivated, you can effectively manage and navigate stressful situations by engaging in the calming habit of deep breathing.

By balancing habit and instinct, you'll learn to master human evolution itself through your leadership and discernment. This is a skill that sets leaders and visionary leaders apart.

Habits _are_ Decisions

Habits feel automatic, but they originate from decisions made in the past. At some point, you chose to act in a particular way and repeat that action consistently until it became second nature to you. The decision to build a habit is always a conscious one, even if you eventually learn to engage in the resulting behavior without thinking about it.

However, habits formed long ago may no longer seem like decisions. Their sheer repetition has obscured your memory of choosing them. Certain habits go back to childhood and may originate from your environment and upbringing. You may have developed these habits before you had full agency or control over your choices and actions.

One could argue, of course, that habits like these were never true "decisions" since you didn't have the informed consent or intention to make them. They were reactive or conditioned responses that you integrated into your behavior before you could critically analyze them. Such habits may feel permanently hardwired and unchangeable as a result.

But even these habits involve an element of choice, however subtle. At any time, you have the power to decide whether to continue or discontinue them through conscious deliberation. You can opt out of long-held habit loops by constructing alternate decision paths and following them consistently. Your circumstances and past conditioning alone do not determine your future habits.

Every habit, no matter how deeply ingrained, remains open to re-evaluation based on present priorities and decisions. While you cannot change the initial choices that encoded old habits in your brain, you can choose new ones going forward. Habits feel involuntary, but you can stop them or perpetuate them based on the decisions you make today.

Ultimately, the view that "habits are decisions" is an empowering one. This view emphasizes your autonomy in creating your habits rather than your powerlessness to changing them. Even the habits you developed before you could choose to do so can be strengthened or weakened through your decision making. You can re-decide and rewire your habits anytime by crafting new choices to override the automatic ones. Habits yield to these choices, not the other way around.

The Philosophy of Habits

The philosophies of habit explored by thinkers like Hume, Aristotle, Epictetus, Nietzsche, and Socrates provide invaluable insight into why we do what we do each day and how small changes to your daily practices can create vastly different results over a lifetime. Understanding habit from these deeper perspectives gives broader context for why habits matter and how they can either be obstacles or vehicles for progress based on awareness and choice.

These philosophers considered habit inextricably linked with ethics, virtue, reason, excellence, and an intentional life lived for purpose and meaning. Constructive habits reinforce values and priorities that shape character and destiny. But habits also depend on continual examination and willingness to adjust based on outcomes and new insights gained over a lifetime. Mastery of habit is essential to mastery and meaning in life.

Let's look at a few philosophers and their points of view regarding habits:

Nietzsche

Nietzsche believed that excellence is achieved only through habit. In his words: "All naturalism in morality, as in all other things, is of no importance whatever. Moral notions too are to be used as cures for habits." Nietzsche advocated cultivating constructive habits and overcoming destructive ones to reach your full potential. He promoted an active life lived with purpose and instinct questioned. Habits shape character and destiny.[3]

Aristotle

Aristotle believed living well means living virtuously. He viewed habits as a means of cultivating virtues and achieving a state of moral excellence. Conversely, he believed engaging in negative habits would result in the formation of a flawed character.[4]

Socrates

Socrates promoted questioning and examining habits of thinking through logic and reason. Habits of thought should withstand rational scrutiny and serve virtue and truth. In Plato's Protagoras, Socrates says, "The only true wisdom is in knowing you know nothing." Habits of continuous learning, openness to being proven wrong, and challenging assumptions lead to wisdom and conscious living. Questioning habits is key.[5]

Epictetus

As a Stoic, Epictetus believed habit and thought are tightly linked. He believed our thoughts shape our interpretations, perceptions, and emotional reactions. The Stoics advocated habits of perception and judgment aligned with reason, virtue, and serenity by accepting what they could control and letting go of what they could not.[6]

Hume

David Hume believed habit is the basis of understanding and identity. In his *Treatise on Human Nature*, Hume wrote,

[3] Anderson, R. Lanier, "Friedrich Nietzsche", The Stanford Encyclopedia of Philosophy (Summer 2022 Edition), Edward N. Zalta (ed.), URL = <https://plato.stanford.edu/archives/sum2022/entries/nietzsche/>.

[4] Kraut, Richard, "Aristotle's Ethics", *The Stanford Encyclopedia of Philosophy* (Fall 2022 Edition), Edward N. Zalta & Uri Nodelman (eds.), URL = <https://plato.stanford.edu/archives/fall2022/entries/aristotle-ethics/>.

[5] Cooper, John M., 'The Socratic Way of Life', Pursuits of Wisdom: Six Ways of Life in Ancient Philosophy from Socrates to Plotinus (Princeton, NJ, 2012; online edn, Princeton Scholarship Online, 19 Oct. 2017), https://doi.org/10.23943/princeton/9780691138602.003.0002

[6] Epictetus. The Discourses of Epictetus: With the Encheiridion and Fragments. WorldCat, 1995.

"Custom, then, is the great guide of human life. It is that principle alone which renders our experience useful to us, and makes us expect, for the future, a similar train of events with those which have appeared in the past." For Hume, habit and custom are the foundations of knowledge, as we base our beliefs about the world on the associations we have built through repeated experiences. Habit shapes our expectations and intuitions.[7]

These enduring concepts teach us that habit is the cornerstone of character and personal development. Whether we are conscious of their impact or not, both our positive and negative habits shape our identity. These habits also grant us the power to intentionally cultivate responses that align with our evolving goals and values and reflect our sense of purpose.

The Biology of Habits

The Purpose of Habits
Habits help you conserve energy by allowing you to operate on autopilot. As you build habits through repetition, you give them the momentum they need to become automatic parts of your routine that won't drain your mental resources. Think of the habit of driving a car, eating, or riding a bike. The first time you learned to ride a bike required immense amounts of focus and energy to balance, pedal, and steer. Now even after years of not riding, you are able to pick up right where you left off. Without habit, these simple activities and actions would exhaust your energy reserve completely. In this way habits are a gift, a way for us to automate some daily tasks to make way for creativity and innovation.

But this conservation of energy not only helps you build good habits, it can lead you to perpetuate inefficient or counterproductive behavioral patterns that gradually deplete

---

[7] Open Text BC. David Hume's (1711–1776) Enquiry Concerning Human Understanding. 2013.

your energy reserves. By repeating these harmful behaviors, you may not only experience a lack of fulfillment, but you may damage other aspects of your life, career, and business. So many people act without thinking, not realizing the results their actions yield can destroy their lives, until it's too late.

In our evolutionary history, this energy was vital for key survival tasks such as hunting and gathering food, escaping from predators, or enduring harsh environmental conditions. By reducing the cognitive 'cost' of routine actions through habit formation, our ancestors could retain energy for these crucial tasks. In the same vein, preserving energy is also essential for procreation - another fundamental aspect of species survival. The process of attracting a mate, procreating, and rearing offspring can be extremely energy intensive. Therefore, any energy conserved through habit-driven efficiencies could contribute significantly to these vital processes.

Today, the importance of energy conservation may not be as apparent as during our early evolutionary history, but it still plays a significant role in how we operate. The tasks we face may not be as physically demanding as hunting or foraging, but our modern world presents its own cognitive challenges that require energy. By automating routine actions and decisions into habits, we save mental 'fuel' to navigate complex problems or innovative tasks that can't be run on 'auto-pilot'.

Habits, in other words, shape your identity and significantly impact the outcomes in your life. While these habits may feel automatic, you always have control over forming new habits or ending existing ones that don't serve you well. While developing strong and positive habits and eliminating negative habits from your routine requires practice and consistency, you have the ability to design habits strategically, so they produce the results you desire.

The Breath

Habits share an important characteristic with one of the most fundamental bodily functions: your breath. Both habits and breathing operate under your automatic control but you can also consciously manipulate them.

Breathing is an autonomic process; your body does it for you subconsciously and effortlessly. However, you can also take deliberate control of your breath by using certain breathing techniques. Similarly, habits become automated behaviors that we perform without awareness or intention, but since they were formed through conscious action in the first place, you never lose the ability to directly shape and influence your habits.

Habits, like breathing, bridge the conscious mind to the subconscious. We build this bridge by consciously reinforcing behaviors over time. Because habits involve specific behaviors and patterns of action, they are primed for conscious optimization, modification, or replacement. You build habits through purposeful repetition, and you break them by consciously interrupting automatic sequences.

No other autonomic function offers this degree of voluntary control or custom design. You cannot directly rewire other automatic processes such as your heartbeat, digestion, or hormone activity through conscious effort alone. But you can reprogram your habits by understanding how to gain identify and redirect them toward success.

The breath provides an instructive metaphor for how to "rewire" habits. Just as you can regulate your breathing, you have the ability to strengthen some habit loops while weakening others. You must make the habit patterns the focus of your awareness to shape them.

Slow, deep breathing activates the relaxation response. When you slow and deepen your breath, it stimulates your vagus nerve and parasympathetic nervous system to reduce arousal, stress, and anxiety. The prefrontal cortex (which we talk more about in this chapter) helps regulate parasympathetic activity and enhances vagus nerve function. Slow breathing in particular helps activate the prefrontal cortex, leading to a state of greater calm and self-control. This state of relaxation makes it easier for you to form and change healthy and unhealthy habits as your prefrontal cortex improves your decision making and willpower. The relaxation response provides mental and emotional equilibrium conducive to overcoming resistance and staying committed to your goals.

The breath extends your window of tolerance. Your window of tolerance refers to your ability to remain composed and in control of your reactions during challenging moments. By practicing mindful, slowed breathing you train yourself to lengthen the time between the stimulus (stressor) and your eventual response (reaction). This gives you more opportunity to choose a constructive response rather than just reacting impulsively. Having a wider window of tolerance supports habit mastery through greater conscious regulation of urges and impulses.

Your breathing pattern influences your habit loop. The pace and depth of your breathing impacts the speed of your habit loop. When you breathe rapidly and shallowly in a stressful state, your brain quickly and unconsciously activates a habit loop in a reactive manner. Slow, diaphragmatic breathing helps you develop awareness of the stages of your habit loop — the trigger, craving, behavior, and reward — allowing you to substitute healthier alternatives for unhealthy behaviors. Your breath controls the speed of your thoughts and actions. Slower breath, slower habit loop.

The benefits of mindful, paced breathing come from its ability to shift the autonomic nervous system into a parasympathetic state via the vagus nerve and regulatory centers in the cortex. By tapping into these parts of the brain through a simple breathing practice, we can experience an array of psychological and physiological benefits.

Like mastering various breathing techniques, optimizing your habits is a learnable skill that takes deliberate practice. The ability to modify habits at will gives you leverage to alter unconscious responses that no longer serve you. By turning awareness into a tool for disrupting automated loops whenever needed, your habits serve as reactions your intentions rather than barriers to progress. Habits may become second nature, but the conscious mind remains in control of programming them. Like the breath, they can achieve autonomy while remaining flexible and adaptable. Understanding this power allows you to revamp and redesign your habits by choice.

Cravings

Cravings influence the motivation and rewards we experience when building and reinforcing habits. Cravings arise when habits activate your brain's reward center, spurring you to seek pleasure or relief through a particular behavior. While cravings feel urgent at the moment, giving in to them can damage your long-term wellbeing and progress.

Negative habits breed more craving, creating cycles that worsen over time. They narrow your focus to instant gratification rather than growth or achievement. Bad habits tax your health, relationships, productivity, and vitality. They limit your potential and development through wasted time and effort.

Imagine you have developed a negative habit of excessive social media scrolling. Whenever you feel bored or stressed, you find yourself reaching for your phone, mindlessly scrolling through social media platforms to seek instant distraction and relief.

> ***Craving:*** In this case, the craving emerges as a strong desire to   escape from boredom or stress by indulging in the mindless scrolling behavior. You experience a sense of urgency and an immediate need for the temporary pleasure or relief that comes from engaging in this habit.

Behavior: The behavior stage involves picking up your phone, opening social media apps, and scrolling endlessly through various posts and updates.

Reward: The reward of this habit lies in the instant gratification and distraction provided by the social media content. However, this reward is short-lived and superficial, as it fails to address the   underlying causes of boredom or stress and does not contribute to your long-term well-being or personal growth.

Over time, the negative habit of excessive social media scrolling reinforces the craving, creating a detrimental cycle. Instead of focusing on personal growth, achievement, or meaningful activities, the habit narrows your focus to instant gratification and distractions. As a result, your health may suffer due to increased sedentary behavior, your relationships may be negatively impacted by reduced engagement, and your overall productivity and vitality may decline.

Addictive habits cause you to lose control as your cravings overtake rational choice. If you can manage to resist the urge to give in to cravings, they begin to lose their power. Pangs of desire arise quickly and will dissipate in time. Be patient and remember they will lose strength. Replace bad habits with positive alternatives that still meet your underlying needs, and you'll learn to manage emotions in a sustainably.

While cravings pass, the rewards of good habits endure. Good habits yield benefits that compound over the days and years. They produce progress and results through consistent action and practice. Positive habits boost creativity, resilience, confidence, and wellbeing. They save time and mental space by operating on autopilot. Good habits express your values and positively shape your identity. Choose your habits well, and they will lead you to fulfillment.

Stress

Stress has a significant impact on your habits, both positive and negative. In moderate amounts, stress can accelerate habit formation by increasing focus and motivation. But excessive or chronic stress weakens your ability to develop habits and makes it harder for you to break existing habits by impairing mental functions involved in learning and willpower.

Some degree of urgency or pressure can activate your stress response and spur you to begin building good habits. However, you must relieve stress to empower your mind to integrate habits into your long-term memory and to automate them. Without periods of low stress, you cannot build sustainable habits.

For breaking habits, chronic stress is detrimental. Constant stress impairs your prefrontal cortex, limiting self-control, awareness and decision making. Stress can also lead you to develop addictive habits as coping mechanisms.

Cortisol is the primary hormone involved in the stress response, and it influences habit formation directly. High cortisol inhibits dopamine production in your brain, making you less responsive to the positive reinforcement you experience when engaging with good habits. It fuels cravings for quick pleasure via addictive habits. Lowering cortisol through stress relief helps restore dopamine sensitivity, so you can experience rewards from positive habits again.[8]

The exact influence of stress depends on its nature and duration. Helpful habit development relies on:

Your habits will thrive when you apply stress strategically and counterbalance it regularly. Short-term stress may drive motivation, but chronic distress erodes results and wellbeing over time. Develop routines for rest, social interaction, mindfulness, and restoration to complement periods of

---

[8] Jentsch, Valerie & Wolf, Oliver & Merz, Christian. (2016). Cortisol alters reward processing in the human brain. Hormones and Behavior. 84. 10.1016/j.yhbeh.2016.05.005.

challenge. With wisdom, stress becomes fuel for progress through the productive habits that emerge from both pressure and calm in optimal proportion. Command them, and no limit can withstand your aim.

The Neurology of Habits

Your brain is a habit-forming machine. Understanding the neurology of how your brain builds and maintains habits provides valuable context for creating positive change.

Your brain is comprised of billions of neurons (specialized cells in your brain that communicate with other cells to transmit information throughout your brain and nervous system) that communicate through electrical and chemical signals. As you repeat behaviors, thoughts, or actions, neurons in your brain form connections to represent the pattern. The more you repeat something, the stronger these connections become. Over time, through repetition, the connections between neurons create neural pathways (think of neural pathways as roads and highways in your brain that guide tendencies toward habitual behaviors) in your brain that encode your habits. Neural pathways are created by neurons communicating with each other repeatedly, which causes the connections between them to become more prominent and efficient. The more you activate a neural pathway, the stronger and more automatic it becomes.[9]

Once a habit pathway is established, your brain can activate it unconsciously in response to cues in your environment. The habit seems automatic and outside your control. But because the brain remains plastic - able to reorganize neural connections based on new experiences - you can reshape habit pathways by building awareness and new routines through

---

[9] Mendelsohn, Alana I. "Creatures of Habit: The Neuroscience of Habit and Purposeful Behavior." Biological psychiatry vol. 85,11 (2019): e49-e51. doi:10.1016/j.biopsych.2019.03.978

continuous practice. Understanding your brain's role in habit formation equips you with insights for change.

Areas of the Brain Associated with Habit Formation

Our brains are wired for efficiency and habits. Several areas of the brain work together as we work to build and change our habits:

The **prefrontal cortex** is responsible for conscious thought and decision making. It is involved in early habit building and in our attempts to break old habits by making deliberate choices. Once we form a new habit, the prefrontal cortex is less active.[10]

The **basal ganglia** store automatic patterns and is involved in habit memory. It creates associations between triggers, craving, behavior, and rewards. The basal ganglia drive us to perform habitual behaviors efficiently and without conscious effort. Breaking habits requires retraining this part of the brain.[11]

The **hippocampus** helps encode and store habit memories. While the hippocampus is initially important during the habit formation process, our brains eventually recall habit memories independent of the hippocampus. This is why old habits seem hardwired. Rewriting habit loops involves recoding new memories and associations within the hippocampus.

Areas of the brain that produce dopamine are related to reward-processing and motivation. Dopamine reinforces habit behaviors by training our brains to associate them with pleasure. Both building and breaking habits requires us to tap into dopamine reinforcements to keep ourselves motivated to change.

---

[10] Arnsten, Amy et al. "This is your brain in meltdown." *Scientific American* vol. 306,4 (2012): 48-53. doi:10.1038/scientificamerican0412-48

[11] Rolls, Edmund T. "Emotion, motivation, decision-making, the orbitofrontal cortex, anterior cingulate cortex, and the amygdala." *Brain structure & function* vol. 228,5 (2023): 1201-1257. doi:10.1007/s00429-023-02644-9

The **amygdala** allows us to process our emotions and habitual behaviors linked to emotions or moods. When we experience an emotion that triggers a craving or behavior, the amygdala is activated and it requires conscious retraining on our parts to reshape how we react to these emotions. Emotional habits often prove the most stubborn.

Neural pathways between these areas become more connected as we repeat behaviors, like paths in a forest becoming more defined and direct with increased use. When we form new habits, we carve new pathways, and when we put a stop to old habits, we pursue the old pathways less and less.

Neurotransmitters

Neurotransmitters are the messengers that allow neurons to communicate with other neurons to influence your thoughts, emotions, and behaviors. By understanding the key neurotransmitters involved in habit formation, you can begin to optimize them for greater success.

Dopamine is the "motivation molecule" and plays a central role in habit development. When you satisfy a need, craving, or desired outcome, neurons produce dopamine that makes you feel pleasure. Dopamine reinforcement teaches your brain to repeat the associated behavior in a cycle that drives habit creation.[12]

To build positive habits, boost dopamine by giving yourself rewards and reinforcement. Provide incentives and track progress to keep motivation high. For negative habits, disrupt dopamine release by avoiding triggers and rewards. Find alternative rewards to replace unhealthy ones. You can retrain your brain to produce dopamine in response to good behaviors by consistently practicing good habits.

---

[12]Wickens, Jeffery R et al. "Dopaminergic mechanisms in actions and habits." *The Journal of neuroscience : the official journal of the Society for Neuroscience* vol. 27,31 (2007): 8181-3. doi:10.1523/JNEUROSCI.1671-07.2007

Serotonin regulates mood and impulse control. Low serotonin is linked to clinical issues such as depression or OCD that can drive those with these conditions to engage in unhealthy behaviors. Boosting serotonin can help you build perseverance and manage addictive habits. Exercise, sunlight, and meditation naturally increase serotonin.[13]

GABA inhibits excess stimulation and promotes feelings of calmness. Healthy GABA levels lead to mental balance conducive to habit formation. Low GABA is associated with anxiety, restlessness, and difficulty maintaining focus or routines. Activities such as yoga, deep breathing, and spending time in nature can help your brain manage GABA.[14]

Acetylcholine impacts arousal, attention, and memory — all of which shape habits. Higher acetylcholine supports habit learning and helps the brain encode new habit loops into memory. Acetylcholine tends to decrease with age, but you can maintain it through regular exercise, a healthy diet, and brain-training activities.[15]

Norepinephrine helps you manage alertness and vigilance. When properly regulated in the brain, it can enhance your perception and wakefulness to help you improve habit learning. Both too much and too little norepinephrine can negatively impact habit change. Manage stress levels, limit stimulants, practice mindfulness, and stay well-rested to keep norepinephrine balanced.[16]

Neurochemistry strongly impacts how you build and eliminate habits in your life by influencing your motivation, mood, focus, and recall. You must gain awareness of your brain's messaging

---

[13] Andrews, Paul W, and J Anderson Thomson Jr. "The bright side of being blue: depression as an adaptation for analyzing complex problems." *Psychological review* vol. 116,3 (2009): 620-54. doi:10.1037/a0016242

[14] Lydiard, R Bruce. "The role of GABA in anxiety disorders." *The Journal of clinical psychiatry* vol. 64 Suppl 3 (2003): 21-7.

[15] https://bebrainfit.com/acetylcholine-neurotransmitter/

[16] https://www.verywellhealth.com/norepinephrine-what-does-or-doesnt-it-do-for-you-3967568

system and determine how to optimize it for habit mastery. Apply strategies to activate and balance neurotransmitters conducive to building positive habits and overcoming negative ones.

While you cannot directly control neurotransmitters, you can shape them through management of your thoughts, environment, and practices. Your habits rely on biochemistry, but biochemistry is also dependent on your daily choices and routines. With insight and intentionality, you hold the power to conduct an orchestra of neurotransmitters to work in harmony, rather than dissonance.

Neuroplasticity

Your brain is continually changing and reprogramming itself based on your experiences, environment, and habits. This is known as neuroplasticity. At any age, you can rewire your brain and nervous system by forming new habits and breaking old ones. Neuroplasticity allows your brain's vast network of neurons to make new connections, strengthen existing ones, and weaken those it no longer uses.

According to Eastern philosophies such as yoga, our habits and patterns of thought create "samskaras" and "vasanas," or impressions and tendencies that shape our unconscious behaviors and reactions. Samskaras refer to past experiences that create deep grooves in the psyche, similar to neural pathways in the brain. Vasanas relate to the habits and behaviors resulting from those grooves. Together they represent the sum of your conditioning and life experiences that drive habit loops.

You can visualize samskaras and vasanas through the metaphor of a stream cutting through rock over time. At first, the stream flows in shallow grooves, like a new habit loop. With repetition, the groove becomes deeper, representing a habit that grows stronger and more automatic over time. Over many years, the stream forms a deep canyon, similar to a lifelong habit or emotional pattern. Constantly reinforcing habits strengthens them and deepens the groove.

But just as a stream can be diverted to carve a new path, you can use neuroplasticity to reroute habit loops by forging new neural connections in your brain. This requires going against the path of least resistance through conscious intention and practice. When you build awareness around habits and consciously substitute alternative behaviors into your routine, you create new samskaras and vasanas. The old habit loop, like the abandoned stream path, gradually weakens without reinforcement.

In this way, both western neuroscientists and eastern spiritual leaders view habits as pathways that you strengthen through repetition that you can change through effort and intention. Your brain's plasticity allows you to choose and strengthen new habit paths at any point. Understanding this power provides motivation for change. While long-held habits may have left deep canyons in your psyche, you always have the ability to start fresh and re-channel the stream.

Emotions

Emotions provide motivation and reinforcement for the habits you build. The feelings a habit evokes, whether positive or negative, embed themselves in your memory and strengthen the habit loop. They do so by strengthening the neural pathway. The stronger the emotion upon the reward, the deeper the connection. Harnessing emotions for habit change means tapping into the satisfaction and rewards of positive habits while deactivating the reinforcement of negative ones.

Addictive habits in particular take root and grow from intense emotions — such as cravings, anxiety, or excitement—and are more challenging to break. Addictive habits activate primal reward centers in the brain, warping motivation and reasoning abilities in favor of habitual behavior. The emotional "high" these habits provide drives you to continue engaging in these behaviors at escalating costs. These habits will ultimately limit your effectiveness as a leader. Conquering addictive behavior requires treating both root emotions and habitual actions simultaneously. Professional support is often needed.

Emotions drive habit choices. Addictions pervert emotions to prevent you from making choices that benefit you. But these mental forces are also tools within your control. You have power to reshape and redesign them.

To master your habits, learn to experience your emotions through a lens of logic rather than reactivity. Recognize and redirect your addictive impulses toward productive habit loops. And take command of your habit memory, revising the stories and experiences you use to define your possibilities.

Your psychology need not determine your habits. Through self-knowledge, intentionality, and practice, you illuminate deeper drivers of behavior that you can reorient toward success. Emotions follow your logic, addictions yield to deliberate habit design, and as you will see in the next section, memory reflects the narrative you choose.

In this way, you are no longer ruled by habits, you're ruling them. You are no longer a servant to instinct but to reason, and where reason leads, habits follow and self-mastery emerges.

Memory

Memory plays a significant role in shaping our habits as it stores the information about past habit loops and reinforces them when triggered by specific cues or circumstances. However, it's important to recognize that memory is not fixed; it can be fallible and subject to change. When we recall memories of how we feel after performing a habit, the act of recalling itself can alter the memory, either increasing the positive associations or decreasing the negative associations we have with the habit. By strategically reframing our habit memories, we can consciously reshape our perception of the habit and influence our future behavior. This requires retelling our memories through new habit stories and experiences, intentionally reinforcing positive associations and diminishing negative ones. Through practice and conscious effort, our minds can re-remember the habit more accurately, supporting the formation of desired habits and the eradication of unwanted ones.

As an example, let's say you have a habit of snacking on unhealthy foods while watching TV in the evenings. Each time you indulge in this habit, your brain forms a memory that associates the act of snacking with relaxation and entertainment. However, over time, you realize that this habit is not aligned with your health goals.

To reshape the memory associated with this habit, you can consciously introduce new experiences and stories. For instance, you decide to replace the unhealthy snacks with nutritious alternatives like fruits or nuts. As you enjoy these healthier options while watching TV, you consciously focus on the positive sensations and satisfaction they provide. By doing so, you create a new habit memory that associates the act of snacking with nourishment and well-being.

Additionally, you may deliberately recall the negative consequences of indulging in unhealthy snacks, such as feeling sluggish or guilty afterward. By revisiting these negative associations each time you have the urge to snack, you weaken the positive memory reinforcement and discourage the unwanted behavior.

Through consistent practice and conscious retelling of your habit story, your mind begins to re-remember the habit accurately, with the new associations and experiences taking precedence. Over time, the revised memory helps strengthen your resolve to choose healthier snacks or even eliminate the habit of snacking while watching TV altogether.

The Psychology of Habits

The Habit Loop

The habit loop is a four-part neurological cycle of *trigger, craving, behavior,* and *reward* that forms the basis for all habits. Understanding your habit loops can give you tremendous leverage for continuous improvement and can help you overcome professional or personal stagnation.

The **trigger** cues the habit loop, signaling your mind to initiate a particular behavior. Triggers can be internal or external and may involve preceding actions. They drive you to engage in a habit automatically outside your conscious control or intention. Let's say, for example, you habitually smoke a cigarette every time you have a cup of coffee. In this example, the trigger may be pouring the coffee into a mug or taking your first sip of it.

The **craving** refers to the motivation or urge to perform a habit behavior in anticipation of a reward. At this stage in the habit loop, you experience a desire to act in your habitual way that feels nearly irresistible. Craving is fueled by dopamine in your brain anticipating the reward associated with your habit from past experiences. Your mind imagines how good you will feel once you get the reward, strengthening your craving through desire and daydreaming. Your brain defaults to the habit pathway, rather than evaluating choices rationally based on future consequences.

The **behavior** is the actual habit in action or within a sequence of steps; here, the behavior is smoking the cigarette, and you engage in this habit as a conditioned response to the trigger. Your mind has little need to devote effort or willpower to the behavior. It has become second nature through repetition over time.

The **reward** provides mental reinforcement that keeps the habit loop cycling. Rewards satisfy your body's needs and cravings, offer relief or pleasure, and incentivize the habit to drive you to repeat the behavior. If a habit fails to reward your brain effectively or frequently enough, it will eventually extinguish on its own. But habits that produce rewards, especially in unpredictable ways, can feel not only compelling, but overwhelming. Let's look to some more examples of habit loops, first negative and then positive.

Negative Habit Loop Examples

Life:

Trigger: Feeling bored or lonely.

Behavior: Mindlessly scrolling through social media for hours.

Reward: Temporary distraction, but ultimately feeling unfulfilled and disconnected.

Career:

Trigger: Feeling overwhelmed by workload.

Behavior: Procrastinating or avoiding important tasks.

Reward: Temporary relief from stress, but increased pressure and decreased productivity in the long run.

Business:

Trigger: Facing a setback or failure.

Behavior: Dwelling on failure and playing the blame game.

Reward: Temporary validation but missed opportunities for growth and improvement.

Positive Habit Loop Examples

Life:

Trigger: Feeling stressed or anxious.

Behavior: Mindful meditation for 10 minutes.

Reward: A sense of calm and relaxation, reduced stress levels.

Career:

Trigger: Receiving a new work assignment.

Behavior: Prioritizing tasks and creating a detailed plan.

Reward: Increased productivity, a sense of accomplishment.

Business:

Trigger: Completing a successful sale.

Behavior: Immediately following up with a personalized thank-you email to the customer.

Reward: Strengthened customer relationships, potential for repeat business.

The habit loops launch and perform seamlessly without conscious thought or effort, just as a well-designed computer program runs efficiently on its own. Like a program or macro, your habit loops remain open to re-design and improvement. You have the ability to re-engineer triggers, introduce new behaviors, and shift rewards to suit your needs as they evolve. You can disrupt the cycle at whatever point you choose to re-write or replace habit loops. Building or breaking any habit is possible through deliberate practice and persistence over time. Remember, lasting change requires establishing a new loop to take place of the old one.

Automaticity

Automaticity refers to your ability to perform actions without conscious thought or effort; when you form a habit, automaticity drives you to perform the behavior automatically.

This allows you to accomplish more while expending less mental energy and willpower. Imagine if you had to think through every small step of your morning routine instead of acting automatically. If you used your mental energy to turn off your alarm, make your bed, get your kids dressed for school, and check your inbox every morning, you probably wouldn't have the mental capacity left to lead your 10 AM stand-up or manage the remaining tasks of the day.

But while automaticity helps you preserve energy, it also makes it harder to break bad habits since they operate below the level of consciousness. The good news is that automaticity can be hacked; with awareness and intention, you can reshape your habits to automatically get the sets of behaviors (and results) you want. Several techniques speed up this process:

- **Repetition**: Repeat the behavior frequently and consistently. With each repetition, you'll perform the behavior more and more automatically.

- **The habit loop:** Cue the automatic habit sequence by initiating the trigger, recognizing the craving, following through with the behavior, and giving yourself the reward. Over time, the loop becomes self-perpetuating.

- **Stacking:** Group a series of steps into one automatic sequence. Your mind processes them as a single unit. This is how complex routines can become habitual.

- **Alignment:** Ensure the habit aligns with your priorities and motivations. Automaticity is strongest when you have internal motivation to achieve the end result. You must find purpose and meaning.

- **Tracking:** Use habit trackers to build awareness of your behaviors and establish a system of self-accountability. Measure adherence to your routine and review these scores to identify strengths and areas for improvement.

By understanding automaticity and techniques for harnessing it, you gain the power to build habits quickly and break old habits for good. You can transform one automatic behavior at a time through consistency and practice. Making positive habits automatic is how you make effortless progress and enact permanent change.

Willpower

To establish positive habits in your life, you'll need willpower which is not a finite resource. To maximize your habit gains, leverage willpower strategically and then lock in new routines until they become self-sustaining.

Willpower is the mental resolve and determination you use to control impulses and make choices that serve your long-term interests rather than your short-term desires. It enables you to form good habits and break bad ones through conscious intention and effort. You deplete willpower through sustained effort in the same way you fatigue muscles through overuse — so use it carefully and consistently rather than attempting radical or extreme changes all at once. It requires rest to recharge and is often strongest in the morning. Use the early morning hours to conquer tasks to which you are most resistant to. Getting exercise in before the workday begins not only crosses it off your habit list, but it also provides the body with revitalizing energy and the mind with clarity and focus. If you were to wait until the workday ended you might become more susceptible to excuses, fatigue, and laziness. Rather than exhausting your willpower through repeated attempts at total habit overhaul, focus it on starting or stopping just one habit at a time. Let motivation and automaticity build from there through repetition and rewards. We recommend using an app to track habits to hold yourself accountable to the behaviors you set goals around.

Examples of Willpower

As a business owner, you harness your willpower, which is the mental resolve and determination, to control impulses and make choices that serve your long-term interests. You understand that willpower is not a finite resource, but rather a capacity that can be strategically leveraged.

> **Strategic Use of Willpower:** To maximize your habit gains, you   decide to use your willpower strategically and focus on making   gradual changes that can be locked in as self-sustaining routines.   Instead of attempting radical or extreme changes all at once, you   choose to start or stop just one habit at a time.

Morning Focus: Recognizing that willpower is often strongest in the morning, you utilize the early hours to tackle tasks that require more willpower and resistance. For example, you prioritize getting exercise before the workday begins. This not only helps you cross it off your habit list but also provides your body with revitalizing energy and your mind with clarity and focus. By addressing challenging tasks in the morning, you reduce the likelihood of succumbing to excuses, fatigue, or laziness later in the day.

Repetition & Rewards: Understanding the importance of repetition and rewards in habit formation, you track your habits using an app. This allows you to hold yourself accountable and monitor progress toward your goals. By setting achievable goals, tracking your habits, and rewarding yourself for successful completion, you build motivation and automaticity over time.

By strategically using your willpower, focusing on one habit at a time, and leveraging tools like habit-tracking apps, you can cultivate positive habits that enhance your productivity and time management as a business owner. Gradual changes and consistent effort, coupled with rest and recharge for your willpower, lead to lasting improvements and sustainable routines.

Activation energy refers to the initial effort or willpower you need to start building a new habit. It is the motivation and determination you use to overcome inertia and get going with a behavior change or learning process. Think of it as the spark that ignites the habit loop cycle and set its progress in motion. This energy emerges from motivation, or the clear sense of purpose that reminds you why developing the habit matters. Activating a new habit loop demands an initial infusion of energy and resolve. It requires gaining enough momentum to push past the point of comfort into new terrain. While you may be able to sustain a habit over the long run, its journey starts with the self-starting force to break from stillness into action.

Limbic Friction

The limbic system drives many of the factors that make us prone to unhealthy habits. It is responsible for governing emotional responses, driving cravings and desires, and activating the release of dopamine. When the limbic system (emotions & cravings) is in misalignment with the intentions set by your prefrontal cortex (rational mind), it causes internal conflict and discomfort. This friction created by unhealthy cravings and desires works against your better goals and judgment. The clash of the "two minds" feels a bit like cognitive dissonance. The argument between the voices "want to" and "have to" create resistance that can make building new habits feel unpleasant, difficult, or tedious at the moment. Limbic friction often makes building new habits feel unpleasant, difficult or tedious in the moment. It is discomfort that must be tolerated for future gain. The emotional pull of old habits must be overcome through greater vision, motivation, and perseverance.

Without understanding limbic friction, you may misinterpret the difficulty you experience in changing habits as personal failings. But in truth, it is a natural result of the neural pathways your mind has strengthened through repetition of habits. Having shaped those pathways once, the brain resists rerouting them unless given cause to do so. Limbic friction provides you an opportunity to strengthen your willpower and discipline to break through resistance into new patterns of thought and action.

As you increase alignment between your desires and rational intentions, the more you reduce limbic friction, and the less energy you need to expel to build or break a new habit. It is important to mitigate limbic friction as much as possible to set yourself up for success.

You can reduce limbic friction using several strategies:

- Rewire reinforcement by attaching rewards and incentives to the new habit routine. Give your limbic system reason to support rather than oppose the change.

- Repeat the new habit loop consistently until it becomes familiar and automatic. Familiarity allows you to overcome discomfort and uncertainty, signaling to the brain that your new approach is valid and worthwhile. Practice and consistency are key.

- Create positive associations and reframe meaning around the new habit to build motivation. The more motivated and committed you are, the less limbic friction impedes your progress. Find purpose and relevance.

- Start small by breaking down the new habit into manageable steps. Don't trigger too much limbic opposition at once, or you'll expend activation energy. Build habits up gradually.

- Leverage tools such as habit tracking to stay accountable to and aware of progress. Monitoring your habit loop helps ensure you follow through on your goals despite discomfort, giving limbic friction less influence over your actions. Awareness limits its impact.

- Reframe the friction as a temporary and normal part of growth rather than a setback. Know that it will pass in time as your neural connections adapt. Stay patient and determined. The more you push through resistance, the weaker it becomes.

With practice, the new habit pattern grows increasingly familiar and automatic to your brain until it no longer elicits friction. Your emotional circuits adapt to the routine, associating it with normalcy and reward.

Self-Awareness, Identity, & Values

Self-awareness, values, and identity are all deeply connected to your habits. Developing insight into these areas allows you to build habits that align with your priorities and advance your potential.

Self-awareness refers to your identification and understanding of your thoughts, emotions, behaviors, strengths, weaknesses, needs, and motivations. It means objectively examining your habits and tendencies without judgment. With self-awareness, you can determine which habits serve you well and which do not based on your goals and circumstances. You recognize how certain habits were formed and identify those you may wish to change or discard going forward. Self-awareness is a prerequisite for habit mastery.

Your values refer to the principles or beliefs that provide meaning or purpose to your life. Values-based habits are those that allow you to honor and uphold your values through action and choice. Examining your habits through the lens of values lets you evaluate whether they contribute to living according to your principles or operate counter to what you deem most important. Values provide motivation and reinforcement for positive habits that align with them.

Your identity consists of the attributes, roles, interests, relationships, and sense of purpose that make up your self-concept. Identity-based habits are those ingrained in who you believe yourself to be. These are routines that match your self-image and support key aspects of your identity, such as habits related to your role as a parent, your professional expertise, or your commitment to health and growth. You can build new identity-aligned habits by expanding your self-concept to include them.

Understanding how these influences shape and interact with your habits gives you power over them. You can accelerate your construction of new habits by continually validating how they map to your most significant values and priorities, match your strengths, and align with an identity you wish to develop. You break negative habits by recognizing how they conflict with your values or self-concept and then revising them to bring all into harmony.

Conclusion

Habits, the automatic behaviors we frequently engage in, are driven by a cycle of triggers, cravings, behaviors, and rewards known as the habit loop. This loop operates like a computer program, becoming automatic over time, so we can preserve our mental energy to focus on higher-level goals. Our ability to form and break habits is a significant tool for mastering our lives, and shaping our productivity, progress, and overall potential.

Key to mastering habits is understanding their architecture. Habit loops, composed of triggers, cravings, behaviors, and rewards, can be modified to suit our needs, and the resulting changes can help in cultivating positive habits, and eliminating negative ones. The behavior, which lies at the heart of the loop, becomes automatic over time through a process called automaticity, conserving cognitive resources.

The brain plays a crucial role in habit formation and modification. Various brain regions (including the prefrontal cortex, basal ganglia, hippocampus, and amygdala) and brain chemicals (such as dopamine, serotonin, GABA, acetylcholine, and norepinephrine), encode, store, and perpetuate our habits. An understanding of these neurological underpinnings can help us optimize them.

Balancing various factors such as stress, willpower, activation energy, and limbic friction is critical for mastering habits. Appropriate stress can enhance focus, motivation, and facilitate habit formation, while excessive stress can impair the process. Willpower and discipline are like muscles that can be fatigued but can also be strategically used to establish a new habit until it becomes automatic.

Furthermore, our habits are a reflection of our self-awareness, values, and identity. They express our choices and priorities. Even though habits feel automatic, they begin as decisions and we can reshape them through continuous conscious choices. Ultimately, we can leverage this power to reshape our habits as well as our understanding of habit architecture for personal development. Having established a framework of knowledge for habit formation, we will now use this knowledge to build our plan in the next chapter, Principle 2: Design Your Habit Plan.

Summary Q & A

1. What are habits?
    Habits are repeated behaviors that tend to occur subconsciously.

2. What factors contribute to the formation of habits?
    Habits are formed through a complex interplay of psychological, neurological, and biological conditions.

3. How do habits impact our brain function and structure?
    Habits are deeply ingrained in our neural pathways through repetition and influencing our brain function and structure.

4. Can habits be both positive and negative?
    Yes, habits can be both beneficial or detrimental to health

5. What is the habit loop?
    The habit loop is a 4-part neurological cycle: trigger, craving, behavior, and reward; which forms the basis for all habits.

6. How does the trigger component of the habit loop work?
    The trigger cues the habit loop and signals the mind to initiate a particular craving or behavior, which can be internal or external.

7. What is the reward component important in the habit loop?
    The reward provides mental reinforcement, satisfying needs and cravings, and incentivizing the habit to drive repeated behavior.

8. How does automaticity help in achieving goals?
    Automaticity allows us to accomplish more while expending less mental energy & willpower, enabling efficient task performance.

9. What techniques can speed up the process of habit formation?
    Techniques such as repetition, habit loops, chunking, alignment with priorities, and tracking can help build habits effectively.

10. How can habit trackers be useful?
    Habit trackers help build awareness of behaviors, establish self-accountability.

Exercises

1. Take a moment to reflect on a habit you would like to change. Identify the trigger, craving, behavior, and reward associated with that habit.
2. Set up a habit tracker to monitor your progress and provide incentives for building positive habits.
3. Experiment with alternative rewards for a negative habit you want to break. Find healthier options that can replace the pleasure or relief associated with the habit.
4. Reflect on Your Current Habits. Make a list of both positive and negative habits that you engage in regularly. Be honest with yourself and consider how these habits impact areas of your life.
5. Habit Replacement. Identify one negative habit that you would like to break. Replace it with a positive habit that aligns with your goals and values. Create a plan of action and commit to practicing the new habit consistently for at least 21 days.
6. Trigger Analysis. Choose a habit and analyze its triggers. Pay attention to the cues that initiate the habit. Are they internal or external? What actions or situations precede the habit? Understanding triggers can help you take control of a habit loop.
7. Habit Loop Redesign. Select a habit loop that you would like to redesign. Identify the trigger, craving, behavior, and reward associated with it. Brainstorm alternative behaviors that can lead to the same reward but in a more positive and beneficial way.
8. Tracking & Accountability. Start tracking your habits using a habit tracker or journal. Record your daily habits and evaluate your adherence to the desired behaviors. Use the tracker as a tool for self-accountability and motivation to stay consistent.
9. Purpose & Motivation Alignment. Reflect on your habits and assess whether they align with your priorities. Identify any habits that are not serving your greater purpose and consider how you can replace them with habits that are more meaningful.

10. Breaking Bad Habits. Choose one bad habit that you want to
    break and analyze its underlying rewards. Explore healthier
    alternatives that can fulfill those needs and provide a similar
    reward. Experiment with different strategies and techniques to
    gradually replace the bad habit with a more positive behavior.

Principle 2:
Design Your Habit Plan

Mapping the Journey to Lasting Transformation

"A clear vision, backed by definite plans, gives you a tremendous feeling of confidence and personal power."
- Brian Tracy

Every great endeavor requires a well-defined plan and the journey to instill positive habits and eradicate negative ones from our lives is no exception. This principle delves into the critical phase of habit transformation: the planning stage. By embracing the power of planning, we set the stage for meaningful and sustainable change in our lives, careers, and businesses. Research indicates that individuals who engage in effective planning are more likely to achieve their desired goals. In a study conducted by the Dominican University of California, researchers found that those who wrote down their goals, created specific action steps, and shared their progress with others were 42% more likely to accomplish their objectives compared to those who did not engage in these planning activities[17]. Why is planning so crucial in the habit change process? Imagine embarking on a long journey without a map or compass. You might find yourself wandering aimlessly, unsure of your destination or the steps you need to take to reach it. Similarly, when endeavoring to transform our habits, a clear plan becomes our compass, guiding us toward success. It provides us with a roadmap to navigate the

---

[17] Matthews, G., et al. (2015). The impact of a goal-setting intervention on academic performance. *Journal of Applied Social Psychology*, 45*(6)*, 329-338.;
https://www.dominican.edu/sites/default/files/2020-02/gailmatthews-harvard-goals-researchsummary.pdf

complexities of habit change and empowers us to make intentional choices along the way.

Key Question:
What are the core elements of a well-defined plan for habit change that will enable us to navigate the journey of habit transformation with clarity and purpose?

In our journey toward personal growth and self-improvement, the power of habits cannot be underestimated. Habits shape our daily routines, influence our actions, and ultimately determine our success in achieving our goals. However, changing habits can be a challenging task that requires careful planning and strategic execution. In this chapter, we delve into the essential elements of planning for habit transformation, exploring key strategies such as brainstorming, establishing metrics, defining clear objectives, leveraging intrinsic and extrinsic resources, utilizing coaching and technology, setting timelines, and creating a comprehensive plan. By understanding and implementing these crucial steps, you will be better equipped to embark on a successful habit transformation journey.

To ensure progress and maintain accountability, it is crucial to establish metrics for measuring your habit transformation. Metrics could include tracking the frequency or duration of the habit, measuring associated outcomes, or assessing subjective indicators such as mood or energy levels. These metrics provide tangible evidence of your progress and allow you to course correct when necessary. Moreover, it is important to leverage both intrinsic and extrinsic resources to support your habit transformation. Intrinsic resources encompass your own internal motivation, discipline, and resilience, while extrinsic resources may include external support systems, such as mentors, friends, or tools that aid in habit formation. By recognizing and utilizing these resources, you create a robust support system that enhances your chances of success. Let's start by defining our goals.

Defining Clear Objectives

Setting specific and measurable objectives is a crucial step in the habit change process. By clearly defining our objectives, we gain clarity on what we aim to achieve and create a solid foundation for success. It allows us to focus our efforts and track our progress effectively.

In the realm of habit change, defining clear objectives involves identifying the desired outcome we seek to attain. Whether it's instilling a positive habit or eradicating a negative one, understanding our desired outcome provides us with a target to work toward. Additionally, it helps us recognize the specific habit behaviors we wish to change. By breaking down the habit into actionable behaviors, we gain clarity on the actions we need to take to achieve our desired outcome.

Examples:

Life Objective: Develop a daily meditation habit. Take the time to reflect on the significance of meditation in your life and consider the potential benefits it can bring you, such as increased mindfulness, reduced stress, or improved focus.

Career Objective: Improve networking skills. Reflect on the importance of networking in your career and the potential benefits it can bring, such as expanding professional connections, unlocking new opportunities, and enhancing your visibility in your industry.

Business Objective: Strengthen risk management practices. Start by conducting a thorough assessment of your current risk management processes to identify areas of vulnerability or gaps in your existing approach. With a clear understanding of the risks involved, establish specific objectives to mitigate these risks. By setting and pursuing these objectives, you will safeguard your business's operations and long-term success.

Establishing Metrics

Selecting appropriate metrics to measure your progress is essential in the habit change journey. Metrics serve as tangible indicators that enable us to evaluate how close we are to reaching our goals and whether we are moving in the right direction. They provide valuable feedback and help us stay accountable to our vision of the future.

When measuring your habit change progress, it is important to use metrics that align with your objectives and provide meaningful insights into your behaviors. These metrics can include frequency, duration, quality, or any other quantifiable measurements relevant to the habit you intend to change. Additionally, exploring different methods and tools for tracking habit-related behaviors and outcomes can enhance your ability to monitor progress effectively. These tools and methods may include using habit tracking apps, journaling, or utilizing technology-driven solutions that align with your preferences and lifestyle.

By setting measurable criteria and establishing effective tracking mechanisms, you empower yourself to monitor your progress and make informed adjustments along the way. This allows you to stay motivated, stay on track, and ultimately achieve your desired habit change outcomes.

Examples:

> *Life Objective:* Develop a daily meditation habit.
>
> **Measurement:** Establish a goal to meditate for 10 minutes every morning. Consider tracking the number of consecutive days you successfully meditate, the total minutes you meditate per week, or even the impact it has

on your overall well-being and stress levels. These metrics will not only provide tangible evidence of your habit transformation but also serve as motivators and indicators of your commitment to your life objective.

Career Objective: Improve networking skills.

Measurement: Branch out to reap the benefits. Set a goal to attend at least one industry networking event per month and establish meaningful connections with at least three professionals. Track your progress by attending a certain number of industry events, actively reaching out to new contacts, or enhancing your online networking presence through platforms such as LinkedIn. These measurements will guide you in your efforts and provide you with a roadmap to continuously hone and expand your networking skills.

Business Objective: Strengthen risk management practices.

Measurement: One key measurement approach is to conduct a monthly risk assessment of your business, thoroughly evaluating the potential risks the organization faces. As part of this assessment, aim to identify and address at least two key areas of potential risk each month. This process could involve implementing a comprehensive risk assessment framework to identify vulnerabilities, enhancing internal controls to minimize the likelihood of risks, or fostering a culture of risk awareness and accountability throughout the organization. By consistently implementing these risk management practices and tracking your organization's progress through regular assessments, you will be better equipped to proactively identify and mitigate risks.

Discovering your Purpose

Discovering your purpose, the reason *why* you want to instill or eradicate a habit in your life, is a vital component of successful habit change. It serves as the driving force behind your commitment to change and your willingness to overcome challenges and obstacles along the way. Understanding your purpose provides you with clarity and serves as a constant reminder of the *rewards* that await you if you succeed, as well as the *consequences* if you fail to take action.

By envisioning the rewards, you tap into the deeper reasons why habit change is important to you. It goes beyond surface-level motivations and connects with your values, aspirations, and long-term goals. This deeper understanding ignites a sense of passion and commitment within you, propelling you forward even when faced with challenges or setbacks.

Additionally, aligning your habits with your values, aspirations, and long-term goals provides a sense of coherence and fulfillment. It creates harmony between your actions and your vision for the future. By consciously connecting your purpose to your habit change efforts, you infuse intention and meaning into your actions, making the process more meaningful and rewarding.

While both pain (i.e., consequences) and pleasure (i.e., rewards) can motivate you to make changes in your life, pain is a more powerful driving force for change. This is because pain, whether physical or emotional, tends to elicit a stronger and more immediate response. When we experience discomfort, adversity, or negative consequences, we are often compelled to take action in order to alleviate the pain and restore a sense of balance.

The power of pain as a motivator lies in its ability to urgently demand our attention. When we encounter discomfort or negative outcomes that result from our habits, it serves as a clear signal that we need to change something in our routines. Pain pushes us out of our comfort zones and propels us toward finding solutions and taking decisive action to avoid further pain.

Moreover, pain can serve as a powerful teacher. It provides us with valuable lessons and insights, highlighting the consequences of our actions or inactions. By experiencing pain, we gain a deeper understanding of what we do not want to experience in our lives and what we need to transform. It serves as a catalyst for growth, pushing us to develop resilience, adaptability, and the willingness to make necessary changes to avoid future pain.

However, it is important to note that the role of pleasure should not be disregarded. Pleasure can serve as an intrinsic motivator, drawing us toward positive habits and reinforcing their benefits. It can provide a sense of joy, satisfaction, and fulfillment when we engage in activities aligned with our values and goals. Striking a balance between the motivational power of pain and pleasure can lead to a holistic and sustainable approach to habit change.

By honestly evaluating the negative impact these habits can have on your life, career, or business, you gain a deeper understanding of the urgency and importance of habit change. Reflecting on the consequences serves as a wake-up call, reminding you of the potential pitfalls and undesirable outcomes that await you if you do not take action.

Consider the ripple effect these detrimental habits may have on your personal life, career, and business. Visualize the missed opportunities, strained relationships, stagnation, missed promotions, decreased satisfaction, financial losses, and loss of competitiveness that may result from clinging to negative habits. Allow yourself to truly comprehend the gravity of the situation and the potential long-term consequences of inaction.

This reflective process is not meant to discourage or overwhelm you, but rather to ignite a sense of urgency within you and reinforce your commitment to change. It becomes a powerful catalyst for transformation, motivating you to take the necessary steps toward instilling positive habits and eradicating negative ones. By fully understanding the potential consequences and the price you may pay for inaction, you are empowered to make deliberate and impactful choices that align with your goals and aspirations.

For the previous examples, we will now add a Purpose Statement:

> *Life Objective:* Develop a daily meditation habit.
>
> *Measurement:* Track days that you meditate for 10 minutes every morning…
>
> **Purpose:** By cultivating a daily meditation practice, I aim to reduce stress, enhance mental clarity, and foster inner peace. This habit will support my overall well-being and help me navigate life with greater calmness and resilience.
>
> *Career Objective:* Improve networking skills.
>
> *Measurement:* Note attendance at least one industry networking event per month and establish meaningful connections with at least three professionals….
>
> **Purpose:** Enhancing my networking skills is crucial for advancing my career. By building a strong professional network, I can gain access to valuable opportunities, collaborate with industry leaders, and stay updated on market trends. This habit will contribute to my professional growth and success.
>
> *Business Objective:* Strengthen risk management practices.
>
> *Measurement:* Conduct a monthly risk assessment and identify and address at least two key areas of potential risk….
>
> **Purpose:** As a business, our success relies on effective risk management. By strengthening our risk management practices, we can mitigate potential threats, protect investor capital, and ensure long-term sustainability. This habit will

contribute to the overall stability and growth of our business.

Brainstorming

One of the fundamental steps in planning for habit transformation, in addition to defining clear objectives, is engaging in a process of brainstorming. Begin by identifying the habits you wish to change or develop and envision the outcomes you hope to achieve. This initial brainstorming phase allows you to explore various possibilities and refine your focus. Once you have a clear vision in mind, it is essential to refer to specific objectives that will guide your efforts. These clear objectives provide you with a sense of direction and purpose, acting as a compass throughout your habit transformation journey.

Brainstorming is a key step in creating your plan. Creative thinking allows you to explore different possibilities and discover innovative approaches to instilling or eradicating habits. By opening your mind to new perspectives, you expand the range of potential solutions and increase your chances of success. Remember, the goal at this stage is quantity over quality. Allow your imagination to flow freely and capture every idea that comes to mind. They will be filtered out later once you have captured all ideas.

To stimulate creative thinking, employ brainstorming techniques. Start by creating a supportive and non-judgmental environment where all ideas are welcome. Encourage yourself to think outside the box and consider unconventional approaches. While creating a plan is a process, brainstorming requires a non-linear approach. Use techniques such as mind mapping, free association, or listing to generate a wide range of ideas. Each technique stimulates your imagination and empowers you to break free from conventional patterns of thinking and discover fresh perspectives. Experiment with these techniques and find the ones that resonate with you, allowing you to unlock your creative potential and uncover innovative strategies for transforming your habits.

Mind Mapping

Mind Mapping is a powerful technique, originally developed by Tony Buzan[18], that allows you to visually organize your thoughts and generate a wide range of ideas. Start by writing down the central concept or problem related to your habit change. From there, branch out and create associations, connections, and subtopics using lines, colors, and keywords. As you explore each branch, let your mind roam freely and capture any new ideas that come to mind. Mind mapping encourages nonlinear thinking and stimulates creative associations, helping you uncover fresh perspectives and generate a rich array of potential strategies for habit change.

Free Association

Free Association is a technique that taps into your subconscious mind to spark new ideas and connections. This technique was created by psychoanalyst Sigmund Freud in the 19th century[19]. Begin by selecting a keyword or prompt related to your habit change goal. Then, without censoring or judging your thoughts, let your mind wander and freely associate words, images, or concepts that come to mind. Allow your thoughts to flow spontaneously, without worrying about coherence or logical sequence. By accessing your subconscious mind, free association can unlock hidden insights and unconventional approaches to habit change.

Listing

Listing is a simple yet effective technique for generating a wide range of ideas quickly. Start by creating a list of ideas, potential strategies, or actions related to your habit change. Write down each idea as it comes to mind, without overthinking or

---

[18] Tony Buzan. "Mind Maps." Tony Buzan Education. Accessed June 13, 2023. URL: https://www.tonybuzan.edu.sg/about/mind-maps/#:~:text=Originated%20in%201970%20by%20Tony,use%20their%20brains%20more%20effectively

[19] Psych Central. "Free Association Therapy." Accessed June 13, 2023. URL: https://psychcentral.com/health/free-association-therapy#history

analyzing. Don't worry about the order or organization at this stage; the goal is to capture as many ideas as possible. By creating a list, you create a tangible record of your thoughts, making it easier to review and evaluate later. Listing allows you to bypass self-censorship and self-editing, enabling you to explore a broad range of possibilities and uncover potential strategies that you may not have considered initially.

Evaluating the Ideas

Once you have generated a pool of ideas from your brainstorming session(s), it's time to evaluate and select the most suitable strategies for your habit change journey. Evaluating strategies involves considering their feasibility, practicality, and alignment with your goals and values. Not every idea generated during brainstorming will be equally effective or applicable to your specific situation, so it's essential to discern which strategies hold the most promise.

As you evaluate strategies, pay attention to how well they help you address the underlying triggers and rewards associated with the habit. Effective habit change strategies go beyond surface-level modifications and target the *root causes* of the habit. They aim to disrupt the triggers that prompt the habit and provide alternative rewards that satisfy the same underlying needs.

Select strategies that resonate with you and align with your values, lifestyle, and circumstances. Consider the resources, time, and effort required for each strategy and choose those that are practical and feasible for your situation. Remember that habit change is a journey, and selecting strategies that you genuinely believe in and are committed to implementing in your life increases your chances of long-term success.

By engaging in a thorough brainstorming process and carefully evaluating and selecting strategies, you set the stage for effective habit change. Embrace creativity, think outside the box, and choose strategies that address the core elements of your habits. With a solid foundation of well-thought-out strategies, you are equipped to embark on your habit change journey with confidence and determination.

Resources

A crucial part of the brainstorming process is to consider the resources available to you that improve your chance of success. When brainstorming on resources, it is important to consider a wide range of options that can support your journey. Resources can provide you with the necessary tools, support systems, and knowledge you need to facilitate habit transformation.

Remember, the specific resources needed for habit change may vary depending on the nature of the habit and individual circumstances. Assess your unique needs and explore additional resources that align with your goals and aspirations for habit transformation.

Intrinsic vs. Extrinsic Resources

When it comes to resources for habit change, it's important to consider both intrinsic and extrinsic factors. These two types of resources play distinct roles in supporting your habit transformation journey. Let's explore them in more detail:

Intrinsic Resources

Intrinsic resources are internal factors that reside within you. They are essential for cultivating the right mindset and providing the necessary energy, discipline, and focus for habit change. Here are some key intrinsic resources to consider:

- *Mindset:* Developing a positive and growth-oriented mindset is crucial for habit change. It involves cultivating self-confidence, resilience, and the belief that change is possible. A mindset shift can empower you to overcome obstacles, maintain motivation, and

embrace the challenges that come with habit transformation.

- *Time Management:* Effectively managing your time is an intrinsic resource that allows you to prioritize your habits amidst other commitments. By establishing time blocks and optimizing your daily schedule, you can allocate dedicated time for habit-related activities, ensuring consistent practice and progress.

- *Energy & Well-being:* Taking care of your physical and mental well-being is vital for habit change. It involves practices such as regular exercise, healthy eating, quality sleep, and stress management. When you have sufficient energy and overall well-being, you are better equipped to engage in habit-related behaviors and maintain consistency.

- *Discipline & Willpower:* Discipline and willpower are internal resources that help you stay committed to your habits, even in the face of challenges or temptations. Cultivating discipline involves setting clear boundaries, creating routines, and developing strategies to overcome distractions and stop patterns of self-sabotage.

- *Focus & Concentration:* Maintaining focus and concentration is crucial for habit change, as it allows you to stay present and engaged when performing desired behaviors. Building focus-enhancing practices such as mindfulness and meditation, or eliminating distractions can support you in changing your habits.

Extrinsic Resources

Extrinsic resources refer to external factors and support systems that can enhance your habit change journey. These resources involve leveraging the power of people and technology to create an environment conducive to habit transformation. Here are some examples of extrinsic resources:

- **Information & Education:** Gather information and educate yourself about the habit you want to change. Books, articles, online resources, and educational programs can provide you with valuable insights, strategies, and techniques to support your habit transformation.

- **Support Networks & Accountability Partners:** Seek support from family, friends, or colleagues who can provide encouragement, understanding, and accountability. Find a mentor or join support groups or online communities for additional and valuable guidance and motivation.

- **Professional Help & Counseling:** If you are struggling with an addiction or deeply-ingrained habit, you may need professional help. Consider reaching out to therapists, counselors, or addiction specialists who can provide you with expert guidance, therapy, and tailored strategies to overcome addiction.

- **Environmental Modifications:** Make changes to your physical environment to support habit change. This may include organizing your workspace, creating visual reminders, or removing triggers that drive you to engage in negative habits.

- **Rewards & Incentives:** Establish a system of rewards or incentives to motivate yourself and reinforce the positive habit changes you make. This can be as simple as treating yourself to a small reward after achieving certain milestones or setting up a reward system with a partner or accountability group.

- **Personal Reflection & Journaling:** Engage in introspection and self-reflection to gain deeper insights into your habits, triggers, and motivations.

Journaling can provide a private space to process thoughts and emotions, track progress, and gain clarity on your habit change journey.

By recognizing and leveraging both intrinsic and extrinsic resources, you can create a supportive ecosystem that strengthens your habit change endeavors. The combination of internal factors such as mindset, time management, energy, discipline, and focus, along with external factors such as social support, coaching, habit tracking apps, and technology, empowers you to optimize your habit change process and achieve sustainable results.

Coaching + Technology
Transforming habits can be challenging, but there are two particular resources that deserve special mention for their invaluable contribution to the process of habit change: coaching and habit tracking software/apps. When used in conjunction, they can accelerate habit transformation and maximize success.

Coaching: Guidance & Accountability
Coaching is a valuable resource you can use to facilitate habit change. A coach provides you with personalized guidance, support, and accountability throughout your habit transformation journey. Here are some key aspects of coaching as a resource:

- ***Expertise & Knowledge:*** A coach offers you specialized knowledge and expertise in habit change methodologies. They have a deep understanding of the psychological, behavioral, and physiological aspects of habits which allows them to provide targeted guidance and strategies to meet your specific needs.

- ***Goal Setting & Action Planning:*** A coach helps you define clear and achievable goals related to habit change. They assist you in breaking down your goals into manageable steps, creating an action plan, and setting realistic timelines. This structured approach ensures that you have a clear path forward and increases your chances of success.

- *Accountability & Support:* A coach serves as a source of accountability and support throughout your habit change journey. They help you stay on track, celebrate your progress, and provide guidance and motivation during challenging times. The coach-client relationship creates a safe and supportive space for open communication and honest reflection. We will discuss accountability in more depth in Principle 3.

- *Personalized Strategies:* A coach works closely with you to identify the underlying triggers and barriers related to your habits. They help you uncover patterns, develop self-awareness, and devise personalized strategies to address those triggers effectively. By understanding your unique circumstances, a coach can offer tailored approaches that resonate with you.

- *Motivation & Resilience:* Habit change can be challenging, and it is common to face setbacks or moments of low motivation. A coach helps you stay motivated and develop resilience in the face of obstacles. They provide encouragement, guidance, and perspective, helping you navigate challenges and maintain a positive mindset.

- *Feedback & Reflection:* A coach offers you constructive feedback, helping you develop insight into your habit change strategies and make adjustments as necessary. They facilitate reflection on your progress, successes, and areas for improvement. This feedback loop allows for continuous learning and growth throughout the habit change process.

- *Positive Reinforcement & Celebration:* A coach recognizes and celebrates your achievements, providing positive reinforcement along the way. They help you acknowledge milestones, both big and small, helping you to foster a sense of accomplishment while boosting your confidence and motivation.

Coaching as a resource can significantly enhance your habit change efforts by providing you with guidance, accountability, and support. By partnering with a coach, you gain access to a dedicated ally and expert who supports you in devising personalized strategies for success. This collaboration empowers you to overcome challenges, maximize your potential, and achieve lasting habit transformation.

Technology: Habit Tracking Apps

Habit tracking apps have gained popularity as valuable resources for habit change. These digital tools provide a convenient and organized way to monitor your habits, track progress, and stay motivated. Here are some key aspects of habit tracking apps as a resource:

- *Habit Monitoring & Tracking:* Habit tracking apps allow you to record and track your habits on a daily, weekly, or monthly basis. They provide a visual representation of your habit progress, making it easier for you to monitor your consistency and identify patterns over time. By regularly revisiting a visual display of your long-term habits, you gain insights into your behavior and can make informed decisions for habit change.

- *Customization & Flexibility:* Habit tracking apps offer customization options to tailor the app to your specific needs. You can create and customize habit categories, set target frequencies or goals, and choose the tracking parameters that align with your habit change objectives. The flexibility of these apps allows you to adapt the tracking process to fit your unique habits and goals.

- **Reminders & Notifications:** Habit tracking apps often include reminder features to help you stay consistent with your habits. You can set up personalized reminders or notifications at specific times or intervals to prompt you to engage in your desired behaviors. These reminders serve as gentle nudges and help reinforce the habit change process.

- **Progress Visualization:** Habit tracking apps provide visual representations of your progress, such as charts, graphs, or streak counters. These visualizations offer a sense of accomplishment and motivation as you witness your streaks or progress building over time. The ability to see your improvement and consistency reinforces positive behavior and further encourages you to stick to your habits.

- **Insights & Analytics:** Many habit tracking apps offer data and analytics features that provide insights into your habit patterns. You can analyze trends, identify correlations, and discover the factors that improve or impede your habit success. These insights enable you to make data-driven adjustments to your strategies and optimize your habit change process.

- **Community & Social Support:** Some habit tracking apps have built-in communities or social sharing features. Engaging with a community of like-minded individuals can provide you with support, motivation, and accountability. Sharing your progress, challenges, and successes with others creates a sense of camaraderie and can inspire you to stay committed to your habit change goals.

- **Integration & Synchronization:** Habit tracking apps often integrate with other platforms or devices, allowing you to synchronize your habit data across multiple devices. This feature ensures that you can access and update your habits seamlessly, whether on your smartphone, tablet, or computer. Integration with other apps or tools, such as calendars or task managers, can also enhance your overall productivity and organization.

Habit tracking apps serve as valuable resources by providing a structured and user-friendly approach to habit monitoring, progress tracking, and motivation. By leveraging the features and capabilities of these apps, you can gain insights, stay accountable, and make positive changes toward your habit transformation goals.

Coaching + Technology: A Powerful Combination

Working with a coach *and* a habit tracking app can be a game-changer in habit transformation. The synergy between these two resources can enhance your journey and increase your chances of success. Here are some reasons why combining a coach with a habit tracking app can be highly effective:

- *Personalized Guidance & Accountability:* A coach provides personalized guidance, support, and accountability tailored to your specific needs. They work closely with you to understand your habits, challenges, and goals. By having access to your habit tracking app data, the coach can gain valuable insights into your progress, patterns, and areas for improvement. This allows them to provide you with targeted and impactful guidance and accountability.

- *Data-Driven Insights:* Habit tracking apps provide data and analytics that offer insights into your habit patterns and progress. With the coach's expertise, they can analyze this data alongside you, helping you identify trends, strengths, and areas that require your attention. The combination of a coach's expertise and the app's data-driven insights allow you a deeper understanding of your habits and facilitates strategic adjustments to your approach.

- ***Continuous Support & Motivation:*** A coach acts as a consistent source of support and motivation throughout your habit change journey. They help you stay focused, navigate challenges, and celebrate your successes. With access to your habit tracking app, the coach can monitor your progress in real-time and provide timely feedback and encouragement. This ongoing support and motivation create a powerful synergy that keeps you motivated and engaged.

- ***Goal Setting & Action Planning:*** A coach assists you in setting clear and achievable goals and developing an action plan for habit change. They work with you to define specific objectives and milestones. By integrating the habit tracking app into the process, the coach can align your goals with the app's tracking features. This ensures that you have a structured plan and a tangible way to measure your progress, making the habit change process more organized and effective.

- ***Enhanced Accountability & Transparency:*** The combination of a coach and a habit tracking app adds an extra layer of accountability and transparency to your habit change efforts. The app provides a visual representation of your habits, streaks, and progress, which the coach can access and review. This transparency fosters open and honest discussions between you and your coach, allowing for deeper insights, problem-solving, and adjustments as needed.

- ***Tailored Strategies & Interventions:*** A coach can leverage the insights from the habit tracking app to develop tailored strategies and interventions. By understanding your habit patterns and triggers, the coach can provide targeted techniques and approaches to address specific challenges or facilitate habit change. This personalized approach ensures that the strategies implemented align with your unique needs and circumstances.

Combining a coach and a habit tracking app creates a holistic and comprehensive approach to habit change. The coach's guidance, expertise, and support, coupled with the data-driven insights and tracking capabilities of the app, provide a powerful framework for success. This combination empowers you to make meaningful and lasting changes, optimize your progress, and achieve your habit transformation goals.

Time

A well-structured plan takes into account the element of time, incorporating elements such as timelines, deadlines, and start lines. These temporal markers provide structure, accountability, and a sense of urgency, propelling us forward on our path to habit transformation. In this section, we delve into the significance of time in our plans, exploring how the strategic utilization of timelines and milestones enhances our ability to cultivate positive habits and eradicate negative ones.

Timelines

Setting realistic timelines is essential when embarking on a habit change journey. While it can be challenging to estimate precisely how long it will take to instill or eradicate a habit, having a general timeline provides you with a sense of direction and purpose. Timelines help you establish a framework for your habit change plan, allowing you to track progress, stay motivated, and assess the effectiveness of your strategies. It's important to be flexible with timelines and adapt them as needed, considering the individual nature of habit change and the potential for variability in the process.

Habit Transformation Duration

Many experts on habit-building have said that it takes 21 days to form a habit. However, research has shown that the time required to establish a habit can vary significantly among individuals. In a 2010 study conducted by Lally and colleagues, researchers examined how long it took participants to develop the habit of walking after dinner; previous research has shown that this health-related behavior helps many people improve glucose clearance and cardiovascular health. The researchers classified habits as fully formed when individuals managed to engage in the behavior approximately 85% of the time with minimal initiatory mental effort. Over the course of the study, the research team determined that it could take anywhere from 18 days to 254 days for different individuals to develop the same habit[20].

The notion of why certain individuals can form habits more easily than others may be attributed, at least in part, to the concept of "limbic friction," discussed in the previous chapter, but it is crucial to recognize that the habit formation timeline isn't one-size-fits-all. We must approach habit formation, then, with patience, persistence, and an understanding that different habits may require different timeframes and levels of effort for successful integration into our daily lives.

Deadlines

Deadlines are specific target dates or milestones within your habit change plan. They create a sense of urgency and help you maintain focus and accountability. Deadlines can be useful for certain kinds of habit change, such as setting a deadline to quit a detrimental habit or achieve a specific milestone in instilling a new habit. By breaking down your habit-change journey into smaller, manageable goals with corresponding deadlines, you create a roadmap that propels you forward. However, it's crucial to set realistic deadlines that correlate with the complexity of the habit and your individual circumstances to avoid subjecting yourself to undue pressure or setting unrealistic expectations.

---

[20] "Habit Formation: The 21-Day Myth" by Jason Selk on Forbes: Selk, J. (2013, April 15). Habit Formation: The 21-Day Myth. *Forbes.* Retrieved from https://www.forbes.com/sites/jasonselk/2013/04/15/habit-formation-the-21-day-myth/?sh=55c894f7debc

Start-lines

The concept of a "start line" is about choosing the right time to begin your habit change plan. It acknowledges that initiating the process is often the most challenging part. Selecting a strategic start line helps build momentum, motivation, and commitment. Consider factors such as personal readiness, external circumstances, and support systems when determining your start line. It's important to choose a time when you have the necessary resources, energy, and mental readiness to commit to the habit change process. By starting at a time that aligns with your circumstances and provides the best opportunity for success, you set yourself up for a strong foundation.

While timelines, deadlines, and start-lines are valuable tools in habit change, it's important to approach them with flexibility and adaptability. Each individual's journey is unique, and the time required for habit change can vary depending on various factors, including the complexity of the habit, personal circumstances, and individual differences. Avoid rigid adherence to arbitrary timelines or deadlines, as this can lead to discouragement or unrealistic expectations. Instead, focus on progress, consistency, and sustainable change over time. Remember that habit change is a continuous process, and embracing a long-term perspective fosters patience, resilience, and a greater likelihood of lasting success.

Categorization

The importance of categorization, or chunking, in a plan cannot be overstated when it comes to effective organization and focused execution. Categorization involves grouping related topics, tasks, or actions together based on their similarities or shared characteristics. By breaking down a plan into distinct categories, we create a structured framework that enables us to prioritize, allocate resources, and maintain clarity in our approach. This organizational strategy not only enhances our understanding of the plan but also facilitates efficient decision-making and targeted action. By identifying key categories and grouping related elements, we streamline our efforts, optimize our time and energy, and increase the likelihood of successfully instilling positive habits or eradicating negative ones. In essence, categorization empowers us to navigate the complexities of our plan with greater ease, focus, and effectiveness.

Actions

Action items play a crucial role in any plan as they represent the specific tasks or steps that need to be executed to achieve desired outcomes. They serve as actionable milestones that propel us forward and keep us accountable to our goals. By clearly defining and listing the action items in a plan, we create a roadmap for progress and ensure that our intentions are translated into concrete actions. Action items provide a sense of direction, focus our efforts, and break down larger goals into manageable tasks. They help us track our progress, maintain momentum, and celebrate small victories along the way. Without well-defined action items, a plan can remain abstract and lack the necessary clarity and structure needed for effective implementation. By incorporating action items into our plan, we establish a tangible path toward habit change, enabling us to move from intention to action and ultimately achieve the desired results.

Prioritization

Prioritization is a critical aspect of creating a plan for habit change as it allows us to focus our time, energy, and resources on the most important and impactful areas. The first step in prioritization is to establish a hierarchy of categories or areas of focus within the plan. By determining which categories hold the greatest significance or have the highest potential for positive impact, we can allocate our attention and efforts accordingly.

Once the categories are prioritized, it is equally important to prioritize the action items within each category. This involves identifying the tasks or steps that will yield the most significant results or contribute to the desired habit change. The 80/20 Rule, also known as the Pareto Principle, comes into play here. It suggests that roughly 80% of the outcomes come from 20% of the inputs or efforts. In the context of habit change, this means that a small number of action items will have a disproportionate impact on the overall results.

By applying the 80/20 Rule to prioritize our action items, we can identify the critical few tasks that will lead to the greatest progress. These tasks should align with the highest-priority categories and address the key factors influencing the desired habit change. By focusing on these high-impact action items, we can maximize our efficiency, make the most of our resources, and accelerate our progress toward habit transformation.

Prioritization not only helps us direct our efforts toward the most impactful areas but also ensures that we make efficient use of our time and avoid getting overwhelmed by an extensive list of tasks. It allows us to maintain focus, clarity, and momentum as we work toward our habit change goals. By prioritizing categories and action items, we create a roadmap that guides our actions, enables effective decision-making, and increases the likelihood of successful habit transformation.

Pre-Situation Plans: Anticipating Challenges

In the pursuit of cultivating or eradicating habits, we often encounter situations that put our willpower and commitment to the test. These challenges can range from everyday temptations to more significant hurdles that require a strong resolve to overcome. That's why pre-situational planning becomes an invaluable tool in our habit journey. By proactively strategizing and preparing for potential obstacles, we set ourselves up for success and ensure that we stay on track even when faced with difficult circumstances.

The essence of pre-situational planning lies in its ability to anticipate and address challenges before they arise. It involves taking a *proactive approach* by envisioning future scenarios in which our commitment to our habits may be tested. By identifying these situations and the potential triggers or temptations they may bring, we empower ourselves to develop effective strategies to navigate them.

When we know that we will be facing difficult challenges that require our willpower to be summoned, pre-situational planning becomes extremely crucial. It allows us to plan ahead and arm ourselves with the necessary tools and mindset to overcome obstacles and maintain our habit game.

The Process
Here's how pre-situational planning can work in practice:

1. ***Identify Potential Obstacles:*** Take some time to reflect on the specific situations or circumstances that may present challenges to your habit cultivation or eradication efforts. It could be social gatherings where unhealthy food choices are abundant, stressful work environments, or even certain triggers in your daily routine.

2. ***Anticipate Triggers & Temptations:*** Once you've identified potential obstacles, delve deeper into the triggers or temptations that these situations may pose. Is it the sight and aroma of tempting treats at a party? Is it the stress and pressure of a demanding project? Understanding the specific triggers will help you devise targeted strategies to counteract them.

3. ***Develop Counteractive Strategies:*** Armed with knowledge about obstacles and triggers, brainstorm

strategies that will help you stay committed to your habits. For example, if you anticipate encountering tempting food at a social gathering, plan to eat a healthy meal beforehand to curb your appetite. If work stress is a challenge, identify stress-relief techniques such as deep breathing exercises or short mindfulness breaks to help you stay centered and focused.

4. ***Rehearse & Visualize Success:*** Visualization is a powerful technique that can enhance the effectiveness of pre-situational planning. Mentally rehearse your strategies and visualize yourself successfully navigating challenging situations while maintaining your desired habits. By repeatedly imagining yourself overcoming obstacles and staying true to your commitments, you strengthen your belief in your ability to succeed.

5. ***Seek Support & Accountability:*** Pre-situational planning becomes even more effective when you involve others in your journey. Share your strategies and challenges with a trusted friend, family member, or accountability partner who can offer support and encouragement. Their presence and understanding can provide an extra layer of motivation and assistance when faced with challenging situations.

Remember, pre-situational planning is not about being pessimistic or expecting failure. Instead, it is a proactive approach that empowers you to be prepared and confident in your ability to handle obstacles along your habit journey. By considering potential challenges in advance, developing effective strategies, and visualizing success, you equip yourself with the necessary tools to maintain your habit game, even in the face of adversity.

Pre-situational planning is a vital component of successful habit cultivation or eradication. It allows us to anticipate and address potential obstacles before they derail our progress. By proactively strategizing, developing counteractive measures, and seeking support, we ensure that our willpower remains strong and our commitment to our habits remains unwavering. Embrace pre-situational planning as a powerful tool in your habit journey, and pave the way for long-lasting, positive change.

Creating a Comprehensive Plan

Creating an effective habit change plan requires integrating all the elements discussed thus far into a cohesive and comprehensive strategy for success. By bringing together the objective, purpose, measurable criteria, brainstormed strategies, and identified resources, you can develop a plan that sets you up for success.

Here are key considerations for integrating these elements into your habit change plan:

- *Creating a Clear Plan:* Start by clarifying your objective and defining the specific habit you want to instill or eradicate in your life. Set clear and measurable criteria for progress, such as the frequency or duration of the habit-related behaviors. These criteria will serve as benchmarks for tracking your progress and the effectiveness of your efforts.

- *Establishing a Timeline:* Develop a timeline that outlines the key milestones and deadlines for your habit change journey. Consider the research findings that habit formation can vary in duration and be mindful that you may need more time to develop some habits than you do to develop others. Align your timeline with your specific habit and allow for flexibility, recognizing that habit change is a gradual process.

- *Action Steps:* Break down your habit change goal into smaller, more manageable action steps. Determine the specific behaviors or actions you need to consistently take to instill the habit, or eradicate it from, your life. Consider the strategies generated during the brainstorming phase and identify the most effective approaches to incorporate into your action steps.

- ***Contingency Plans:*** Anticipate challenges and obstacles that may arise along your habit change journey. Develop contingency plans to address these hurdles and maintain your progress. Consider potential triggers, temptations, or situations that may undermine your efforts, and strategize how to navigate them effectively. Having contingency plans in place increases your resilience and prepares you to overcome setbacks.

By integrating all these elements into your habit change plan, you create a roadmap that provides clarity, structure, and flexibility. Your plan should serve as a guide, helping you stay focused, motivated, and adaptable as you navigate the challenges and opportunities that arise during the habit change process. Regularly review and update your plan as needed, ensuring that it continually aligns with your goals and aspirations. Remember: a well-designed habit change plan increases your chances of success and empowers you to transform your habits effectively.

Conclusion

In this chapter, we have explored the essential elements of habit analysis and planning as integral parts of achieving successful habit change. We discussed the importance of setting measurable criteria for progress, establishing clear objectives, and selecting appropriate strategies. We also emphasized the value of integrating intrinsic and extrinsic resources into our habit change plans. By creating a comprehensive plan with a clear timeline, action steps, and contingency plans, we set ourselves up for success in transforming our habits.

Understanding the distinction between the plan and the process is crucial. While the plan serves as a roadmap, outlining the specific actions and strategies, the process itself encompasses the broader journey of habit change. By following the principles outlined in this book, we engage in a comprehensive process that empowers us to instill positive habits in our lives and eradicate negative ones from it, leading to personal growth, career advancement, and business success.

As we transition to the next chapter, we will delve into practical techniques for habit conditioning and management. These techniques will provide us with valuable tools to initiate smaller actions, understand the role of triggers, and reinforce positive habits. By incorporating these techniques into our habit change process, we can further strengthen our ability to align our behaviors with our desired outcomes.

In conclusion, habit analysis and planning are critical components of successful habit change. By setting measurable criteria, generating effective strategies, and utilizing available resources, we lay the foundation for transformative habit change. As we continue our journey, let us embrace the power of habit conditioning and management to further enhance our progress.

Summary Q & A

1. Why is planning crucial in the habit change process?
   Planning helps us navigate the complexities of habit change and make intentional choices.
2. What are the benefits of defining clear objectives?
   Defining clear objectives helps us focus our efforts.
3. Why is it important to establish metrics for measuring habit transformation?
   Metrics serve as tangible indicators that provide feedback and guide us toward our habit change goals.
4. How can leveraging intrinsic and extrinsic resources support habit transformation?
   They create a robust support system that enhances our chances of success in habit transformation.
5. Give an example of an extrinsic resource you can use for habit change.
   Some examples include coaching and support networks.
6. How can habit tracking apps support habit change?
   They allow you to record and track your habits, set reminders, visualize progress, and gain insights into your behavior.
7. What is the role of coaching in habit change?
   Coaching provides you with personalized guidance, support, & accountability throughout your habit transformation journey.
8. What should you consider when evaluating strategies for habit change?
   Consider their feasibility, practicality, and alignment with your goals and values.
9. What role do deadlines play in habit change?
   Deadlines create a sense of urgency, help you maintain focus, and provide you with self-accountability.
10. How can a coach and a habit tracking app complement each other in habit change?
    By providing you with personalized guidance, accountability, and data-driven insights.

Exercises

1. Choose one habit you wish to change or develop in your life. Create a clear plan outlining the specific steps you will take to achieve this habit transformation.

2. Identify three specific objectives related to the habit you want to change. Ensure these objectives are measurable and provide a clear target for your efforts.

3. Determine three measurable metrics that you can use to track your progress in transforming the chosen habit. Consider factors such as frequency, duration, quality, or subjective indicators related to the habit.

4. Identify two intrinsic resources and two extrinsic resources that you can leverage to support your habit transformation.

5. Reflect on the potential negative consequences of maintaining the current habit you wish to change. Write down three specific consequences that highlight the urgency and importance of habit change in your life, career, or business.

6. Think of a complex routine or set of behaviors that you would like to make automatic. Break down the routine into smaller, manageable chunks.

7. Choose a habit you would like to change or eliminate. Identify the triggers or cues that lead to this habit and develop a plan to avoid or modify those them.

8. Select a habit that you struggle to maintain consistently. Set up a habit tracking system, such as a habit tracker app or a physical calendar, to monitor your progress.

9. Pick a habit that requires a specific environment or setup. Create a designated space or area that supports the habit. Organize the necessary tools or materials in a way that is easily accessible.

10. Identify a habit you would like to develop and associate it with a positive reward. Determine a small reward that you will give yourself each time you successfully perform the habit.

Principle 3:
Embrace Accountability

Building a Supportive Environment for Growth

"Accountability breeds response-ability."
— Stephen Covey

Assuming responsibility for our actions and behaviors grants us the power to consciously address a wide range of challenges, events, and stimuli that we encounter in our lives. This includes not only external difficulties and circumstances, but also internal struggles, societal pressures, diverse perspectives, cultural differences, and various forms of stimuli that shape our experiences and interactions. By taking accountability, we cultivate the capacity to navigate and respond thoughtfully to the vast array of situations and influences that shape our personal growth and collective well-being. In this chapter, we explore how accountability and support shape the process of changing habits. When it comes to forming or modifying habits, we should never go it alone. We need external reinforcement and guidance to navigate the challenges we will encounter on our way to success.

Key Question:
How can accountability and support enhance habit change and empower individuals to overcome obstacles and achieve lasting results?

Accountability ensures we remain consistent and persistent as we work toward our goals, even in the face of discomfort or obstacles. By measuring and monitoring the progress we are making in building and maintaining habits, we bridge the gap between our intentions (or our desire for change) and our actions (or the changes themselves). Moreover, accountability provides us with consequences and rewards for our behavior. Whether we are struggling to implement a new habit in our lives or reaching habit milestones we never thought possible, accountability reinforces our setbacks and successes.

However, accountability alone is not enough for habit mastery. When combined with accountability, support helps us manage the challenges that we face in building or breaking habits. The encouragement, feedback, and mentorship of others drives our commitment to progress. We must leverage this support for motivation and guidance, particularly during moments when our willpower wanes. We must also engineer environments that help us succeed instead of working against us. Together, accountability and support transform the habit-building process from an arduous battle against ourselves to a triumph of partnership and teamwork. With their collective strength backing our every effort, no challenge appears insurmountable and progress becomes an inevitable reality.

Accountability & Why It is Necessary

Accountability is the willingness to accept responsibility for your own behavior — and it can make or break the habit-building process. Accountability ensures you follow through and remain committed to your own success despite obstacles or discomfort along the way. People who practice accountability measure and monitor their habits so they can stay on track toward their goals. This provides them with external support — whether that support comes from other people or through habit tracking software — that empowers them to stay motivated when their habits change.

Accountability provides you with consequences when you fail to stick with your habits and rewards when you succeed. It helps you identify slip-ups or backsliding quickly so you can course correct, and it highlights milestones you achieve to inspire you to make continued progress. For your habits to flourish, it is essential you have accountability systems in place that involve comprehensive planning, record-keeping, and support from others in your community.

Types of Accountability

Accountability is the key to building better habits. There are two main types of accountability:

External
External accountability involves making commitments to others who can track your progress and check-in on milestones. When others are invested in your success or work with you toward a shared goal, it creates a sense of responsibility that is hard to ignore or make excuses for. You have to show up and deliver due to not wanting to let others down or be perceived as unreliable.

Internal
Internal accountability means holding yourself responsible for your progress and actions. It is the ability to set goals and ensure you follow through with expectations you've set for yourself. For most, this type of accountability is rarely effective. The ability to generate high internal willpower to push through discomfort or obstacles and stay focused on goals is extremely difficult. Internal accountability is challenging to establish or maintain, especially when motivation is low or willpower is depleted.

In some cases, self-accountability can also be dangerous. Internal motivation alone is rarely enough to overcome powerful addictive habits due to impaired self-control and judgment, lack of meaningful consequences, susceptibility to excuses and discouragement, and a tendency toward wishful thinking.

Even if you think you have strong internal accountability, it is still beneficial to leverage an external accountability source. For example, if you always exercise alone, you may avoid adding intensity or stay complacent at a certain level. But with a trainer pushing you, you rise to meet the challenges and endure the temporary discomfort for the long-term rewards of mastering a healthier and stronger body.

Accountability Strategies

The most effective approach is to establish both internal and external accountability. There is a certain amount of internal resolve that is necessary even with an external accountability strategy. You strengthen your chances of accomplishment by leveraging both. Whatever method you choose, accountability means building expectations with consequences. Define specific and realistic targets, share them with others, and establish rewards and repercussions if you do or do not follow through. While success lies within you, let's look at some effective strategies you can use to improve your motivation and discipline as you work to change your habits.

Coaching

Unlike most kinds of therapy, coaching provides you with results-focused support for habit change. Therapy is most suitable for individuals dealing with complex emotional and mental health conditions that affect their ability to cope with life experiences. When it comes to habit formation or modification, however, many people turn to coaching. Coaching allows you to zero in on the precise skills and strategies you need to master your habits and gives you access to guidance from an expert dedicated to your progress and success. A coach helps you outline your plan, holds you accountable to your milestones, and gives you feedback or encouragement to keep you on track toward your goals. Coaches energize you and equip you with proven techniques to forge or break habits at will. Coaches employ several methods to maintain client accountability, keeping them on track toward their goals:

1. ***Clear Goal Setting:*** Coaches work with clients to define clear, measurable, and realistic goals. This provides a concrete target for the client to aim for and allows both parties to track progress objectively.

2. ***Regular Check-Ins:*** Regular meetings or check-ins provide an opportunity to discuss progress, address concerns, and re-adjust plans as needed. This keeps the client's progress at the forefront and facilitates timely course corrections.

3. ***Action Plans:*** Coaches help clients create action plans, breaking down larger goals into manageable tasks. This makes the process less overwhelming and provides a clear path forward.

4. ***Progress Reports:*** Regular reporting of progress helps clients see their achievements and areas needing improvement. This can be highly motivating and serves to reinforce the coaching process.

5. ***Feedback & Reflection:*** Coaches provide constructive feedback and encourage clients to reflect on their experiences. This helps clients understand their strengths and weaknesses, and learn from their experiences.

6. ***Assigning Homework:*** Assigning tasks or exercises for clients to complete between sessions can reinforce what was learned during coaching and encourage consistent effort.

7. ***Encouragement & Motivation:*** Coaches serve as cheerleaders, providing positive reinforcement and encouragement to keep clients motivated, especially during challenging times.

8. ***Using Tools & Technology:*** Using tools like coaching apps or platforms can facilitate tracking of goals, tasks, and progress, and provide a visual representation of the client's journey.

9. ***Creating Consequences:*** Some coaches may arrange consequences (either positive or negative) related to progress. For example, rewarding achievements or creating repercussions for not meeting commitments can increase motivation.

10. ***Peer Accountability:*** Coaches may encourage group coaching sessions or buddy systems where clients can hold each other accountable, providing another layer of motivation.

Remember, accountability should be collaborative and supportive, not punitive. The main goal is to empower clients to take ownership of their goals and actions.

Technology

Technology platforms provide users tools for tracking, measuring, and staying accountable to their habits. Habit trackers record your progress, provide you with visual data of your behavioral patterns, and notify you when it's time to take action. When used in combination with a coach, accountability software can dramatically improve your outcomes as you work to change your habits. Habit tracking apps, such as Arootah's Habit Coach app, also deliver feedback and reinforcement 24/7 so you always know where you stand and what you need to change to reach your goals.

Environment

Your environment and community can either empower you to succeed or lead you to stumble during your journey to change your habits. For example, if you are trying to build a habit of walking around your neighborhood every evening, leaving your sneakers beside the front door provides you with a visual cue to lace up your shoes as soon as you arrive home from work.

Design environments that are conducive to habit-building then surround yourself with people who share your priorities and values.

Your Peer Group
The company you keep can determine your destiny and they are a window into your future self. This idea was popularized by motivational speaker, Jim Rohn, who famously asserted: You are the average of the five people you spend the most time with. These people have an influence over your mindset, values, priorities, habits, and outcomes. This influence is known as "social contagion" or "mirroring". By surrounding yourself with people who challenge and inspire you, you'll begin to strengthen your habits through collaboration and teamwork. Likewise, by surrounding yourself with negative people, you may find yourself swimming upstream while fighting against bad habits and routines. Choose your company wisely.

Public Commitments
Announcing your habit goals on social media or sharing them with colleagues and friends can strongly motivate you to follow through with them. Nobody likes to be a hypocrite and — when your pride and integrity is on the line —it's much easier to stay on track. Share updates on your habit goals, milestones and wins via social media platforms. Let others cheer you on and ask you about your progress. The social support and potential embarrassment you might experience if you slip up will keep you striving toward success.

Team Accountability
Team accountability works in part because no one wants to be the weakest link or let their team down. When you commit to shared goals or habits with others, you feel obligated to follow through and do your part due to social pressure and the desire to avoid embarrassment. If you struggle or fail to meet expectations, you risk being seen as unreliable or not pulling

your weight by those who depend on you. This motivates you to show up and succeed for the good of the team.

Groups that work well together begin to identify as a collective, rather than as separate individuals. Your success and progress become intertwined with the success of your peers and partners. You feel driven to achieve not just for yourself but for others who share in your experience and results. You become accountable to contributing value and doing whatever work is required to accomplish goals or form habits, not wanting to be perceived as the weak link jeopardizing shared aims or outcomes.

Competition

Competition ignites motivation by leveraging your drive to outperform others or surpass your previous success. When accountability depends on internal factors alone, it is easy to make excuses or rationalize poor performance without consequences. Competition introduces external accountability by comparing your progress to objective measures and the achievements of your peers.

There are many forms of competition you can use to boost accountability:

- *Metrics or Key Performance Indicators:* Many people use metrics or KPIs to compare their progress with pre-established targets, budgets, or ratings. When they fall short of these metrics, they may then adopt new strategies to improve their chances of success. When they meet or surpass a metric, they may feel motivated to make continuous improvement. This is known as competing against yourself.

- *Rivals:* Competition against your rivals can spur you to prove your team's or organization's superiority through measurable wins and advancement. The desire to outperform your teammates can also be a friendly rivalry that keeps everyone operating at their full potential. Peer competition demands that you change strategies for success on an ongoing basis so you can stay ahead of the pack.

- *Leaderboards or Rankings:* Many leaders and organizations use platforms that publicly compare and rank them against their peers or rank their organizations according to key metrics. Your position on the leadership board depends on how you measure up with your competitors and you can use these measurements as a form of accountability as you strive to earn the recognition that comes with taking over a top spot on the board.

- *Past Performances:* If you believe you are your own worst critic, you may find self-competition productive. When you begin performing against your own past performances, you may feel compelled to hold yourself accountable to your previous achievements and make continuous progress.

Competition powerfully reinforces accountability during the habit building process by providing you with external pressure and consequences for unproductive behaviors. Consider using various forms of competition to accelerate your habits and meet your goals. Compete against metrics, peers, rankings, and your own historical best/s to beat your self-imposed limitations and redefine what you can accomplish. Championship is contagious and competition brings out the best in you — and those around you — driving you toward progress.

Quantifying Progress

To determine whether your actions are helping you accomplish the outcomes and transformation you desire, be sure to use measurable systems of accountability. When it comes to habits, you must quantify your progress to gain insights into your behavior that fuel your motivation and continued advancement. Measurement makes the intangible tangible through metrics connected to your priorities and goals.

Numbers do not lie and provide you with an objective reflection of reality that enables you to course correct and persevere through challenges.

To begin measuring your progress, select the indicators you will use to evaluate your habit and performance *wins* over both short and long periods of time. For daily habits, track frequency, duration, or other indicators of your progress. You can even broaden your system of measurement to include the benefits or rewards you experience from habitual practice to drive your motivation. Review how you feel before, during, and after the habit to determine if it aligns with your values and you need to make any adjustments. Below, we explore how you can measure your progress in life, career, and business:

Life: If your goal is to improve your fitness level, use metrics such as the number of workouts you complete, the distance you run, or the weight you lift each week. By tracking these metrics over time, you can objectively evaluate your progress, identify areas for improvement, and stay motivated to achieve your desired fitness outcomes. Additionally, monitoring how you feel before, during, and after engaging in healthy habits provides valuable insights into the positive impact they may have on your overall well-being, enabling you to make necessary adjustments and sustain motivation.

Career: To track progress and gauge the effectiveness of your career-related habits, you can measure key performance indicators (KPIs) and milestones relevant to your field. For example, if you aim to increase your sales performance, you may track metrics such as the number of leads generated, conversion rates, and revenue. By quantifying these indicators, you can identify patterns, areas of improvement, and adjust your strategies accordingly. Measurement empowers you to set specific goals, track your progress, and make data-driven decisions to enhance your performance and advance in your career.

Business: Managers rely on various metrics to quantify their fund's performance, such as the rate of return, risk-adjusted metrics (such as the Sharpe ratio), and portfolio composition. These measurements provide managers with insight into their fund's profitability, risk exposure, and alignment with investment objectives. By carefully tracking and analyzing these indicators, managers can make informed decisions about portfolio adjustments, risk management strategies, and potential investment opportunities.

Once you have a better understanding of how close you are to changing your habits and how your habits make you feel, revise targets or metrics that are unrealistic or that fail to motivate you to deliver maximum effort and output. Make evidence-based decisions quickly by relying on data that signals the need for course correction or innovation. Compare your progress against key performance indicators and industry benchmarks to ensure you are optimizing outcomes.

Accountability requires measurement to determine if you are making progress at the rate and scale you desire. Select metrics that quantify your habit development, performance, and key wins or milestones. Track obstacles and how you navigate them over time. Score your strengths and opportunities for improvement. Compare progress against targets and external benchmarks. These metrics will set you up for sustainable success.

Deadlines

Deadlines are important for building new habits and breaking old ones. Without deadlines, habits are hard to start or stick with because there's nothing keeping you accountable. Setting start and end dates makes your habits concrete and gives you a goal to work toward. Deadlines also provide you with a structured time period that keeps you from procrastinating and introduces you to consequences, such as disappointment, if you do not achieve your goals. To use deadlines well, you need to plan ahead and review them regularly to stay on track.

Setting an end date won't help you unless you map out the milestones to reach it, however, and that's where scheduling comes in.

Scheduling

Scheduling gives your habits traction by turning them into concrete actions. A schedule turns a vision into reality. Once you've landed on a deadline, set aside time to practice your habits and anchor those practice sessions to your calendar. Begin with just minutes at a time and stick to that schedule until it becomes second nature. Let your progress and small wins drive you toward change, rather than unrealistic ideas of instant perfection. Increase the time you spend working on your habits as you improve your motivation through long-term repetition and results.

As you work toward your priorities, analyze how you spent your time. See what did and didn't work, then make changes to your deadlines and schedule as needed to keep yourself on track. Learn from your wins and failures to create a better plan next time. The life you want is built one day and habit at a time. Progress comes from persistence, not exhaustion and, when you map your daily, weekly, and yearly schedules around your persistence, you set yourself up for success.

Conclusion

In conclusion, accountability emerges as a non-negotiable element of achieving habit mastery, providing us with the necessary motivation, consequences, and rewards to ensure consistent follow-through. By anchoring our habits to external sources of accountability, such as record-keeping, goal setting, deadlines, and the support of coaches or communities, we create a strong framework for sustained progress. Accountability and support offer us the leverage we need to overcome obstacles and continue our journey toward habit transformation.

Our environment and social connections play a pivotal role in shaping our habits. By consciously designing our surroundings to support positive behaviors and surrounding ourselves with individuals who uplift and inspire us, we create an environment conducive to progress. Conversely, removing triggers and negative influences safeguards us against unhealthy habits. Recognizing the power of social contagion, we must choose our relationships wisely and seek communities that align with our goals.

Technology platforms and habit trackers provide invaluable support, offering tools for heightened awareness and accountability. Coaching apps stand as virtual mentors, offering guidance and reinforcement around the clock, enabling us to achieve more. Public commitments provide us with external social pressure that bolsters our commitment to follow through on our habits.

In answering the key question of how accountability and support can enhance habit change and empower individuals to overcome obstacles and achieve lasting results, we find that accountability forms the bedrock of habit mastery, while support provides the necessary reinforcement, guidance, and motivation to navigate the challenges that arise. Together, they create a framework for sustained progress, transforming aspirations into reality. Through the power of accountability and support, we harness the strength to forge new paths, break free from unhealthy habits, and unlock the potential for lasting transformation in our lives. Now that we've learned how accountability can keep us on track toward our habit change goals, we will learn how triggers — both good and bad — can influence our behavior.

Summary Q & A

1. What is accountability and why is it necessary for habit change?
   It provides external support and consequences for sticking with or failing to follow through with your habits.

2. How does coaching contribute to accountability?
   Coaching provides us with targeted support and personalized guidance for habit change.

3. In what areas can coaching be beneficial?
   Coaching can be beneficial in personal development and life improvement, as well as in the context of business and career development.

4. How does environment influence habits?
   Your environment and community can either enable or sabotage your habits.

5. How can technology support accountability in habit formation?
   A habit tracking app, provides tools for tracking, measuring, and staying accountable to your habits.

6. Why are deadlines and schedules important for habit formation?
   Deadlines and schedules make habits concrete by driving us to set goals and establish boundaries around our time.

7. How does the hyper-rewarding nature of certain foods affect our eating habits?
   They activate the reward centers in our brain, causing us to experience cravings.

8. Why is measurement important for accountability?
   It allows you to quantify progress and gain insights that fuel motivation, revision, and continued advancement.

9. How can changing our environment support building healthier eating habits?
   It helps reduce exposure to cues that trigger unhealthy habit loops while providing alternatives to meet our underlying needs.

10. Why is it important to set up our environment for success when building new habits?
    It helps make the healthy choice the easy choice.

Exercises

1. Write three accountability strategies that support habit change.

2. Think of a specific habit you want to develop. How can you leverage support from others to reinforce this habit?

3. Create a plan outlining your habit goals and milestones.

4. Identify one positive environment or community that aligns with your habit aims.

5. Sign up for a habit tracking app that can help you stay accountable to your habits.

6. Think of a habit you want to publicly commit to. Share it with a friend, family member, or on social media.

7. Take a look at your kitchen or pantry and identify and remove any unhealthy foods that might be triggering unhealthy eating habits.

8. Make a list of alternative snacks or foods that you can keep on hand for moments when cravings strike. Include nutritious options that satisfy your cravings without derailing your progress.

9. Create a daily schedule for your week. Account for all of your priorities, making sure to also include time for self-care, family, friends and fun.

10. Reflect on your daily routines and identify any environmental cues or triggers that lead to unhealthy habits.

Principle 4:
Harness the Power of Triggers

Leveraging Catalysts for Lasting Evolution

*"The power to control your habits lies in
understanding the triggers that initiate them."*
- Gretchen Rubin

Have you ever found yourself suddenly craving something intensely? Perhaps something that you wish you weren't craving because deep down you knew it wasn't good for you? How did that happen? You were triggered! The importance of mastering triggers cannot be overstated. Triggers can either propel us toward our goals and aspirations or drag us into the realm of unwanted habits and behaviors. By developing awareness and control over them, we can effectively initiate positive habits and break free from detrimental patterns of behavior. Triggers profoundly influence the habit change process, serving as the catalysts that set our behaviors into motion. They possess the remarkable ability to shape our choices, actions, and ultimately, the trajectory of our lives. In this chapter, we embark on an exploration of triggers, aiming to unravel the "how" and "why" behind their potent impact on our habits and behaviors. By understanding the definition and significance of triggers as well as strategies to effectively manage them, we can also learn how to harness their power for positive habit change and personal transformation.

Key Question:
*How can we effectively manage triggers to initiate and shape habit
formation, as well as eradicate unwanted habits?*

A trigger is an internal or external stimulus that prompts us to initiate habitual behavior. It can be as simple as a sound, a visual cue, a particular time of day, an emotional state, or even a preceding action. Triggers can also be thoughts! Triggers have a remarkable ability to kick-start our habits, leading us down familiar paths of behavior without conscious effort. By recognizing, understanding, and learning to manage these triggers effectively, we gain the power to consciously shape our habits to transform our lives, careers, and businesses. Whether we aspire to cultivate productive habits in our lives, enhance our professional performance, or optimize the operations of our businesses, unraveling the mysteries of triggers is essential for sustainable and successful habit change.

Every time a trigger precedes a habit, our brains strengthen the association between a habit and its trigger. This associative process is described in neuroscience as Hebbian learning, and can be summarized by "neurons that fire together, wire together." As an association between a habit and a trigger increases, the habit becomes more and more ingrained until we can perform our habits on full auto-pilot.[21]

Throughout this chapter, we will explore various facets of triggers and their role in habit formation and eradication. We will revisit the science behind triggers, understanding how they interact with our brains and influence our behaviors. Additionally, we will discuss the practical strategies and techniques you can use to manage triggers, empowering you to take charge of your habits. By the end of this chapter, you will have the knowledge and tools to identify, analyze, and navigate triggers effectively, paving the way for positive habit change and personal growth.

---

[21] Forcing Function. "Triggers: The Key to Building and Breaking Habits." *Medium*, 15 Dec. 2019, medium.com/@ForcingFunction/triggers-the-key-to-building-and-breaking-habits-fa8ed153ab0c.

The First Stage of the Habit Loop: Trigger

The Habit Loop is a cycle of behavior with four key players: the trigger, the craving, the behavior, and the reward. Each step in the cycle influences the next step, creating the flow that keeps our habits alive and kicking. At the start of the Habit Loop is the trigger.

Triggers are the cues or signals that initiate our habitual behaviors, setting the stage for what follows. They can be external stimuli, such as a ringing phone or the smell of freshly baked cookies, or internal cues, such as a specific thought or emotion.

Just like running a macro or launching a computer program, triggers set off a series of automatic actions. Once triggered, our brains go on autopilot, driving us to execute the familiar routine we associate with the trigger without conscious effort.

Types of Triggers: Biology & Neuroscience

In the habit loop, the trigger works by influencing our behaviors and shaping our daily routines. To fully comprehend its impact, let's examine the two types of triggers, external and internal, and then delve into the biology and neuroscience that underlies their mechanisms. By understanding the intricate workings of our brains and their response to triggers, we can gain deeper insights into the formation of our habits.

External Triggers

Environmental Cues

External triggers, such as environmental cues, and preceding actions activate specific neural pathways in our brains. When we encounter visual, auditory, or olfactory cues in our surroundings, they stimulate certain regions of the brain associated with habit formation.[22] When we perform certain actions, such as brushing our teeth, we may automatically reach for dental floss or mouthwash. Many actions are linked together in this habitual way — remember, neurons that 'fire together, wire together'. These cues act as signals that prompt our brains to drive us to perform behaviors automatically without conscious effort or decision making. Through repeated exposure to these environmental cues, our brains form strong associations between the cues and the corresponding habits, leading to their automatic activation.

Examples:

> **Life:** Whenever you see your running shoes placed beside the front door, they serve as a visual cue that triggers your habit of going for a daily run.

> **Career:** When you enter the office and see your desk neatly organized with your computer turned on, it signals the start of your work routine.

> **Business:** When you walk into a meeting room with multiple chairs facing a projector screen, the arrangement of the objects in the room triggers the habit of conducting client presentations and pitches.

Time-Based Triggers

Time-based triggers rely on our brain's ability to perceive and track time. Our brains have an internal clock, known as the circadian rhythm, which regulates our sleep-wake cycle and other physiological processes. Time-based triggers align with our brain's perception of time and can activate specific habits based on the timing of events or activities. This synchronization between external cues and our brain's internal clock contributes to the formation and execution of time-based habits.

---

[22] Graybiel AM. Habits, rituals, and the evaluative brain. Annu Rev Neurosci. 2008;31:359-87. doi: 10.1146/annurev.neuro.29.051605.112851. PMID: 18558860.

Examples:

> **Life:** When the clock strikes 6:00 AM, it serves as a time-based trigger for your morning meditation practice.

> **Career:** When you receive an email notification at 4:00 PM indicating the release of a new market report, the alert on your phone triggers your habit of reviewing and analyzing market trends.

> **Business:** Every Monday morning at 9:00 AM, you schedule a team meeting, which serves as a time-based trigger for discussing investment strategies and setting goals.

People-Based Triggers

Our interactions with other individuals also have a neural basis when it comes to triggers. Our brain is highly social, and when we observe or engage with others, it activates regions associated with empathy, imitation, and social learning. People-based triggers can influence our habits through social norms, peer pressure, or our desire for social acceptance. The neural processes involved in social cognition and influence play a significant role in shaping our behaviors based on the cues we receive from others.

Examples:

> **Life:** Meeting a friend at the gym who is always enthusiastic about fitness motivates and triggers your habit of pushing yourself during workouts.

> **Career:** Attending a conference and hearing a renowned hedge fund manager speak about their investment strategies triggers your desire to learn and implement similar approaches in your own career.

> **Business:** Having a discussion with a successful entrepreneur who has built a thriving business inspires you

and triggers you to take calculated risks and pursue growth opportunities.

Internal Triggers

Emotions and Mood

Internal triggers, such as emotions and mood, involve intricate neural networks in our brains. Emotions result from the interplay of various brain regions, including the amygdala, prefrontal cortex, and insula.[23] Different emotions can act as triggers for specific habits as our brains seeks to regulate and respond to these emotional states. The activation of emotional circuits in our brains prompts the execution of habits that provide relief, comfort, or a sense of control.[24]

Examples:

> **Life:** Feeling stressed after a long day triggers you to engage in the habit of eating comfort food to alleviate tension.

> **Career:** Experiencing excitement and anticipation before a crucial client meeting triggers you to engage in the habit of reviewing and rehearsing your presentation to ensure you speak confidently and persuasively.

> **Business:** Feeling a sense of urgency and determination after encountering a new investment opportunity triggers you to engage in the habit of conducting thorough research and analysis to evaluate its potential.

---

[23] Šimic G, Tkalcic M, Vukic V, Mulc D, Španic E, Šagud M, Olucha-Bordonau FE, Vukši☐ M, R Hof P. Understanding Emotions: Origins and Roles of the Amygdala. Biomolecules. 2021 May 31;11(6):823. doi: 10.3390/biom11060823. PMID: 34072960; PMCID: PMC8228195.

[24] Jordan E Pierce , Julie Péron, The basal ganglia and the cerebellum in human emotion, *Social Cognitive and Affective Neuroscience*, Volume 15, Issue 5, May 2020, Pages 599–613, https://doi.org/10.1093/scan/nsaa076

Thoughts and Mental Associations

Our thoughts and mental associations have a basis in the neural connections within our brains. When we think about specific concepts, memories, or ideas, various regions of our brains become active and establish connections.[25] These neural connections become stronger with repetition and reinforcement, creating pathways that facilitate the retrieval and execution of associated habits. Thoughts and mental associations act as triggers that activate the neural circuits responsible for habit enactment.

Examples:

> **Life:** Thinking about a relaxing beach vacation triggers you to engage in the habit of practicing deep breathing exercises to reduce stress and promote relaxation.

> **Career:** Reflecting on successful trades and positive investment outcomes triggers you to engage in the habit of approaching new investment opportunities with a confident and strategic mindset in your hedge fund career.

> **Business:** Associating networking events with opportunities for business growth triggers you to engage in the habit of preparing informative elevator pitches and engaging in meaningful conversations to expand your network and attract potential investors to your business.

Identifying Triggers

Why is it Important to Identify Triggers

Identifying triggers requires a curious mindset, keen observation, and a willingness to delve into the details of our habits. By developing self-awareness and mindfulness, tracking, and analyzing our habits, and recognizing patterns and common triggers, we sharpen our detective skills and uncover the hidden cues that prompt our behaviors. This detective

---

[25] Wood, Wendy and Dennis Rünger. "Psychology of Habit." *Annual review of psychology* 67 (2016): 289-314 .

work equips us with the knowledge we need to intervene and modify our responses to triggers, ultimately empowering us to shape our habits and create positive behavior changes.

Self-Awareness and Understanding
By identifying triggers, we gain a deeper understanding of ourselves and our behaviors. Triggers provide valuable insights into why we engage in certain habits and the circumstances that prompt us to do so. This self-awareness allows us to recognize patterns, tendencies, and vulnerabilities that influence our habits.

Examples:

> **Life:** You may discover that, when feeling stressed or overwhelmed, you often turn to unhealthy coping mechanisms such as emotional eating. This self-awareness allows you to understand your emotional patterns and the circumstances that lead you to engage in the habit, enabling you to make better nutritional choices and find healthier ways to manage stress.

> **Career:** Receiving critical feedback or facing tight deadlines may help you recognize that you often react to criticism with self-doubt or perfectionism. Understanding these triggers can help you develop strategies to build resilience, manage your emotions, and maintain confidence in your work.

> **Business:** Changes in market conditions or high-pressure client interactions can provide businesses insights into how these external factors impact decision-making and team dynamics. Understanding these triggers can lead to more informed and strategic responses to challenges and opportunities in the business environment.

Behavior Prediction and Control
Once we identify triggers, we can predict and anticipate our behavioral responses more effectively. By understanding the

cues that prompt our habits, we gain a sense of control over our behaviors. This awareness empowers us to make conscious choices and exert intentional effort in managing our responses to triggers.

Examples:

Life: Identifying triggers, such as scrolling through social media or seeing junk food in the kitchen, can help you predict and anticipate your impulsive behaviors. With this awareness, you can exercise control by implementing strategies to manage these behaviors such as setting phone usage limits or keeping healthy snacks readily available.

Career: Recognizing triggers, such as receiving praise or positive feedback from colleagues, can help you predict your behavioral responses and ensure they align with your professional goals. By being aware of how external recognition impacts your motivation and work habits, you can consciously steer your actions toward continued growth and improvement.

Business: Identifying triggers, such as encountering changes in the competitive landscape or industry trends, enables business leaders to anticipate their organizations' response. This prediction and control allow for strategic decision-making, timely adjustments, and the ability to seize opportunities in a rapidly evolving business environment.

Targeted Habit Intervention

Identifying triggers helps us focus our efforts on the specific cues that initiate habits. Instead of trying to change a habit in its entirety, we can intervene at the trigger level to disrupt the automatic response. By addressing triggers, we can implement targeted strategies and interventions to modify or redirect our behaviors.

Examples:

> **Life:** Identifying triggers, such as feeling bored or lonely, can prompt you to engage in unproductive habits such as excessive social media scrolling. By addressing these triggers, you can redirect your behaviors toward more fulfilling activities by practicing targeted and alternative habits like reading a book or connecting with friends.

> **Career:** Recognizing triggers, such as encountering challenging tasks or uncertain situations, can help you design interventions to boost your confidence and competence. Implementing strategies such as seeking support from mentors, acquiring new skills, or breaking tasks into manageable steps can help you effectively address these triggers to enhance your professional growth.

> **Business:** Identifying triggers, such as changes in customer preferences or disruptive technological advancements, allows businesses to develop targeted interventions to stay competitive. This may involve diversifying product offerings, investing in research and development, or adopting innovative strategies to adapt to the changing market landscape.

Habit Change and Transformation

Triggers play a critical role in habit formation, maintenance, and change. By identifying triggers, we can actively work on replacing negative or unwanted triggers with positive ones that align with our desired habits. This intentional modification of triggers contributes to the rewiring of our neural pathways and the establishment of new and healthier habits.

Examples:

> **Life:** By identifying triggers such as negative self-talk, you can work on replacing them with positive triggers. This is also true of associating certain environments with

unhealthy behaviors; you can avoid or change unhealthy environments. For example, consciously practicing self-affirmations or creating a supportive environment at home can contribute to the rewiring of your neural pathways and the establishment of healthier habits.

Career: Recognizing triggers, such as procrastination or perfectionism, can be instrumental in initiating habit change. Developing strategies such as setting realistic goals, breaking tasks into smaller steps, or practicing time management techniques can help rewire your behavior and foster professional growth.

Business: Identifying triggers, such as resistance to change or a culture of complacency, allows businesses to initiate transformative efforts. Implementing strategies like fostering a culture of innovation, empowering employees through training and development, or embracing agile practices can lead to a fundamental shift in the organization's habits and drive long-term success.

Prevention of Unwanted Behaviors

Identifying triggers helps us become proactive in avoiding or managing situations that may lead to undesirable habits. By recognizing the specific cues that precede our unwanted behaviors, we can take preventive measures to minimize the occurrence of these triggers or create strategies to counteract their influence.

Examples:

Life: By identifying triggers such as socializing in certain environments that may lead to excessive alcohol consumption, you can take preventive measures to stop yourself from drinking too much. This may involve choosing alternative social activities or attending events that align with your desire to reduce alcohol intake, thus minimizing your chance of encountering the trigger and reducing your risk of engaging in unwanted behaviors.

Career. Recognizing triggers such as unproductive meetings or time spent on non-essential tasks can help you proactively prevent inefficiencies in your work. Implementing strategies such as setting clear meeting agendas, prioritizing tasks, and utilizing time management techniques allows you to counteract these triggers and optimize your productivity.

Business: By implementing preventive measures such as fostering open and transparent communication channels, establishing clear expectations, and providing ongoing feedback and support, businesses can mitigate the occurrence of these triggers and promote a positive work environment.

How to Identify Triggers
Being a detective in identifying triggers requires a curious mindset, keen observation, and a willingness to delve into the details of our habits. By developing self-awareness and mindfulness, tracking and analyzing our habits, and recognizing patterns and common triggers, we sharpen our detective skills and uncover the hidden cues that prompt our behaviors. This detective work equips us with the knowledge we need to intervene and modify our responses to triggers, ultimately empowering us to shape our habits and create positive behavior change.

Self-Awareness and Mindfulness
Developing self-awareness and cultivating mindfulness are essential aspects of identifying triggers. To uncover the cues that drive us to perform specific habits, we must attentively observe our thoughts, emotions, and behaviors. Self-awareness allows us to step back and objectively observe ourselves in various situations, noticing the patterns and triggers that prompt our habits. Through mindfulness practices such as meditation, we sharpen our ability to be fully present in the

moment, enabling us to notice subtle cues and triggers that may go unnoticed otherwise without judgment.

Examples:

Life: By consciously observing your thoughts and emotions, you can become aware of these triggers and their impact on your well-being. Practicing mindfulness techniques such as meditation or journaling can enhance your self-awareness and enable you to recognize and address these triggers more effectively.

Career: By being present in the moment and observing your thoughts and emotions without judgment in high-pressure work environments, you can recognize these triggers and take proactive steps to manage stress, such as implementing relaxation techniques or seeking support from colleagues or mentors.

Business: By cultivating a reflective mindset and paying attention to our mental and emotional states during decision-making, we can recognize our biases and knee-jerk reactions as well as the external pressures that may influence our choices. This awareness enables us to make more informed and intentional decisions so we can avoid potential pitfalls and align our actions with the goals of the business.

Tracking and Analyzing Habits

Tracking and analyzing our habits provides us with valuable clues about the triggers that prompt their activation. By keeping a habit journal or using habit tracking apps, we create a record of each habit occurrence, noting relevant details such as time, location, emotional state, and the actions that result from these details. This data becomes evidence of our emotions and behaviors, allowing us to analyze and detect patterns and correlations. By examining the entries in our habit journal or reviewing the data from habit tracking apps, we can uncover triggers that commonly precede habit enactment.

Examples:

> **Life:** Tracking your exercise habits may reveal that hearing energizing music consistently triggers you to think about working out. By analyzing the data and patterns in your habit tracking, you can gain insights into the specific cues that prompt your desired behaviors.

> **Career:** By documenting your work habits and noting factors such as interruptions, task complexity, or specific work environments, you can identify triggers that decrease your focus and motivation. This awareness allows you to implement strategies to modify or manage these triggers effectively.

> **Business:** By tracking team performance and noting patterns in communication, decision-making, or conflict resolution, leaders can identify triggers that influence team effectiveness. This insight can guide them in implementing strategies to address or modify these triggers for improved collaboration and productivity.

Recognizing Patterns and Common Triggers

In our quest to identify triggers, it is crucial that we pay attention to recurring patterns and triggers that prompt us to engage in different habit behaviors. For example, we may find that stress is a common trigger for various unhealthy coping habits such as emotional eating or nail-biting. By recognizing these patterns and common triggers, we gain a deeper understanding of the cues that shape our behaviors and drive us toward habit change.

Examples:

> **Life:** Many people find that feeling fatigued triggers excessive caffeine consumption, procrastination, or unhealthy snacking. Recognizing these patterns allows you to address the underlying trigger of fatigue by developing

healthier coping mechanisms or making lifestyle adjustments.

Career: Tight deadlines or unclear project requirements may consistently trigger you to experience feelings of stress or anxiety. By recognizing these triggers, you can develop strategies to manage your stress and improve time management, or seek support to mitigate their impact on your performance.

Business: Identifying that certain customer inquiries frequently trigger frustrations or challenges in communication can prompt businesses to develop training programs or implement systems to improve customer service and satisfaction.

Harnessing Triggers for Habit Change

Harnessing triggers for habit change while employing effective strategies to manage and modify them enables us to create a supportive environment for positive behavior change. The following techniques empower us to leverage the power of triggers to reinforce desired habits while navigating the influence of negative triggers to transform our habits for good.

Creating Cue-Action Associations

To link a specific trigger with a desired habit, we must create cue-action associations between them. When we repeatedly and consistently establish a clear connection between a trigger and a corresponding action, we are more likely to perform the desired action in response to that trigger. Over time, the association between the trigger and the habit becomes stronger, making it easier for us to perform the habit behavior in response to the trigger.

Examples:

> **Life**: You can establish a trigger for gratitude by placing a gratitude journal on your bedside table and committing to writing three things you are grateful for every night before going to sleep. The act of seeing the journal serves as a trigger for the habit of expressing gratitude.
>
> **Career**: If you set a reminder on your calendar or phone to review and prioritize tasks at the beginning of each workday, the trigger of the reminder can prompt you to plan and prioritize tasks that help you improve your productivity and efficiency.
>
> **Business**: In a business setting, creating a cue-action association can be used to foster effective communication. For instance, before team meetings, team members can review the meeting agenda and prepare any relevant materials to trigger themselves into active participation in the discussion that follows. This practice can enhance communication within the team.

Designing a Trigger-Rich Environment

Designing a trigger-rich environment involves strategically arranging our surroundings to provide cues that prompt us to engage in our desired habits. By intentionally placing reminders, visual cues, or environmental prompts around ourselves, we create an environment that supports and motivates us to cultivate the habits we desire. For example, if we want to develop a habit of reading more, we can place books in visible locations or create a dedicated reading space in our home. This trigger-rich environment acts as a constant reminder and source of reinforcement to follow-through on habitual behaviors, making it easier for us to get started on a new book.

Examples:

Life: Placing a water bottle on the desk or in prominent locations throughout the house serves as a visual cue and a reminder to drink water regularly and stay hydrated.

Career: Creating a dedicated space in the office with a bookshelf filled with industry-related books or subscribing to relevant newsletters and placing them in visible locations provides employees with visual cues and reminders to engage in continuous learning activities.

Business: Setting up collaborative spaces with whiteboards, sticky notes, and other creative tools motivates businesses to spontaneously generate ideas and facilitates collaborative problem-solving.

Keystone Habits

Keystone habits are powerful habits that have a ripple effect, positively influencing other areas of our lives, careers, or businesses. They act as catalysts for change, leading to the development of other beneficial habits and transforming our overall lifestyle. Keystone habits have the unique ability to create a domino effect, where small changes in one area trigger a cascade of positive behaviors in other areas.

Process of Choosing Keystone Habits:

1. **Identify Areas for Improvement:** Start by identifying the areas of your life where you would like to see positive change. It could be related to health, productivity, relationships, personal growth, or any other aspect that is important to you.

2. **Consider Impact & Alignment:** Evaluate potential habits based on their potential impact and alignment with your desired goals. Look for habits that have the potential to influence multiple areas of your life and align with your values and aspirations.

3. **Reflect on Your Current Routine:** Reflect on your current routine and identify any existing habits that already have a positive influence on other areas. These habits may serve as a foundation for identifying potential keystone habits.

4. **Assess Interconnectedness:** Consider how the habit you are considering can have a domino effect on other behaviors. Will it naturally lead to positive changes in other areas? For example, a keystone habit of regular exercise can improve physical health, mental well-being, and productivity.

5. **Start Small & Build Momentum:** Choose a keystone habit that is attainable and manageable. Starting small allows you to build momentum and make the habit easier to integrate into your daily routine.

Examples of Keystone Habits:

1. **Sleep:** Developing a healthy sleep routine can be a keystone habit with far-reaching effects. Prioritizing sufficient sleep and establishing a consistent sleep schedule can enhance overall well-being. A good night's sleep improves cognitive function, boosts mood, increases energy levels, and supports physical health. By prioritizing sleep, you may find that other areas of your life, such as productivity, concentration, and emotional balance, are positively influenced.

2. **Mindful Eating:** Cultivating a habit of mindful eating can act as a keystone habit for improved nutrition and overall health. Mindful eating involves paying attention to your body's hunger and fullness cues, savoring each bite, and making conscious food choices. This habit can lead to better nutritional choices, improved digestion, and a healthier relationship with food. Additionally, it can create a positive ripple effect on

other areas, such as self-care, body awareness, and mindful decision-making.

3. ***Daily Gratitude Practice:*** Engaging in a daily gratitude practice can serve as a keystone habit for cultivating a positive mindset and enhancing overall well-being. Taking a few moments each day to reflect on what you are grateful for can shift your perspective, increase happiness, and foster a sense of contentment. This habit can influence other areas of life, such as relationships, resilience, and self-esteem.

Keystone Habits can also be Bad Habits

It's important to note that keystone habits can also be negative or detrimental. For example, excessive alcohol consumption can act as a keystone habit with adverse effects. Alcohol may initially serve as a way to cope with stress or socialize, but it can lead to a cascade of negative behaviors, impacting physical health, relationships, productivity, and overall well-being. Recognizing and addressing these keystone habits is crucial for creating positive change and breaking free from harmful patterns.

Remember, the key to choosing keystone habits is to focus on those that have a broad positive influence and are aligned with your goals and values. By implementing and nurturing these habits, you create a ripple effect of positive change that extends beyond the specific habit itself, transforming various aspects of your life along the way.

Habit Stacking

Habit stacking involves linking a new habit with an existing one by specifying a *specific trigger* that prompts the desired behavior. For example, if you're already in the habit of brushing your teeth each night, you can add a new habit of flossing by stating, "After I brush my teeth, I will floss." This way, the existing habit serves as the trigger for the new habit.

Examples:

> **Life:** Habit stacking can be applied to personal habits such as incorporating stretching into a morning routine. By linking the habit of stretching to an existing habit (such as making the bed), you can establish the trigger for stretching by stating, "After I make the bed, I will do a five-minute stretching routine."

> **Career:** After finishing a task or completing a phone call, you can implement a trigger in your routine to review and organize your emails by stating, "After I finish a task or a phone call, I will spend 10 minutes organizing my inbox." This habit stacking serves to enhance your productivity.

> **Business:** After conducting a team meeting, a project manager can establish a trigger for updating project documentation by stating, "After every team meeting, I will review and update the project documentation with the latest decisions and action items." In this way, project management is enhanced.

Implementation Intentions

Implementation intentions, on the other hand, involve creating a specific plan for *when and where* to perform the desired habit. By setting a clear intention and specifying the trigger event, we are more likely to follow through with the desired action. For instance, by stating, "When I arrive home from work, I will immediately change into my workout clothes and go for a run," you establish a clear trigger and plan for engaging in the habit of exercise.

Examples:

> **Life:** You can apply implementation intentions to personal habits such as practicing mindfulness. For instance, you can set a specific plan by stating, "When I wake up in the morning, I will spend five minutes practicing mindful breathing before getting out of bed." This clear trigger and

plan increases the likelihood that you will follow through with the habit.

Career: In a career context, you can use implementation intentions to improve your presentation skills. For example, you can state, "Before every presentation, I will spend 10 minutes rehearsing and visualizing a successful delivery." This implementation intention establishes a clear trigger and plan that prepares you to deliver effective presentations.

Business: In a business setting, you can use implementation intentions to enhance customer service. For instance, you can state, "When a customer reaches out with a complaint, I will listen attentively, empathize, and offer a resolution." This implementation intention establishes a clear trigger and plan that empowers you to deliver exceptional customer service.

Avoiding or Modifying Triggering Situations

To effectively manage triggers, it is important to identify and avoid situations that may lead you to engage in unwanted habits. If certain environments, people, or activities consistently trigger you to engage in negative habits, it may be beneficial to modify or remove those triggering elements from your life. By proactively avoiding or altering triggering situations, we create environments that are conducive to positive habit change.

Examples:

Life: If you are trying to improve your sleep quality, limit your screen time before bed and avoid using electronic devices at least one hour before sleep. Additionally, try replacing the triggering activity with a routine that calms you, such as reading a book or taking a bath, to help yourself fall asleep more quickly.

Career: To reduce workplace distractions, use noise-canceling headphones. Set specific office hours dedicated for uninterrupted work. This adjustment can help you manage interruptions to enhance your focus and productivity.

Business: If a particular client or business partner consistently triggers you to engage in unhealthy coping skills to manage your stress, you may need to reevaluate the business relationship and consider modifying or terminating the partnership to create a more positive and harmonious working environment.

Substituting Positive Triggers for Negative Ones

When confronting negative triggers, it may be helpful to identify alternative positive triggers with which to replace them. By consciously choosing and incorporating new cues that elicit positive responses, we can redirect our behavior toward healthier habits.

Examples:

Life: Instead of reaching for unhealthy snacks whenever you feel stressed, you might try using the trigger of stress to solicit a new behavior that offers positive rewards such as deep breathing exercises, going for a walk, or practicing meditation to promote relaxation and well-being.

Career: Rather than succumbing to the trigger of boredom or lack of motivation and engaging in time-wasting activities, you can substitute your habitual reaction with a positive alternative, such as breaking tasks into smaller and more manageable steps or using a productivity hack such as the Pomodoro Technique. This helps you manage the bad habit of procrastination.

Business: Instead of letting failure or setbacks trigger demotivation or a negative atmosphere, leaders can encourage their team to pivot into a growth mindset. Using the trigger to train the mind to see failure as a learning opportunity allows businesses to overcome any obstacle. In this way, they can strengthen the team dynamics and support team morale.

Implementing Strategies to Resist or Redirect Triggers

In managing and modifying triggers, it is important to have strategies in place to resist or redirect their influence. These strategies can include techniques such as distraction, mindfulness, or cognitive reframing. By practicing mindfulness, we can become aware of triggers as we experience them and consciously choose a different response. Additionally, employing distraction techniques or reframing our thoughts can help us redirect our attention away from the triggering cues and toward more positive behaviors.

Examples:

Life: Using smartphone apps or built-in features that limit screen time, setting phone-free zones and times during the day, or keeping the phone in a different room can help you resist the trigger of phone notifications and help you redirect your attention to more meaningful activities.

Career: Techniques such as practicing deep breathing exercises, taking short breaks for physical activity or relaxation, or engaging in stress-reducing activities (such as listening to calming music) can help you resist the trigger of stress and redirect your focus toward maintaining well-being and productivity.

Business: Using active listening techniques, seeking common ground, or reframing perspectives can help you resist the trigger of confrontation and redirect conversations toward constructive problem-solving and collaboration.

Overcoming Trigger-Related Challenges

On the journey of habit change, we encounter various challenges that test our commitment and resilience. By understanding how to navigate unexpected triggers, build resilience, and maintain awareness and control, we can overcome these challenges and keep moving forward on the path to habit modification. Let's explore practical techniques and insights we can use to overcome trigger-related challenges and continue our transformative journey of habit change.

Dealing with Unexpected Triggers

When we face unexpected triggers arise during your habit change journey, it's important to be prepared and equipped with strategies to navigate them effectively. One approach is to *pause* and observe the trigger without judgment, allowing ourselves to become aware of the thoughts, emotions, and sensations that we are experiencing. By practicing mindfulness in these moments, we can create space to choose a response aligned with our desired habits rather than falling into old patterns. Additionally, having contingency plans in place, such as alternative actions or coping mechanisms, can help us proactively address unexpected triggers.

Examples:

> **Life:** When faced with an unexpected trigger, such as a stressful event, you can pause and observe the trigger without judgment. By practicing mindfulness, you can choose a response better aligned with your health goals (such as deep breathing exercises) instead of falling into old patterns of emotional eating.

> **Career:** When faced with an unexpected trigger, such as an urgent task or a last-minute request, pausing to assess the situation and prioritize tasks can help you manage the trigger effectively. Having contingency plans in place, such as flexible work schedules or resources for delegating tasks, allows you to proactively address unexpected triggers so you can adapt more easily.

> **Business:** When faced with an unexpected trigger such as a supply chain disruption, businesses can pause to evaluate

alternative suppliers or develop contingency plans to minimize the impact. This proactive approach allows businesses to navigate unexpected triggers and maintain operational resilience.

Building Resilience to Triggers

Triggers often exert a powerful influence over our emotions that can make it challenging to resist old habits. Building resilience involves developing strategies to withstand the emotional pull of triggers and maintain our commitment to change. One effective technique is *cognitive reframing*, which involves consciously challenging and replacing negative thoughts or beliefs associated with triggers. *Emotional regulation techniques*, such as deep breathing or engaging in calming activities, can help us manage the emotions triggered by certain situations. Additionally, cultivating a *strong support network* and *seeking accountability* can provide the encouragement and motivation we need to stay resilient in the face of triggers.

Examples:

Life: When you find yourself battling triggers, such as feelings of overwhelm or a lack of motivation, building resilience involves consciously challenging and replacing the negative thoughts or beliefs you associate with those triggers. Practicing cognitive reframing techniques, such as reframing tasks as opportunities for growth or breaking them down into smaller and more manageable steps, can help you overcome procrastination triggers. Engaging in calming activities such as meditation or exercise can help you maintain focus on your desired habits.

Career: When you're dealing with triggers at work, such as confrontational conversations with colleagues or negative feedback, you can consciously challenge the negative thoughts or beliefs you associate with those triggers by practicing cognitive reframing techniques, such as seeking alternative perspectives or finding opportunities for learning and growth. These techniques can help you navigate triggers in a constructive manner. Additionally, seeking support from a strong professional network or mentorship can provide you the encouragement and accountability you need to remain committed to your goals.

Business: When you find yourself confronting triggers in your business, such as financial challenges or changes in customer demand, building resilience involves consciously challenging negative thoughts or beliefs associated with those triggers. Emphasizing adaptive strategies, exploring alternative solutions, and seeking guidance from industry experts or business mentors can help businesses navigate unexpected triggers and maintain resilience in the face of adversity.

Strategies for Maintaining Awareness & Control

Maintaining awareness and control over triggers is crucial for successful habit change. *Habit tracking* is a valuable strategy that involves recording our habits, including the triggers associated with them, to gain insights into patterns and behaviors. By keeping a habit journal or using *habit tracking apps*, we can identify specific triggers and their impact on our habits. This awareness allows us to anticipate potential triggers, develop strategies to manage them, and reinforce positive behaviors. Accountability systems, such as sharing our progress with a trusted friend or joining a support group, can also help us stay mindful and maintain control over our habits.

Examples:

Life: Habit tracking is a valuable strategy that involves recording your habits, including the triggers associated with them, to gain insights into patterns and behaviors. Keeping a habit journal or using habit tracking apps can help you identify specific triggers and their impact on your habits. This awareness allows you to anticipate potential triggers and develop strategies to manage them, such as mindfulness meditation or exercise.

Career: You can use habit tracking to record work-related habits and their associated triggers. Keeping a work-life balance journal or using productivity apps can help you identify specific triggers that may affect that balance. This awareness allows you to develop strategies to maintain control over your personal and professional life, such as setting boundaries, prioritizing self-care, and practicing time management techniques.

Business: Implementing habit tracking methods for tracking key business activities and their triggers can provide you with insights into patterns and behaviors. This awareness allows you to identify triggers that may impact your productivity or performance and develop strategies to manage your schedule, such as optimizing workflows, delegating tasks, or implementing systems for monitoring and improving efficiency.

Personalizing Triggers for Individual Habits
Personalization is key when it comes to triggers. What works for one person may not work for another. Let's explore the importance of customizing triggers, aligning them with specific habit goals, and adapting them as our habits evolve, empowering us to create a personalized and dynamic trigger system for lasting habit change.

Customizing Triggers Based on Personal Preferences
By customizing triggers based on our personal preferences, we can increase their effectiveness. Consider identifying sensory cues or activities that resonate with you personally and align them with your desired habits.

Examples:

Life: If you find the scent of lavender to be calming, you can use it as a trigger for relaxation by lighting a lavender-scented candle or using lavender essential oil when meditating or taking a bath.

Career: If having a clean and organized desk space helps you concentrate better, you can make it a habit to declutter and arrange your workspace before starting work to create an environment that aligns with your personal preferences and triggers a productive mindset.

Business: If vibrant colors and stimulating visuals spark your team's creativity, you could use visual cues such as colorful artwork or inspiring images in brainstorming sessions to create a visually stimulating environment that triggers innovative thinking.

Aligning Triggers with Specific Habit Goals

To optimize the power of triggers, it's important we align them with our specific habit goals. This involves intentionally selecting triggers that directly relate to the desired habit. By creating a clear association between the trigger and the behavior we want to cultivate, we strengthen the connection and make it easier to engage in the habit.

Examples:

Life: If you have a goal to read more books, you might choose to establish a comfortable reading spot in your home, such as a cozy reading nook, and designate it as the trigger for your reading habit. Every time you sit in that spot, it signals to you to pick up a book and begin to read.

Career: If you want to enhance your productivity during focused work sessions, you can select a particular time, such as the early morning when distractions are minimal, as a trigger for deep work. Setting a consistent routine in which you prioritize deep work during a specific period of time reinforces the habit and realigns you with your career goals.

Business: If a business sets a goal to foster better team communication, leadership can designate a daily stand-up meeting to trigger the team members to share updates, discuss challenges, and collaborate on projects. As the team begins to associate the stand-up meetings with communication, they reinforce the habit in alignment with the business's goal of improving collaboration and productivity.

Adapting Triggers as Habits Evolve

Habits are dynamic and evolve over time and so should our triggers. Regularly reviewing and adapting triggers to match the ever-changing nature of our habits is essential for long-term success. As we progress and develop new habits or modify existing ones, it's important to ensure that our triggers continually align with our current goals. By adapting triggers, we keep them relevant and maintain their potency in reinforcing our desired behaviors.

Examples:

Life: If you initially used a specific song as a trigger to start your workout but are finding the song no longer energizes you, you might choose to adapt the trigger by creating a new playlist or changing the trigger altogether. This ensures that the trigger remains relevant and motivational as your fitness habits evolve.

Career: If you initially used a specific time of day, such as the end of the workday, as a trigger to begin journaling, but are finding your energy and focus is more potent in the morning, you could adapt the trigger by shifting your journaling practice to the morning. This adjustment ensures the trigger aligns with your changing preferences and optimizes the habit's effectiveness.

Business: If a business initially used a specific meeting format as the trigger for decision-making discussions but later found decision-making to be too complex, they could adapt the trigger by implementing a different approach, such as a structured decision-making framework. This adaptation ensures that the trigger remains aligned with the evolving needs and challenges of the business.

Conclusion

In conclusion, triggers play a pivotal role in habit conditioning and have a profound impact on our ability to create lasting behavioral change. Throughout this chapter, we explored the various aspects of triggers, from understanding their types and identifying them to harnessing their power for habit change. We learned that triggers serve as catalysts that initiate and reinforce habits, making them essential elements in our journey toward personal transformation. By recognizing the importance of triggers and developing strategies to manage and customize them, we empower ourselves to maintain long-term habit change.

Triggers not only shape our daily routines but also contribute to the formation of new habits and the eradication of old ones. They provide the cues that prompt our brains to engage in automatic behaviors, making them key drivers of sustained behavioral change. By understanding the role of triggers, we can create intentional cue-action associations, design trigger-rich environments, and utilize techniques such as habit stacking and implementation intentions to solidify new habits and replace unwanted ones.

Now, armed with the knowledge and strategies discussed in this chapter, it is up to you to apply them in your life, your career, and your business. By becoming more aware of your triggers, customizing them to your preferences, and harnessing their power, you have the ability to create a trigger system that supports and sustains your desired habits. Remember, habit change is a process, and consistency is key. With each deliberate choice and conscious action, you move closer to the life you envision.

As we transition to the next chapter, it is important to recognize that triggers are just one piece of the puzzle. In the upcoming chapter on habit beliefs, we will delve into the powerful role that our beliefs and mindset play in shaping our habits. By exploring the beliefs we hold about ourselves and our ability to change our thoughts and behaviors, we can unlock new possibilities and overcome any internal barriers that may hinder our progress. The journey of habit change is multi-faceted, and by integrating our understanding of triggers into our exploration of habit beliefs, we pave the way for profound and lasting transformation.

Summary Q & A

1. What is the role of triggers in shaping our habits?
    Triggers are cues or signals that prompt us to engage in habitual behaviors.

2. How do triggers interact with our brains?
    Triggers activate specific neural pathways in our brains.

3. What are the two types of triggers discussed in the chapter?
    The two types of triggers discussed are external triggers and internal triggers.

4. Give examples of external triggers.
    Examples of external triggers include environmental cues, time-based triggers, and people-based triggers.

5. Why is it important to identify triggers?
    Identifying triggers allows us to gain self-awareness and understanding.

6. What is a trigger-rich environment?
    One that involves strategically arranging our surroundings to provide cues that prompt the desired habit.

7. What is habit stacking?
    It involves linking a new habit with an existing one.

8. What are Keystone Habits?
    They are habits that act as triggers for other habits.

9. What are implementation intentions?
    They involve creating a specific plan for when and where to perform the desired habit.

10. How can implementation intentions be used to improve customer service in a business setting?
    By setting a clear intention and plan for how to respond to customer complaints.

Exercises

1. Reflect on your personal habits and identify one habit you would like to cultivate. Design a trigger-rich environment by strategically placing reminders or visual cues that prompt the desired behavior.

2. Choose an existing habit and link a new habit to it using habit stacking. Specify the trigger that prompts the new habit and write it down.

3. Select a career-related habit you would like to develop. Create an implementation intention by specifying when and where you will perform the habit.

4. Identify a triggering situation that often leads to an unwanted habit in your personal life. Come up with a plan to modify or remove that situation to support positive habit change.

5. Think about a negative trigger that often leads to unproductive behavior in a business setting. Brainstorm alternative positive triggers that can replace it and note how you can incorporate them into your work routine.

6. Create a habit stacking statement for a personal habit of your choice. Link the new habit with an existing one by specifying a trigger.

7. Think of a bad habit or habits that serves as triggers that lead to other undesirable habits. Do the same for habit triggers that leads to positive habits.

8. Imagine you are trying to resist the trigger of checking social media frequently during work hours. Brainstorm and list 3 strategies you can implement to resist or redirect this trigger.

9. Consider a personal habit that you are currently working on changing. Explain how you can apply the concept of overcoming unexpected triggers to navigate challenges related to the habit.

10. Think about a habit goal you have set for yourself. Describe how you would personalize the triggers associated with that habit based on your personal preferences.

Principle 5:

Rewire Your Mind

Transforming Mindsets & Beliefs

"The only thing that's keeping you from getting what you want is the story you keep telling yourself."
— Tony Robbins

In this chapter, we explore how our beliefs impact our habits and our lives. Beliefs serve as the foundation on which we build our habits, and they ultimately determine our outcomes. They influence our choices, expectations, and resilience in the face of challenges. As we delve into Principle 5, we'll shed light on the distinction between limiting beliefs and empowering mindsets to learn how they can propel us toward our habit goals or keep us from them.

Key Question:
How can the development of mindset empower individuals to make well-informed decisions, overcome challenges, and drive success in their personal life, professional endeavors, and business pursuits?

As we investigate the tenets of Principle 5 below, we'll not only present you with the tools you need to turn setbacks into progress, but also cultivate a growth mindset that aligns your habits with your vision.

Have you ever wondered how changing your thoughts can reshape your beliefs? If so, read on as we unravel how our beliefs impact our motivation and how we can transform them to cultivate an empowering growth mindset and develop optimistic expectations for our future.

A study published in the Journal of Experimental Psychology found that individuals with a growth mindset — that is, those who believe they can develop abilities through dedication and hard work — are more likely to embrace challenges and persist in the face of setbacks, leading to higher levels of achievement.[26]

Beliefs

Beliefs form the foundation on which we build and modify our habits. Beliefs represent our assumptions and attitudes, the lens through which we interpret the world and the stories we tell ourselves *about* ourselves. When it comes to habits, our beliefs either limit or empower us.

Limiting beliefs drain our momentum and self-confidence. They lead us to view setbacks through a lens of our personal flaws or inadequacies rather than our circumstances. As a result, we learn to adopt a fixed mindset, convinced that our abilities, intelligence, and qualities are unchangeable traits. Over time, limiting beliefs become a self-fulfilling prophecy that sets the upper limit for what we can achieve as well as how we can transform them to transform our lives.

Empowering beliefs, on the other hand, help us build motivation and resilience as we work toward our goals. They help us view setbacks as temporary and remind us that effort and consistency will pay off over the long run. Empowering beliefs lead to a growth mindset and by cultivating a that mindset, we can begin to approach habit modification with optimism, resilience, and a willingness to learn from our setbacks and successes.

Limiting Beliefs
Limiting beliefs are self-imposed mental barriers that restrict our potential and hinder our personal growth. They are

---

[26] Dweck, C. S. (2007). Mindset: The new psychology of success. Random House Digital, Inc.

negative assumptions or perceptions we hold about ourselves, others, or the world around us that limit what we believe we can achieve. These assumptions sap our courage and determination and condition us to expect failure regardless of the efforts we make to change our lives. Research conducted by my alma mater, the Wharton School of the University of Pennsylvania, revealed that individuals with a mindset of self-doubt and fear of failure tend to make more conservative and risk-averse decisions, potentially missing out on valuable opportunities for growth and success.[27] The self-imposed mental walls we build for ourselves, then, do not merely insulate us from risk; they prevent us from exploring what may lie beyond the walls.

Personal Perspective:

1. "I'll never be successful because I don't have a college degree."

2. "I'm not talented enough to pursue my dream career."

3. "I can't achieve work-life balance; it's impossible in my industry."

4. "I'm too old to switch careers and start something new."

5. "I'll never earn a six-figure salary because I come from a modest background."

6. "I'm not confident enough to speak up and share my ideas at work."

7. "I'll never be as successful as my peers; they have better connections."

8. "I'm destined to stay in my current position; I don't have what it takes to move up."

---

[27] Grant, A. M., & Schwartz, B. (2011). Too much of a good thing: The challenge and opportunity of the inverted U. *Perspectives on Psychological Science*, 6(1), 61-76.

9. "I'm not skilled enough in technology; it's too late for me to adapt."

10. "I'll never find a job that aligns with my passion and pays well."

Career Perspective:

1. "I'm not qualified enough to apply for that promotion; I don't have the necessary experience."

2. "I'll never be able to reach a higher position in my field; there are already so many experts."

3. "I don't possess the right skills to pursue my dream career; it's too specialized."

4. "I'm afraid to take risks and explore new career opportunities; I might fail."

5. "I can't negotiate for a higher salary; they'll reject my request."

6. "I'll never find a job that aligns with my passions and interests; I have to settle for what's available."

7. "I don't have the network or connections to advance my career; I'll always be overlooked."

8. "I'm too old to switch careers or make a significant change; it's too late for me."

9. "I can't pursue a fulfilling career and maintain work-life balance; it's an either-or situation."

10. "I'm not confident enough to showcase my accomplishments and skills during interviews; I'll be overshadowed."

Business Perspective:

1. "Our company can't compete with larger corporations; we're too small."

2. "Investing in new technologies won't benefit our bottom line; it's too risky."

3. "We can't expand internationally; the market is too saturated."

4. "Our industry is too traditional; innovative ideas won't be embraced."

5. "We can't attract top talent without offering high salaries and lavish perks."

6. "We can't increase our prices; customers will choose cheaper alternatives."

7. "We can't achieve significant growth without taking on substantial debt."

8. "Entering new markets will stretch our resources too thin; it's not worth the effort."

9. "We can't innovate because we're tied down by our existing processes and procedures."

10. "Our business will always be limited by the economic cycles; we can't thrive in a downturn."

If any of the limiting beliefs above feel familiar to you, you may have developed a fixed mindset, convinced that you cannot change your habits or your circumstances. Limiting beliefs, however, are neither set in stone nor true and, by replacing them with empowering beliefs, you can begin to transform your thinking and your life one good habit at a time.

Empowering Beliefs

Empowering beliefs are beliefs we have about ourselves that are helpful, positive, and accurate. They give us power because they affect our thoughts, feelings, and behaviors, helping us to take positive action and feel good about ourselves. These beliefs drive growth, help us meet our goals, and make us into the best possible versions of ourselves. By adopting empowering beliefs, we can overcome limiting beliefs, achieve success, and lead a more fulfilling life.

An important skill to master in the process of habit transformation is the ability to transform limiting beliefs into empowering beliefs.

- **Awareness:** The first crucial step in transforming limiting beliefs is to become aware of them. Without conscious awareness of our thoughts, it is impossible to address and overcome these beliefs. Once you have identified a limiting belief, you can begin the process of eradicating or replacing it with more empowering perspectives. For example, if you have a limiting belief that you are not capable of public speaking, becoming aware of this belief allows you to challenge it and replace it with a belief that you have the ability to learn and improve your public speaking skills. Mindfulness acts as a powerful tool for recognizing and dismantling limiting beliefs, paving the way for personal growth and the development of more empowering mindsets.

- **Consequences:** Identify all of the consequences (the pain) that this limiting belief is causing you. Holding onto the limiting belief of fear of public speaking can have a range of consequences. It can lead to avoidance of speaking opportunities, self-doubt, limited personal and career growth, social anxiety, negative self-talk, missed chances for influence and personal branding, and a lack of fulfillment. These consequences collectively hinder you from fully expressing yourself, seizing opportunities, and realizing your potential as an effective communicator and leader. Overcoming this limiting belief is crucial for your personal and professional development, enabling you to embrace public speaking with confidence and unlock the doors to growth and success.

- **Challenge:** Challenge limiting beliefs with evidence that contradicts them. Look for examples that prove your perceived limits or inadequacies false. Look for examples of successful public speakers who have faced similar fears and overcome them. Perhaps you have had some success in the past. Look at those examples, too. Find stories of individuals who have delivered impactful speeches despite initial doubts. Recognize that public speaking is a skill that can be learned and improved through practice and experience. By actively challenging the belief and gathering evidence that contradicts it, you can shift your mindset, build confidence and growth, and cultivate a more empowering belief system.

- **Reframe:** Reframe the belief into an empowering belief. Instead of viewing public speaking as a daunting and potentially failure-ridden experience, reframe the limiting belief to see it as an opportunity for growth and personal development. Embrace the belief that public speaking is a chance to share valuable insights, connect with others, and inspire positive change. Recognize that it's natural to feel nervous and vulnerable, and that you can channel these emotions into passionate and engaging presentations. Reframing the belief allows you to approach public speaking with a sense of excitement, curiosity, and a willingness to learn from each experience. In doing so, you empower yourself to embrace the challenge and unlock your full potential as a confident and effective public speaker.

- **Reinforce:** Repeat and reinforce the new beliefs. Continually recite them to yourself and share them with others for accountability and support. Translate them into action and use any progress you make as evidence that the beliefs are true and are propelling you toward success. With consistency, we transform our beliefs from hopeful assumptions into habitual ways of thinking. They become second nature in how we motivate ourselves and maintain determination through difficulties or setbacks.

Examples:

1. *Limiting belief:* "I'll never be successful because I don't have a college degree."

   Empowering belief: "My unique skills, experiences, and determination can lead me to success, regardless of my educational background."

2. *Limiting belief:* "I'm not qualified enough to apply for that promotion; I don't have the necessary experience."

   Empowering belief: "I have valuable skills and knowledge that can contribute to my success in this role, and I am capable of learning and growing to meet new challenges."

3. *Limiting belief:* "Our company can't compete with larger corporations; We're too small."

   Empowering belief: "Our company's size allows us to be agile, innovative, and responsive to customer needs, giving us a competitive advantage over larger corporations."

The ability to transform a limiting belief into an empowering belief is a valuable skill that can significantly impact your life. By recognizing and challenging our limiting beliefs, we can replace them with empowering beliefs that drive personal growth, enhance our self-confidence, and help us achieve our goals. This transformation not only leads to a more fulfilling life but also enables us to overcome obstacles and reach our full potential. As Aristotle, Hume, and Nietzsche explored the nature of habit and its role in human behavior, they emphasized the importance of understanding and shaping our beliefs to create a positive impact on our lives. By mastering the art of transforming limiting beliefs into empowering ones, we can unlock our true potential and lead a life filled with success and happiness.

Negative Self-Talk

Negative self-talk and limiting beliefs are closely related but represent different aspects of our inner dialogue and belief systems. While limiting beliefs are the deeply ingrained assumptions we hold about ourselves, negative self-talk refers to the critical or unconstructive thoughts we direct toward ourselves. Let's look at some signs and examples of negative self-talk below.

Signs of Negative Self-Talk

- A harshly critical inner voice that calls you inadequate, stupid, lazy, and so on. It berates you for perceived mistakes, flaws, and imperfections.

- A "fixed mindset" inner voice that tells you that you "can't change" and that your abilities and potential are static.

- An anxious or pessimistic inner voice that constantly voices worst-case scenarios and sees more limitations than possibilities. It fills your mind with worries and doubts rather than inspiration or determination.

- An inner voice that blames your lack of progress on your personal faults or shortcomings rather than your environment or strategy.

How to Overcome Negative Self-Talk
Defeating negative self-talk is key to building a foundation of
empowering beliefs that help us to achieve our goals. Here's
how you do it:

- **Build self-awareness.** Notice the thoughts and
  beliefs your inner voice expresses, especially following
  a perceived failure or setback. Look for recurring
  beliefs you need to address. Awareness is the first step
  to quieting the inner voice.

- **Challenge those thoughts.** Look for evidence that
  contradicts negative self-talk. Question any limiting
  beliefs you have about your aptitude for improvement;
  you can change and grow through practice.

- **Adopt a self-compassionate inner voice.** Speak to
  yourself with encouragement, empathy, and praise for
  your efforts and perseverance. Forgive yourself for
  imperfections and mistakes. Learn from them and use
  them as tools to motivate yourself to continue
  working toward your goals.

- **Reframe struggles or failures.** Rather than harshly
  judging them, view them as indicators that you need a
  new plan or approach. They provide you with an
  opportunity to develop grit and learn resilience
  strategies for overcoming frustration or
  discouragement. See them as steppingstones, not stop
  signs.

- **Limit negative beliefs.** Identify habitual thoughts
  such as, "I can't change" then reframe them by
  changing your thoughts to, "I can change and improve
  through consistent practice and learning." Change
  "Failure means I'm inadequate" to "Failure means my
  strategy was inadequate and needs improvement."
  With repetition, these new beliefs will replace the old
  ones.

- **Elevate your mental habits.** Cultivate habits of positive self-talk, mindfulness, optimism, and a solutions-based focus. Start each day reviewing your goals and accomplishments to reinforce an empowering mindset. Let motivation flow from progress rather than perfection. Your thoughts shape reality, so habituate them through constant practice and ongoing revision.

- **Identify cognitive biases.** Cognitive biases are ways of thinking that lead us to make inaccurate judgments of our circumstances. In the next section, we outline the cognitive biases that may shape our thinking about our ability to change.

Mindsets

Mindset refers to the overall attitude, perspective, or mental framework we adopt based on our beliefs. It is the lens through which we interpret and respond to the world around us. When considering habits, it's important to recognize that our ways of thinking — our mindsets — can also be seen as habitual patterns. Just like our behaviors, our cognitive habits greatly influence how we interpret and engage with the world around us. Let's explore some contrasting mindset habits: "crisitunity," growth mindset, fixed mindset, abundance mindset, and scarcity mindset.

The *"crisitunity" mindset* exemplifies a positive habit of perceiving setbacks or challenges as opportunities for growth and innovation. Individuals with this mindset automatically train their minds to seek the silver lining within adversity, fostering resilience, adaptability, and proactive problem-solving skills.

The *fixed mindset* represents a negative habit where individuals believe that their abilities and qualities are fixed traits. They may view challenges as threats to their self-worth, avoiding risks and hindering personal development and growth. On the other hand, the *growth mindset* serves as a positive mindset habit. It embodies the belief that abilities can be developed through dedication and effort. Embracing challenges as opportunities to learn, individuals with a growth mindset cultivate resilience, a love for learning, and a willingness to take on new challenges.

Similarly, the **scarcity mindset** represents a negative habit where individuals perceive resources, opportunities, and success as limited and fixed. This mindset fosters a sense of lack and fear, leading to a mindset of competition and hoarding. It can hinder collaboration, creativity, and abundance in various aspects of life. Conversely, the *abundance mindset* is a positive mindset habit that acknowledges the abundance of resources, possibilities, and opportunities available. It cultivates a sense of gratitude, generosity, and a belief in the potential for growth and abundance in all areas of life.

By recognizing mindsets as habitual patterns, we can bring awareness to our thought processes and intentionally cultivate positive mindset habits similar to transforming limiting to empowering beliefs. Through practice and repetition, we can shift from a fixed to a growth mindset, and from a scarcity to an abundance mindset. By embracing the "crisitunity" mindset, we unlock our potential for personal growth, resilience, and a greater sense of fulfillment in life.

Cognitive Biases

Cognitive biases influence our beliefs and mindset and, therefore, our habits. Let's look at a couple of the most common cognitive biases.

Confirmation bias: favoring information that supports what we already believe and ignoring anything that contradicts it. This bias reinforces our limiting beliefs and habits, leading us to dismiss evidence that we can improve or change our circumstances. We can challenge confirmation bias by seeking out different perspectives and facts that challenge our assumptions.

Sunk cost fallacy: sticking with something that no longer works just because we've already invested in it. This bias leads us to repeat poor habits or stay in unhealthy situations because change makes it seem like our previous efforts have been a waste of resources. We can challenge this bias by remembering that our past choices don't determine our future ones and by doing what we know to be most effective, regardless of the time or resources we have invested in other strategies.

These and other cognitive biases often operate outside our awareness, influencing our habits and outcomes in unseen ways. If we fail to identify the biases that might be leading us in the wrong direction, we limit our potential. Let's look at an example:

> *Life:* If you strongly believe that exercise is ineffective for weight loss, you may selectively pay attention to and remember studies or anecdotes that support this belief while ignoring or dismissing evidence that suggests otherwise. This *confirmation bias* can limit your personal growth and prevent you from exploring new possibilities for change.

While cognitive biases strongly influence our habits by operating outside our awareness, they can lead us to ways of thinking and sets of beliefs that may limit our motivation, optimism, and resilience unless we examine or consciously challenge them. But by developing insight into the common biases that fuel our self-doubt, unhealthy choices, or discouragement in the face of setbacks, we gain the ability to reframe our thoughts and develop empowering habits of mind instead.

Diet & How it Impacts Mindset

While caring for our minds is critical to changing our habits, it is equally important that we care for our bodies. This is because our food affects our mindset. How we eat impacts how we think.

- Your blood sugar impacts your willpower and self-control. By stabilizing it, you can better maintain an optimistic, solutions-focused mindset. When your blood sugar drops, it depletes your willpower. Eating a balanced diet across regular mealtimes can prevent blood sugar spikes or crashes that can sap your motivation and make it more difficult for you to maintain habits.[28]

- Inflammation can impact your ability to engage in deductive reasoning and maintain a growth mindset. Chronic inflammation is linked to decreased cognitive flexibility, pessimism, and a belief that your abilities are fixed.[29] An anti-inflammatory diet rich in nutrients such as fatty acids, turmeric, and broccoli sprouts helps you cultivate a growth mindset that makes you open to new learning and possibilities.

- Low levels of serotonin (a hormone in your brain that regulates mood) can limit your impulse control and make it difficult for you to sustain attention or effort.[30] Eating foods that support healthy levels of serotonin in your brain, such as fatty fish, eggs, nuts, seeds, and complex carbs can help you with the habit-building process.

- Low levels of dopamine (a hormone in your brain that regulates how you experience pleasure) may make it

---

[28] Gailliot, Matthew T, and Roy F Baumeister. "The physiology of willpower: linking blood glucose to self-control." *Personality and social psychology review : an official journal of the Society for Personality and Social Psychology, Inc* vol. 11,4 (2007): 303-27. doi:10.1177/1088868307303030

[29] Culley, Deborah J et al. "Systemic inflammation impairs attention and cognitive flexibility but not associative learning in aged rats: possible implications for delirium." *Frontiers in aging neuroscience* vol. 6 107. 10 Jun. 2014, doi:10.3389/fnagi.2014.00107

[30] J.W. Dalley, J.P. Roiser. Dopamine, serotonin and impulsivity. Neuroscience, Volume 215, 2012, Pages 42-58, ISSN 0306-4522, https://doi.org/10.1016/j.neuroscience.2012.03.065. (https://www.sciencedirect.com/science/article/pii/S0306452212003983)

harder for you to feel motivated or resist cravings. Meanwhile, excess dopamine from substance use may impair habit gains.[31] Eat foods that provide dopamine support without triggering spikes or crashes, such as dark leafy greens, broccoli, apples, bananas, and dairy.

- Gut bacteria release neurotransmitters that affect motivation, wellbeing, hopefulness, resilience, and willpower, so gut health can influence your habit-building success, positivity, and perseverance.[32] Improving gut health may help you develop a "grit" mindset built on sustained passion and a commitment to achieving meaningful goals. Eating a probiotic-rich diet with prebiotic fiber feeds the good gut bacteria that release neurotransmitters for optimal physical and mental health.

- Nutrient deficiencies hamper habit formation. Being low in nutrients such as B vitamins, iron, zinc, magnesium or essential fatty acids impairs cognition, focus, and motivation.[33] Address nutritional deficiencies through diet and/or supplements to give your brain what it needs for learning, emotional regulation, and higher reasoning. Stay nourished for habit gains.

- Hydration gives your brain the fuel it needs to forge habits and make progress. Staying properly hydrated leads to clearer thinking, better emotional regulation, and a more positive mindset. Dehydration leads to

---

[31] Poisson Carli L., Engel Liv, Saunders Benjamin T. Dopamine Circuit Mechanisms of Addiction-Like Behaviors. Frontiers in Neural Circuits, Vol. 15. 2021 . https://www.frontiersin.org/articles/10.3389/fncir.2021.752420. 10.3389/fncir.2021.752420. 1662-5110

[32] Chen, Yijing et al. "Regulation of Neurotransmitters by the Gut Microbiota and Effects on Cognition in Neurological Disorders." *Nutrients* vol. 13,6 2099. 19 Jun. 2021, doi:10.3390/nu13062099

[33] Maureen M. Black. Micronutrient Deficiencies and Cognitive Functioning. The Journal of Nutrition.
Volume 133, Issue 11, 2003. Pages 3927S-3931S. ISSN 0022-3166, https://doi.org/10.1093/jn/133.11.3927S.

fatigue, cognitive decline, pessimism, emotional reactivity, and a loss of motivation. Aim for 8–10 glasses of water per day to power your brain, flush out toxins, and transport neurotransmitters essential for habit building throughout your body.

In summary, diet significantly impacts your mindset, assumptions, and quality of thinking in both positive and negative ways. Staying nourished and hydrated provides you with the biological support you need to maintain optimism, motivation, cognitive flexibility, and progress — all of which fuel empowering beliefs and habits of mind that manifest in your choices, behaviors, and outcomes. When you give your body the care it needs to meet you habit goals each day, willpower becomes a sustainable source of energy you can rely on through any challenge.

Locus of Control: Internal vs. External

Your beliefs about how much control you have over your life have a direct impact on your habits and success. An internal locus of control means you *believe* you can influence your circumstances through your choices and effort. It means you see progress or setbacks as the results of the strategies you choose. With an internal locus of control, you feel confident you can build good habits and break bad ones with enough determination.

An external locus of control means you *believe* life's outcomes are determined more by luck, fate, or others around you than by your choices. You may feel unable to change your habits since you feel you have little control over your circumstances. An external locus of control leads you to feel stuck or to blame external circumstances when you face problems.

Your habits reflect whether you have an internal or external locus of control. Those with an internal locus of control build habits and make continuous progress through practice and a commitment to self-improvement. They believe outcomes reflect their choices over time. Those with an external locus of control react to what happens around them, either succeeding or struggling to commit to their habits based on conditions beyond their influence. They may feel unable to start or stop habits since they feel powerless to external circumstances.

While some life events are unavoidable, your thinking effects your locus of control. You can choose how much power you retain over your outcomes or give away to external factors. An internal locus opens up possibilities; an external one restricts them, driving you to focus on obstacles rather than options.

Conclusion

Your beliefs, mindset and ways of thinking determine your habits and potential for progress. Limiting beliefs and cognitive biases often operate automatically, influencing your choices and resilience in unseen ways. But you can gain freedom from unhelpful thought patterns by building insight and awareness into the assumptions and expectations that shape your reality.

Pay attention to thoughts that make you feel stuck or inadequate and replace them with more empowering alternatives. Adopt an optimistic mindset that you can expand your abilities and opportunities through determined effort. Challenge biases, such as confirmation bias and scarcity thinking, before they steer you into making poor decisions or engaging in unhealthy habits.

Staying properly nourished also provides you biological support for motivation, cognitive flexibility, and a belief in your capacity for change. Give your body and mind the fuel they need to strengthen habits and routines that will move you closer to your goals. Developing healthier ways of thinking takes practice and patience but can lead you to outcomes beyond what you once believed was impossible.

While life's events themselves are often out of your control, you retain the power to choose your response and beliefs about what those events mean. Your potential unfolds and habits form from the expectations and perspectives you cultivate rather than your circumstances alone. You steer your own course through the thoughts you habituate and nourish each day. You transform your reality as you transform your mind. Break free of unhelpful beliefs and thought patterns now and discover your true capacity for change. Question assumptions, open your mind, and feed your body, beliefs, and actions with purpose. Your habits follow your thoughts, so command your mind to unlock your potential for transformation. As we continue that journey toward transformation with Principle 6, we'll explore how to use rewards and consequences to shape our behaviors and create habits that benefit our lives.

Summary Q & A

1. How do beliefs and mindset influence your habits?
   They shape your choices, expectations, and perseverance.
2. How can you overcome negative self-talk?
   You can build self-awareness, challenge negative thoughts, and adopt a self-compassionate inner voice.
3. How can you identify limiting beliefs?
   By examining your thoughts, especially during difficult or distressing times.
4. How can you transform limiting beliefs into empowering ones?
   By challenging them with contradictory evidence, adopting a growth mindset, and revising them in an empowering way.
5. What is the difference between an internal locus of control and an external locus of control?
   An internal locus means believing that you can influence outcomes through your choices and effort, while an external locus attributes outcomes to luck, fate, or others.
6. How can you develop an internal locus of control?
   By cultivating optimistic and empowered thinking, and reframing setbacks as temporary.
7. Why is it important to challenge your thoughts and beliefs?
   Unexamined thoughts may sustain limiting beliefs that hinder your progress.
8. How can we challenge confirmation bias?
   By actively seeking out different perspectives and facts that challenge our assumptions.
9. How can we develop a growth mindset and overcome a fixed mindset bias?
   We can start by embracing the belief that we can improve through consistent effort and view struggles as opportunities for learning and growth.
10. What is scarcity bias?
    Scarcity bias focuses our attention on lack or loss, which can lead us to experience anxiety, stress, and a negative mindset.

Exercises

1. Reflect on your beliefs, potential, and your ability to change. Write down at least five empowering beliefs that you currently hold and five limiting beliefs that you would like to transform.

2. Create a list of five common negative thoughts or self-criticisms that you often experience. For each negative thought, challenge it by providing evidence that contradict its validity.

3. Think about a recent struggle or failure you experienced. Write a short reflection on how you initially viewed the situation. Then, identify the lessons learned, the opportunities for growth, and the new strategies you can implement going forward.

4. On a scale of 1-10, rate your internal locus of control. Write down three actions you can take to strengthen it.

5. Spend a day intentionally practicing positive self-talk. Whenever you catch yourself engaging in negative self-talk or self-criticism, immediately counter it with a positive statement.

6. Visualize yourself achieving a significant goal or overcoming a major obstacle. Focus on the empowering beliefs and mindset you need to accomplish it; write them down.

7. Evaluate when and where you've invested a significant amount of time and effort to reach a goal that no longer serves you. Write a journal entry to let go of this old goal, accept the sunk cost fallacy, and how to move on.

8. Set aside 10–15 minutes each day for a week to journal about your efforts and progress in developing new skills or habits.

9. Form a small accountability circle to share the empowering beliefs you want to cultivate and the limiting beliefs you want to transform. Discuss strategies to support each other.

10. Determine whether you tend to make choices based on an internal or external locus of control. Identify three specific areas in your life where you can shift toward an internal locus of control. Write down actions you can take to increase your sense of control and influence in those areas.

Principle 6:
Unlock Rewards & Consequences

Leveraging Incentives for Positive Behavior Shifts

"Every reward you receive is the consequence of your own actions."
- Napoleon Hill

Have you ever wondered why some habits stick while others fade away? If so, know that the answer lies in the power of rewards and consequences. In the intricate dance of habit formation and transformation, rewards and consequences play a vital role. They shape our behaviors, reinforce our habits, and influence the outcomes of our efforts. In this chapter, we explore the power of rewards and consequences in the context of habit change. We delve into the fascinating dynamics of the Habit Loop, in which rewards drive the formation and reinforcement of habits. We examine the various types of rewards and consequences associated with our habits, exploring both their immediate and long-term impacts on our behavior. Furthermore, we unravel the significance of intrinsic and extrinsic motivation and how understanding these concepts can sustain our commitment to habit transformation. By understanding the intricate relationship between rewards, consequences, and habits, we can unlock the keys to effective habit change and pave the way for lasting transformation.

Key Question:
How can the rewards and consequences associated with habits
assist us in transforming them?

145

Our brains are wired to seek rewards (pleasure) and avoid negative consequences (pain), and this innate drive plays a central role in how we form and maintain habits. It's no wonder, then, that learning how to harness the power of rewards and consequences is crucial to changing our habits. To begin that learning process, let's revisit the Habit Loop.

In a study of more than 1,808 workers, people attributed nearly 46% of their career success to having the right habits, which was more than twice as critical to their success than even the decisions they made[34]

The Role of Rewards & Consequences

Rewards (Pleasure)
The brain rewards us in order to drive us toward behavior that it perceives as beneficial for our survival and well-being. Throughout human evolution, our brains have developed intricate systems to reinforce behaviors that ensure our survival, such as finding food, seeking shelter, forming social connections, and reproducing. This reward mechanism is deeply rooted in our biological and psychological makeup.

From a biological perspective, the brain's reward system is closely tied to the release of neurotransmitters, particularly dopamine. When we engage in behaviors that the reward system perceives as beneficial or pleasurable, such as eating nutrient-rich food or engaging in social interactions, the brain produces dopamine. Among neuroscientists, dopamine is known as the "feel-good" neurotransmitter because it produces sensations of pleasure, satisfaction, and motivation.

When we experience pleasure or a sense of accomplishment from a particular action, our brains learn to associate that action with the positive outcome. This association provides us with a source of intrinsic motivation to repeat the behavior to

---

[34]https://www.prnewswire.com/news-releases/resolving-to-find-career-success-in-2020-new-study-says-habits-trump-alleven-decision-making-and-talent-300975979.html

obtain the rewarding experience once again. Let's look at some examples of rewards:

Life: If you have consistently engaged in exercise for a certain period, being in good shape makes you feel better about yourself. This feeling is your reward. You may also receive compliments on your appearance. As your brain learns to associate the reward with the behavior of exercising, you reinforce the habit of remaining physically active.

Career: If an employee consistently meets or exceeds their sales targets, their employer may issue them a commission or bonus. As the employee's brain learns to associate the financial reward with the behavior of hitting and exceeding sales targets, they feel motivated to continually improve their professional performance.

Business: If a business consultant improves a business's bottom line, the business may reward them with a performance fee. As the consultant learns to associate the financial incentive with the work they do for the organization, they feel motivated to improve their performance.

The brain's reward system also plays a role in shaping habits. As we repeat a behavior and receive a reward, the brain begins to anticipate the reward and automates the process through the formation of habit loops. This automation allows us to conserve mental resources and execute behaviors more efficiently. The brain learns to link the cue that triggers the behavior, the routine itself, and the rewarding outcome, creating a seamless loop that promotes habit formation.

Consequences (Pain)

Just as the brain rewards us for behaviors it deems beneficial to us, it also responds to negative consequences or pain to prevent us from engaging in behaviors that may be detrimental to our well-being. Consequences serve as feedback to the brain, signaling that a behavior may have negative implications for our survival, health, or overall functioning.

From a biological perspective, pain or negative consequences activate neural pathways in our brains associated with discomfort, fear, or aversion. These pathways involve various brain regions, including the amygdala, anterior cingulate cortex, and insula, which are involved in processing negative emotions and threat detection. As these regions of our brains are activated, we learn to recognize behaviors we should avoid or modify to prevent further harm.

Psychologically, negative consequences generate emotions such as disappointment, guilt, or regret. These emotions serve as internal feedback mechanisms that make us less inclined to repeat the behaviors in the future to prevent us from experiencing the unpleasant emotions and experiences linked to it. In the context of habit formation and change, understanding the role of consequences is crucial. By recognizing the negative outcomes associated with unhealthy or unwanted habits, we can leverage this knowledge to break the habit loop.

Examples of consequences vary across different aspects of our lives, careers, and businesses. Let's examine some of these consequences below:

Life: If you were to consume a diet high in processed foods, sugars, and unhealthy fats, you may experience weight gain, decreased energy levels, and an increased risk of chronic diseases such as diabetes, heart disease, or obesity. These negative consequences could impact your overall well-being, self-esteem, long-term health, and quality of life.

Career: If you consistently failed to prioritize tasks, meet deadlines, or allocate time effectively, you would miss deadlines, decrease your productivity, and increase your stress. These negative consequences could lead to a decline in work performance, strained professional relationships, and missed opportunities for career advancement.

Business: If a business leader made ill-informed investment decisions, they would incur significant losses for their business. These negative consequences could cause them to lose credibility front of their employees and damage their reputation in their industry.

By understanding the potential negative consequences of certain behaviors, we can evaluate their impact on our well-being, success, and overall goals. This awareness allows us to make informed choices and consciously align our actions with positive outcomes while avoiding or modifying behaviors that lead us to unfavorable consequences. Ultimately, recognizing the role of consequences and their impact on our behavior empowers us to make intentional changes and cultivate habits that contribute to our overall growth.

The Role of Rewards in the Habit Loop

Within the habit loop, rewards play a vital role in shaping our behaviors and reinforcing the formation of habits. Psychologically, rewards serve as positive reinforcements that motivate us to continue engaging in a particular habit. When we receive a reward after completing a behavior, our brain perceives it as a success and this perception strengthens the neural pathways associated with that behavior. This reinforcement ultimately strengthens the habit loop, making the behavior more automatic and ingrained over time.

To illustrate the role of rewards in different domains, let's consider examples of rewards that create a positive feedback loop and reinforce the benefits of certain habits:

Examples:

Life: After going for a morning run, you feel a sense of accomplishment as your brain is flooded with endorphins that boost your mood and energy levels throughout the day. This positive feeling serves as a reward that reinforces the habit of regular exercise.

Career: By completing thorough market research and analysis, you achieve investment success, generating higher returns, and receiving recognition from colleagues and superiors for making informed decisions. These rewards reinforce the habit of conducting thorough research.

Business: By engaging in networking activities and building your professional connections, you expand your network of potential investors, secure partnerships or collaborations, and gain access to valuable industry insights. These rewards reinforce the habit of networking.

Why Reward Negative Habits?

Certain behaviors, such as smoking or drinking alcohol, can still flood our brains with feel-good hormones despite the negative consequences they have on our long-term health. This results from a complex interplay of evolutionary factors, cultural influences, and the brain's response to immediate rewards. As discussed previously, from an evolutionary perspective, our brain's reward system is wired to *prioritize immediate gratification* and short-term benefits over long-term consequences. This bias is rooted in our ancestors' need to ensure survival in environments where resources were scarce and unpredictable. Behaviors that provided immediate rewards, such as consuming calorie-dense foods or seeking pleasurable experiences, offered a survival advantage in those contexts.

However, in today's modern world, with readily available resources and altered cultural norms, this evolutionary programming can work against us. Addictive substances such as nicotine or alcohol hijack the brain's reward system, triggering the release of neurotransmitters such as dopamine, which create pleasurable sensations and reinforce the behavior. The brain associates the immediate rewards with the behavior, leading to a reinforcement loop that can be challenging to break.

Additionally, cultural and social factors play a significant role in shaping our behaviors, including those related to substance use. Cultural norms, peer influence, and societal acceptance can override the potential long-term consequences associated with certain behaviors. Vaping or drinking alcohol, for example, may be influenced by social contexts, peer pressure, or the desire to fit in or cope with stress.

It's important to note that the brain's reward system is not perfect or foolproof. While it evolved to ensure survival in ancestral environments, it can be susceptible to being exploited by modern influences. The brain's reward response isn't suited to accurately assess the long-term consequences of certain behaviors, leading to the rewarding nature of habits that are detrimental to our health and well-being.

Understanding these factors can help us develop strategies to overcome these challenges. By increasing awareness of the long-term consequences and health risks associated with behaviors like vaping or excessive alcohol consumption, we can consciously engage our prefrontal cortex — the part of the brain responsible for rational decision-making — to override the immediate rewards offered by these habits. Seeking support from healthcare professionals, implementing behavior change techniques, and leveraging social support networks can also aid in breaking the reward cycle and fostering healthier habits.

In summary, the rewarding nature of behaviors that are not beneficial for our survival, such as smoking or drinking alcohol, can be attributed to a combination of evolutionary programming, cultural influences, and the brain's response to immediate rewards. By understanding these factors and their impact, we can take conscious steps to counteract the reward-driven nature of these behaviors and make choices that prioritize our long-term well-being.

Examining Rewards & Consequences of Habits

In the journey of habit formation and transformation, understanding the rewards and consequences associated with our habits is essential. In this section, we examine the rewards we derive from our current habits and the consequences, both positive and negative, that result from them. By evaluating the overall impact of our habits on our well-being and desired outcomes, we gain valuable insights that can empower us to make informed decisions and drive positive behavior change. Logic would have us eliminate habits where the negative consequences outweigh the rewards. We will explore this concept further throughout this chapter.

Identifying the Rewards Associated with Current Habits

To truly grasp the power of habits, it is crucial to identify the rewards they provide us. Whether our habits make us happy, help us manage stress, or help us wind down before bed, recognizing these rewards helps us understand why certain habits have become ingrained in our daily lives.

Examples:

> **Life:** After engaging in a meditation practice, your brain rewards you with a sense of relaxation.

> **Career:** After successfully completing a challenging project at work, you feel a rewarding sense of accomplishment and positive recognition from others.

> **Business:** After implementing effective marketing strategies, your company is rewarded with financial gains or increased market share.

Recognizing the Negative Consequences of Current Habits

Alongside rewards, habits also come with negative consequences. These consequences can have a significant impact on our desired outcomes and may decrease our well-being, hinder our progress, or negatively impact our connections with others. By examining these consequences, we gain a clearer understanding of the effects our habits have on various aspects of our lives.

Examples:

> **Life:** If you engage in excessive screen time, you experience the negative consequences of decreased productivity, strained relationships, and diminished mental well-being.

> **Career:** If you procrastinate, you may miss deadlines, decrease your performance, and increase your work-related stress.

> **Business:** If you provide your customers with poor service, you will decrease customer satisfaction, receive negative reviews, and lose business.

Assessing the Overall Impact of Habits

By examining the rewards and consequences of our habits, we can assess their overall impact on our well-being and our desired outcomes. This assessment allows us to make informed decisions about which habits serve us well and which may need modification or elimination. It provides us with an opportunity to align our habits with our long-term goals, values, and aspirations. Understanding the bigger picture helps us prioritize habits that contribute positively to our well-being and take steps to modify or let go of habits that hinder us from making progress or improving our well-being.

One way to approach this evaluation is to weigh the rewards against the consequences so we can make informed decisions about whether to maintain or eradicate our current habits. By using predetermined, weighted criteria to score both the rewards and the consequences, we can create a logical process for assessing the value and significance of our habits.

The Scoring Process

To objectively assess the impact your habits have on your life, use the following process:

1. **_Identify Criteria:_** Begin by identifying the criteria you'll use to score the benefits of the rewards and the drawbacks of the consequences of practicing a habit. Consider the specific aspects that are most important to you in evaluating the impact of the habit on your life, career, or business. These criteria could include factors such as health, productivity, personal growth, financial impact, alignment with values or goals, and overall well-being. Assign weights to each criterion based on their relative significance in your decision-making process.

2. **_Develop a Rubric:_** Create a rubric that provides clear guidelines and scoring parameters for each criterion. The rubric should define different levels or categories of performance within each criterion, indicating the range of scores that can be assigned. For example, if one of the criteria is "health," the rubric may have categories such as "excellent health," "good health," "average health," and "poor health." Each category should be accompanied by specific descriptions that align with the respective criterion.

3. **_Score Rewards & Consequences:_** Evaluate each reward and consequence separately, applying the rubric to assign scores based on the defined criteria. Assess the benefits of the rewards and rate them according to the rubric, considering the extent to which the habit positively impacts the identified criteria. Similarly, evaluate the drawbacks or negative consequences of the habit, assigning scores according to the rubric. This step involves honest reflection and careful consideration of the actual impact of the habit on your life, career, or business.

4. **Calculate Total Scores:** Once you have scored each reward and consequence based on the rubric, calculate the total scores for rewards and consequences separately. Sum up the scores assigned to all the rewards to obtain a total rewards score. Similarly, add up the scores assigned to all the consequences to obtain a total consequences score. These totals represent the cumulative evaluation of the rewards and consequences for the habit.

5. **Compare Scores:** Compare the total rewards score against the total consequences score to determine the balance between the two. If the total rewards score outweighs the total consequences score, the habit has more positive benefits than drawbacks and it may be worth continuing. On the other hand, if the total consequences score outweighs the total rewards score, it suggests that the habit has more negative consequences than positive rewards, indicating the need for modification or eradication.

By following this process, you can assess the rewards and consequences of a habit in a systematic and objective manner. It allows you to consider various aspects of the habit's impact, weigh them based on their significance, and make a rational decision based on the cumulative evaluation. Remember that this process provides a framework for informed decision-making, helping you prioritize habits that align with your desired outcomes and well-being.

As an example, let's assess the habit of running based on six criteria: short-term energy usage, long-term energy benefits, time commitment, disease prevention, the risk of knee injury, and the risk of other injuries. We will assign each criterion a weight based on its importance and a score based on its impact on the habit.

In the consequences section, we consider the short-term energy usage as a consequence rather than a reward, as it represents the energy expended during running. We assign it a score of 8 out of 10, indicating a relatively high impact. The risks of knee injury and other injuries are also taken into account, with scores of 4 and 6, respectively.

In the benefits section, we focus on the long-term energy benefits of running, the time commitment required, and the disease prevention aspect. We give the long-term energy benefit a score of 9, indicating its significant positive impact. We score the time commitment at 7, reflecting that it is only slightly less beneficial. We assign disease prevention a score of 8, indicating that running has a positive effect on our overall health.

CRITERIA	SCORE	WEIGHT	WEIGHTED SCORE
Consequences			
Short-Term Energy Usage	8	5X	40
Risk of Knee Injury	4	2X	8
Risk of Other Injury	6	1X	6
Total Consequences Score			**54**
Rewards			
Long-Term Energy Benefits	9	5X	45
Time Commitment	7	4X	28
Disease Prevention	8	3X	24
Total Rewards Score			**97**

By totaling the scores separately, we find that the consequences section has a score of 54, while the benefits section has a score of 97. This suggests that the benefits of running, such as long-term energy, time commitment, and disease prevention, outweigh the short-term energy usage and risks of knee injury and other injuries.

It's important to note that this scoring process is subjective and may vary depending on your preferences and circumstances. You can adjust the weights and scores according to your personal priorities and advice from experts. We always recommended consulting professionals when evaluating the risks and benefits of any habit.

Leveraging Rewards for Motivation

In the journey of habit transformation, rewards play a crucial role in motivating and reinforcing positive change. By strategically leveraging rewards, we can incentivize ourselves to stay committed and motivated on the path of habit transformation. In this section, we will explore the power of rewards and how we can utilize them to foster successful habit transformation. We will delve into two types of rewards — intrinsic and extrinsic — to explore how they influence our motivation and persistence in changing habits. By understanding the dynamics of rewards, we can design effective strategies to harness their power and facilitate lasting habit change.

Differentiating between Intrinsic & Extrinsic Rewards

It is essential to understand the distinction between intrinsic and extrinsic rewards. Intrinsic rewards originate from within us. They are tightly bound to our personal values, satisfaction, and sense of accomplishment. On the other hand, extrinsic rewards are external incentives within our environment, such as financial gain or praise from others. By recognizing and differentiating between these two types of rewards, we can effectively leverage their power in habit motivation and persistence.

While extrinsic rewards can provide us with immediate gratification and motivation, their impact may be more short-lived and dependent on external factors in our environment. They are often tied to specific outcomes or achievements and may provide us with only short-term contentment. Intrinsic rewards, on the other hand, can provide us with a greater sense of long-term fulfillment than extrinsic rewards. It's important to note that the value and significance of rewards can vary for individuals based on their unique preferences and motivations. While intrinsic rewards are generally considered to be more valuable, striking a balance between the two types of rewards can help us maintain motivation, sustain habit change, and foster a sense of fulfillment along the habit transformation journey.

Strategies to Leverage Intrinsic & Extrinsic Rewards

To maximize the power of rewards in habit reinforcement, it is crucial to develop strategies that effectively leverage both intrinsic and extrinsic rewards. For intrinsic rewards, we can align our habits with our core values, set meaningful goals, and focus on personal growth and self-improvement. Creating a sense of autonomy, competence, and purpose within our habits enhances intrinsic motivation. As for extrinsic rewards, we can establish external incentives that align with our desired habits, such as rewards systems, accountability partners, or public commitments. By combining intrinsic and extrinsic rewards strategically, we create a robust system of reinforcement that helps us build and maintain good habits.

Examples:

> **Life:** To motivate yourself to practice mindfulness meditation, you might set up an *extrinsic* reward system where you purchase a small treat every week that you practice meditation. As a result of this practice, you'd also earn the *intrinsic* rewards of inner peace, improved self-awareness, and enhanced emotional well-being.

Career: To motivate yourself to acquire new skills in a professional field, you might work toward an *extrinsic* bonus or promotion. As a result of this work, you'd also earn the *intrinsic* rewards of increased confidence and professional competence.

Business: To motivate yourself to change company policies surrounding sustainability, you might work toward the *extrinsic* rewards of certifications for sustainability and new, environmentally conscious customers. As a result of these changes, you'd also earn the *intrinsic* rewards of aligning company policies with company values and making a positive impact on the environment.

Consequences as Motivation for Habit Change Success

It is often said that pain can be a powerful motivator, and painful consequences can indeed motivate us to transform our habits. Negative consequences can provide us with a sense of urgency that drives us to change our habits to avoid undesirable outcomes. They can serve as reminders of the impact our habits have on our well-being, personal growth, relationships, and overall success. Let's look at how negative consequences can motivate us to make changes.

Examples:

Life: Failing to address unhealthy habits can have negative consequences on your personal health, including a higher of chronic disease and a lower quality of life. To avoid these consequences, you may choose to engage in regular exercise.

Career: Maintaining stagnant habits and resisting change in the professional sphere can limit your career growth. To avoid the negative consequence of career stagnation, you may choose to learn new technologies or fails and adapt to evolving industry trends.

Business: Failing to adapt to changing market dynamics or neglecting customer needs can lead to loss of market share, decreased revenue, and diminished competitive advantage. To avoid the negative consequence of poor financial performance and a loss of competitiveness, a business may choose to modernize and adopt digital technologies.

Immediate Gratification vs. Delayed Rewards

One of the most significant challenges we face is the allure of immediate gratification. As noted earlier, our brains are wired to seek instant rewards and prioritize short-term pleasure over long-term benefits. This biological preference for immediate gratification can pose obstacles to lasting habit change.

Emphasize Delayed Gratification

To overcome the challenges of immediate gratification and stay committed to long-term habit change, it is essential we develop strategies that help us resist short-term temptations and maintain focus on our desired long-term outcomes. One effective strategy is to reframe our mindset and *shift our perspective from seeking instant rewards to valuing delayed gratification.* By recognizing the long-term benefits and envisioning the positive impact of our habits on our lives, we can increase our motivation to persist with habit transformation. We will discuss this in some depth in Principle 7 as we bring our Current and Future Selves into conversation about the consequences of seeking immediate gratification.

Examples:

Life: Imagine you want to lead a healthier lifestyle by incorporating regular exercise into your daily routine. However, you often find yourself succumbing to the immediate pleasure of lounging on the couch after a long day of work instead of going for a run. The allure of immediate relaxation outweighs the long-term benefits of exercise. To overcome this challenge, you can employ strategies such as setting clear goals, creating a structured workout schedule, and finding a workout buddy for accountability. By focusing on the delayed rewards of improved fitness, increased energy levels, and long-term well-being, you can overcome the temptation of immediate gratification and stay committed to your fitness habit.

Career. Let's consider the challenge a hedge fund professional faces in choosing immediate gratification over long-term investment strategies. They may face pressure to achieve short-term gains to meet quarterly targets or appease impatient stakeholders. However, succumbing to immediate rewards at the expense of long-term investment strategies can undermine their career success. To address this challenge, they can emphasize the importance of disciplined decision-making and align their actions with their long-term investment objectives. By reframing their mindset to prioritize steady and sustainable growth over short-term gains, they can navigate the demands of immediate gratification and make informed investment decisions that contribute to long-term career success.

Swap Bad Habits for Good Habits with the Same Reward

Replacing a bad habit (i.e., a habit that generates negative consequences) with a good habit (i.e., one that generates positive consequences) *that delivers the same reward* is a powerful strategy for habit transformation. This approach leverages the underlying motivation behind the habit, acknowledging that *it is often the reward that drives our behavior*. By identifying a healthier alternative to the behavior that provides a similar reward, we can redirect our actions towards positive habits while satisfying our underlying needs or desires.

The first step in this strategy is to gain a deep understanding of the reward you associate with the bad habit. It could be emotional relief, stress reduction, or a sense of pleasure. Once we have identified the core reward, we can explore alternative habits that offer the same or similar benefits.

To successfully replace a bad habit with a good habit, it is important to make the alternative habit as easily accessible and appealing as possible. Create an environment that supports the new habit by removing triggers and cues associated with the old habit and incorporating cues that prompt the desired behavior. For instance, if the bad habit is excessive screen time, you can make it a habit to keep a book by your bedside or designate a specific time for reading to replace the habit of mindless scrolling.

Consistency and repetition are key to solidifying the new habit and rewiring the neural pathways associated with the old habit. Practice the new habit consistently, ideally in the same context or situation where the old habit used to occur. Over time, the new habit will become automatic and replace the old habit, leading to positive behavior changes.

When implementing this strategy in different areas of life, career, and business, the principles remain the same. For personal habits, such as improving fitness, replacing the habit of sedentary behavior with regular exercise can provide the same sense of accomplishment and physical well-being. In a career context, replacing the habit of procrastination with effective time management techniques can lead to increased productivity and career advancement. In a business setting, replacing inefficient or outdated processes with streamlined and innovative approaches can deliver similar rewards in terms of operational efficiency and profitability.

By consciously replacing a bad habit with a good habit that delivers the same reward, we can transform our behaviors in a positive and sustainable way. This strategy empowers us to harness the underlying motivations behind our habits and channel them towards actions that align with our goals and values.

Conclusion

In conclusion, rewards and consequences play a pivotal role in the process of habit formation and transformation. Understanding the power of rewards and consequences can help us master the intricate dance of habit change. By recognizing the role of rewards in the Habit Loop and identifying the rewards associated with our current habits, we can gain insights into why certain behaviors stick and others fade away. Additionally, assessing the overall impact of our habits, both positive and negative, empowers us to make informed decisions and drive positive behavior change.

Leveraging rewards strategically becomes a key element in sustaining motivation and reinforcing positive habit transformation. By differentiating between intrinsic and extrinsic rewards, we can tap into their respective strengths and align them with our personal values and goals. Combining both types of rewards, we create a robust system of reinforcement that supports consistency and facilitates long-lasting behavior change.

Furthermore, consequences serve as effective motivators for habit transformation, highlighting the impact our habits have on our well-being, personal growth, relationships, and overall success. Understanding the allure of immediate gratification and emphasizing delayed gratification can help us overcome obstacles and prioritize long-term goals over short-term desires.

As we reap the rewards and escape the consequences, we lay the groundwork for successful habit transformation. By leveraging the twin forces of pleasure and pain, we pave the way for lasting change and align our future selves with our current selves. Transitioning to Principle 7, we will explore how consulting with our future self and aligning our actions with our future goals can further enhance our habit transformation journey.

Summary Q & A

1. What role do rewards and consequences play in habit formation?
    They shape our behaviors, reinforce habits, and influence the outcomes of our efforts.

2. What is the significance of dopamine in the brain's reward system?
    Dopamine, known as the "feel-good" neurotransmitter, is released when we engage in pleasurable or beneficial behaviors, reinforcing them and motivating us to repeat them.

3. How do negative consequences contribute to habit change?
    Negative consequences serve as powerful motivators in behavior modification and habit transformation by signaling that change is necessary to avoid further harm or dissatisfaction.

4. How do rewards strengthen the habit loop?
    Rewards trigger the release of neurotransmitters such as dopamine, reinforcing the neural connections associated with a habit and making it more likely to be repeated in the future.

5. Why do certain behaviors that have negative consequences still feel rewarding?
    Evolutionary factors, cultural influences, and the brain's response to immediate rewards can make negative behaviors feel rewarding despite their long-term harm.

6. How can understanding the potential negative consequences associated with habits help us make informed choices?
    Awareness of negative consequences allows us to evaluate the impact of behaviors on our well-being, success, and goals, enabling us to consciously align our actions with positive outcomes.

7. How can we break reward cycles associated with negative habits?
    Increasing awareness of long-term consequences, engaging the prefrontal cortex for rational decision-making, seeking support,

implementing behavior change techniques, and leveraging social networks can help break the reward cycle.

8. What is the purpose of assigning scores to rewards and consequences in habit assessment?

   Assigning scores to rewards and consequences allows us to create a logical framework for evaluating the value and significance of our habits. It helps us objectively compare the positive benefits against the negative consequences.

9. How can we determine the criteria for scoring the rewards and consequences of habits?

   We can identify criteria based on factors important to us, such as health, productivity, personal growth, financial impact, alignment with goals, and overall well-being. Assigning weights to each criterion helps prioritize their significance.

10. What should we do if the total consequences score outweighs the total rewards score in habit assessment?

    If the total consequences score is higher, it indicates that the habit has more negative consequences than positive rewards, suggesting the need for modification or eradication.

Exercises

1. Reflect on a habit you have successfully formed or transformed in the past. Identify the rewards and consequences associated with that habit and explain how they influenced the change.

2. Choose a specific habit you would like to change or develop. List three potential rewards that could reinforce this new habit and motivate you to continue it.

3. Conduct a self-assessment of your daily routines and habits. Identify one habit that provides immediate rewards but has negative long-term consequences. Develop a plan to replace this habit with a healthier alternative.

4. Take a habit you want to assess and identify five criteria that are important to you in evaluating its impact. Assign weights to each criterion based on their relative significance.

5. Develop a rubric for one of the criteria identified in Exercise 1. Define different levels or categories of performance and provide specific descriptions for each category.

6. Evaluate the benefits of a habit you want to assess using the rubric. Assign scores to each level/category based on the habit's impact on the criterion.

7. Evaluate the drawbacks or negative consequences of the same habit using the same rubric. Assign scores based on the consequences' impact on the criterion.

8. Calculate the total rewards score and the total consequences score for the habit assessed.

9. Compare the total rewards score against the total consequences score for the habit. Determine whether the habit has more positive benefits or negative consequences.

10. Choose one habit that has more positive benefits than negative consequences based on the assessment. Reflect on how you can further enhance or optimize this habit to maximize its impact.

Principle 7:
Consult Your Future Self

*"The ability to discipline yourself to delay gratification
in the short term in order to enjoy greater rewards in the long term
is the indispensable prerequisite for success."*
- Brian Tracy

Have you ever found yourself making what you believed to be a sound decision, only to regret that choice at a later point? If so, you may be dealing with a conflict of interest between your present self and your future self. Our present selves often prioritize immediate rewards and take the path of least resistance, while our future selves are driven by purpose, meaning, and long-term goals. Balancing the needs and desires of our current and future selves is essential in aligning our actions and creating a fulfilling life. However, this balance is often elusive as our brains are wired to seek instant gratification and short-term gains. Our ancient survival instincts, coupled with the influence of modern culture and technology, make it challenging to delay gratification and prioritize long-term rewards. In this chapter, we explore the concept of consulting our future selves, understanding our present selves' drives, and bridging the gap between them through strategic habit-building and the use of pleasure as a tool for progress.

Key Question:
*How can we bridge the gap between our present and future selves,
and cultivate a sense of harmony between our short-term
desires and long-term goals?*

167

The ability to think in the abstract and envision future rewards does not come naturally to anyone; it is a skill we must develop through consistent practice over time.

> *Research conducted by psychologists Oettingen and Gollwitzer demonstrated that utilizing a strategy called "mental contrasting" increased individuals' motivation to pursue their goals by vividly imagining both the positive future outcome and the potential obstacles they might face. This technique improved goal attainment rates by 30-40%.*[35]

Although visualizing our future selves can be a source of motivation, the allure of instant pleasure often surpasses the appeal of long-term benefits. This is because activities offering immediate gratification activate dopamine responses in our brain, reinforcing our desire to engage in those behaviors repeatedly. In contrast, delaying gratification necessitates a higher level of mental exertion and cognitive resources.

To overcome this present-future struggle, then, we must reframe our habits and choices to provide immediate rewards that also benefit our future selves. By finding ways to satisfy our present needs while progressing toward our long-term goals, we can "hack" our brain's tendency for immediate rewards and build better habits that align with our desired future.

The Current Self: Immediate Gratification

Our brains and behaviors evolved in environments where scarcity and uncertainty were the norm and the future was unpredictable. During this time, we needed to seize on immediate rewards and resources whenever possible to ensure we survived. Today, we still tend to overvalue short-term rewards and discount future rewards that might be more meaningful or life-enhancing.

---

[35] Wang, Guoxia et al. "A Meta-Analysis of the Effects of Mental Contrasting With Implementation Intentions on Goal Attainment." *Frontiers in psychology* vol. 12 565202. 12 May. 2021, doi:10.3389/fpsyg.2021.565202

Here is why we often choose immediate gratification over future rewards:

Evolutionary Purpose

Because our ancient ancestors immediately took advantage of survival resources, we evolved drives for instant gratification and short-term thinking as an adaptive mechanism. Those drives ensured we met our immediate needs of survival and reproduction, even if bigger rewards came later.

Our obsession with immediate gratification can be traced back to our evolutionary history. Human beings have an innate desire to meet their basic needs, and this desire has been shaped by our ancestors' experiences of near-extinction due to starvation. In such situations, prioritizing immediate rewards and satisfying cravings right away was crucial for survival. This evolutionary bias toward immediate gratification has been passed down through generations and still influences our behavior today.

Another aspect of our evolutionary history that contributes to our preference for immediate gratification is procreation. The act of procreation was designed to be pleasurable, ensuring that humans would continue to reproduce and pass on their genes. Pleasure-seeking behaviors — such as indulging in delicious food, engaging in sexual activities, or spending time with others — are deeply ingrained in our biology and often lead us to seek instant gratification in various aspects of our lives.

However, it is essential to recognize that our modern environment is vastly different from the one our ancestors faced. The abundance of resources and opportunities available today can make it challenging to resist the temptation of immediate gratification, even when doing so may be detrimental to our long-term well-being.

By understanding the evolutionary roots of our desire for instant gratification, we can develop strategies to resist these urges and focus on long-term fulfillment instead.

Brain Development

The human brain evolved over millions of years into a complex system, but the older and more primal parts of our brain still drive us to pursue pleasure and avoid pain. These drives are tied to dopamine responses for motivation and reinforcement.

The Prefrontal Cortex

The prefrontal cortex is the reasoning part of our brain. It is responsible for self-control, long-term thinking, and delayed gratification, and didn't evolve until more recently. It regulates and moderates the older parts of the brain and helps us manage their strong dopamine responses to immediate rewards. Dopamine is the feel-good hormone that drives us to engage in instant gratification by associating it with positive feelings we want to experience again.[36] Self-control and delayed gratification, however, require mental effort and resources. When we are depleted, fatigued, or stressed, it is difficult for the prefrontal cortex to override the more primal brain regions and behaviors.[37] Our present self's desire for instant rewards dominates in these states, but developing an understanding of the power of instant gratification can make us aware of how it impacts our choices and can lead us to self-mastery.

Why Immediate Gratification Often Wins

While our brains crave dopamine and strive for efficiency, there are both psychological and genetic factors at play that influence our ability to think long-term and align our habits with our best interests.

---

[36] Bromberg-Martin, Ethan S et al. "Dopamine in motivational control: rewarding, aversive, and alerting." *Neuron* vol. 68,5 (2010): 815-34. doi:10.1016/j.neuron.2010.11.022

[37] Clear, James. *Atomic Habits: Tiny Changes, Remarkable Results : An Easy & Proven Way to Build Good Habits & Break Bad Ones*. New York: Avery, an imprint of Penguin Random House, 2018.

When we resist short term gratification, this is what we are fighting against:

Lack of Abstraction

Long-term thinking and delayed gratification involve abstract reasoning — that is, being able to envision and value rewards that do not exist in the present moment. This kind of reasoning is dependent upon neural connections and skills that we must develop over time. Young children in particular struggle with delayed gratification because they do not have the brain maturity adults do. For some, developing strong abstract thinking and self-control skills takes considerable time and practice into adolescence and even early adulthood.

Habitual Mindlessness

Over time, we develop habits of choosing instant gratification without much conscious thought. We form these habits through the frequent reinforcement of dopamine rewards and they become automatic responses to triggers. To break habits of instant gratification, we must develop awareness of triggers and make a conscious effort to make alternative choices that align better with our long-term goals or values. Mindless reactions must become mindful and strategic responses.

Learned Expectations

We have learned to expect instant results and quick fixes for our problems or desires. Modern culture in particular has taught us to value speed, efficiency, convenience, and consumption. This primes us to demand immediate gratification rather than working or waiting for more meaningful rewards or experiences. We must learn to challenge these unrealistic expectations of an easy fix.

Here are some examples of choosing immediate gratification over long-term satisfaction:

> **Life**: After a hard day at work, you may opt to binge-watch TV shows instead of going for a run, or indulge in

unhealthy fast food instead of sticking to the more nutritious food you've already meal-prepped.

Career: In the realm of career development, prioritizing immediate gratification may involve procrastinating on important tasks by engaging in non-work-related activities, such as excessive social media scrolling or entertainment, instead of focusing on professional growth and advancement.

Business: Within the context of any business, succumbing to the allure of short-term gains and overlooking long-term investment strategies can lead to risky decisions and potential negative consequences for the overall stability and success of the organization.

Genetics

Your ability to delay gratification and maintain a future-oriented mindset depends in part on your genetics and innate behavioral tendencies. Some people are born with a higher capacity for self-control, patience, and long-term thinking. Their biology and brain functioning support willpower reserves, dopamine regulation, and prefrontal cortex development that enable them to balance their present and future interests more easily.

However, anyone can strengthen these skills and cultivate habits of delaying gratification through continuous practice and work. For those born with a stronger tendency to seek immediate rewards or act without forethought, developing future orientation may require extra conscious effort, strategy, and persistence. But progress is possible when we build awareness, motivation, and mental habits that serve our purpose and priorities over our passing impulses.

Understanding how our natural tendencies, temperament, and biology impact our decision making can help us in several key ways:

- It helps us develop self-compassion. We see that some of our struggles with delaying gratification arise from factors outside our control rather than personal flaws or inadequacies alone. This understanding enables us to cultivate a growth mindset, where we perceive abilities as malleable through effort and dedication.

- It guides us to devise strategies tailored to our needs. If we struggle with impulsiveness or lack natural patience, we can focus on habit strategies that help us regulate dopamine and cultivate optimism, start very small, limit our choices, increase our accountability, build environmental supports that empower us to succeed, and review our progress to motivate us during that process.

- It helps us maintain motivation despite difficulties. Once we understand that our challenges with delaying gratification are based on our biology, we'll begin to anticipate obstacles and see them as normal fluctuations that we can manage with alternative strategies rather than signs of failure or reasons to give up. Motivation comes from expecting challenges and working to navigate them. Understanding and accepting ourselves helps us develop trust in our dedication to continuous learning and progress.

While genetics contribute to behavioral tendencies that impact our present and future orientations, continuous dedicated effort and a commitment to understanding ourselves provides us with resources to strengthen our self-mastery in line with our purpose. Insight into biology can help us develop the strategies we need to ensure advancement despite the inborn influences that can accelerate or hinder our progress.

Overcoming the Struggle: Bring the Rewards Forward

The key to overcoming our tendency for immediate gratification is not to deny ourselves any reward or pleasure, but rather to find ways to satisfy our present self that also benefit our future self. We need to reframe our habits and choices so that they provide us small sources of reinforcements in the short-term while still moving us closer to our long-term goals. In doing so, we can train our brains to value the process of working toward our goals and develop the self-control necessary to resist instant gratification.

For example, imagine you are trying to break the habit of sleeping in late and running behind schedule each morning. Your immediate reward for hitting the snooze button is getting a few more minutes of rest, but this means your future self suffers the consequences of rushing around and being late for work. You can reframe this habit, however, to provide yourself with an immediate reward that also benefits your future self. If you wake up and get out of bed 15 minutes earlier each day, you reward yourself by drinking a hot cup of coffee or listening to an upbeat playlist as you get ready. This provides you with an immediate incentive to get out of bed, but also means your future self will start the day on time with less stress.

Similarly, you can give yourself immediate an incentive to get into the habit of exercising. Let's say you want to start an exercise routine but struggle with motivation. You know that exercising regularly will provide you with long-term health benefits, but you crave more instant rewards. To satisfy your present and future selves, you can start very small and commit to just 10 minutes of exercise a day, 3 days a week; then you can give yourself an immediate reward after each short workout, such as a favorite snack or TV show. Over time, as exercise becomes a habit, you can build up the time and frequency, but still maintain those short-term reinforcements to keep your present self engaged while your future self reaps the rewards of better fitness.

The key in both examples is reframing the habit to provide smaller upfront rewards that lead to bigger rewards and benefits over time through consistency and progress. This allows you to satisfy your need for instant gratification in the short term, while still serving your future self interest in the long run. This is how you can outsmart your brain's tendency for immediate rewards and build better habits.

Akrasia

The word 'akrasia' comes from ancient Greek and means "without command (over oneself)" or "lack of self-control." In a psychological and philosophical sense, akrasia refers to the state of acting against one's better judgment or good sense. It is the failure to follow through on our intentions, plans, or resolutions due to a lack of self-restraint. The concept of akrasia dates back to Aristotle and Plato, who wrote about the challenge of acting with knowledge of what is good but what goes against one's virtue and long-term best interests.

Akrasia refers to acting against your better judgment. It happens when your present self's wants outweigh your future self's priorities in the moment of choice. To gain freedom from akrasia, use strategies that empower you to act on your values and long-term goals over temporary desires or impulses.

Several strategies can help you overcome akrasia:

Pre-commitment means committing to your future self's choice in advance. It could involve telling a friend you will exercise to stay accountable, putting your alarm across the room so you have to get up to turn it off, or only keeping certain snacks at home to stop yourself from eating too much sugar or salt. Pre-commitment makes the right choice easier and the wrong one harder. It empowers you to use future-minded thinking during times of the day when your willpower is strong to help your present self make good decisions later on.

Design your ***environment*** to activate your future self. Keep reminders of your goals visible. Put workout clothes and equipment in plain sight. Only buy groceries for healthy meals. Make cues for distraction-free work or family time. Environment influences your choices, so optimize it to fit your priorities. When your future self's vision automatically comes to mind, you gain freedom to choose what really matters over passing urges alone.

Build **accountability** to others who share your values and priorities. Let them know your goals so they can check-in on your progress. Consider hiring a coach. Accountability partners provide you with motivation and encourage you to make future-oriented choices. They see your potential and insist you persist despite obstacles or excuses. Accountability ignites your sense of determination to avoid disappointing those who believe in and support you.

Notice beliefs that make it harder for you to choose what you really want. Thoughts such as "I don't have enough self-control" or "My circumstances won't allow change" fuel akrasia by discouraging you or teaching you to believe your choices don't matter. Look for evidence that proves these beliefs are too extreme. Develop a growth mindset by viewing abilities as improvable through practice. Although you will inevitably face external circumstances beyond your control, remember that you always retain the power to choose your response and take gradual steps toward change. Challenge your limitations and embrace empowering beliefs by acknowledging even the smallest signs of progress. Each win expands your freedom and control.

Examples:

> **Life:** Instead of succumbing to the temptation of spending the evening watching TV, you choose to go for a jog and prioritize your health and fitness goals. You pre-commit by scheduling the jog in advance and informing a friend who will check on your progress. By making this better choice, you align your actions with your long-term vision of a healthy and active lifestyle.

> **Career:** Instead of procrastinating on an important project, you choose to break it down into smaller tasks and

tackle them systematically. You pre-commit by setting specific deadlines for each task and sharing your plan with a trusted colleague who will hold you accountable. By making this better choice, you prioritize your long-term career growth and demonstrate a proactive approach to achieving professional success.

Business: Instead of cutting corners to meet short-term financial targets, you choose to invest in research and development to improve product quality and innovation. You pre-commit by establishing strict quality control measures and involving a team of experts who will monitor adherence. By making this better choice, you prioritize the long-term success and reputation of your business, ensuring sustainable growth and customer satisfaction.

The Future Self: Long Term Fulfillment

Imagine that a powerful ally resides within you, a wise and experienced guide who knows the outcomes of your choices and the impact they have on your life. This ally is your Future Self, a version of you who has journeyed through time and gained invaluable insights. When it comes to building and changing your habits, consulting with your Future Self becomes essential. Before instilling new habits or eradicating old ones, pause and envision the person you aspire to become. Consider how your Future Self would respond to the habits you are contemplating engaging in in the present moment. Do these habits lead you closer to the vision of who you want to be? Do they provide you with fulfillment and growth? Your Future Self holds the key to making wise decisions. By seeking their guidance, you tap into a reservoir of wisdom that empowers you to bridge the gap between where you are now and where you want to be. Embrace the power of your Future Self as you navigate the path of habit formation, knowing that each choice you make in consultation with them propels you toward a future of your own design.

Future Selves: Timeframe

Your future self is not just a distant vision years from now; it encompasses the person you will become in the next hour, day, or week. The choices you make today shape the reality and possibilities for your future self, whether they lead to improvement or detriment. Your vision of who you want to be and what you aspire to achieve or experience, in the long run, serves as a guiding force for your present choices. It acts as a compass, directing your current decisions and habits. Your ability to imagine and reason abstractly empowers you to set meaningful goals and make choices that align with your vision of a better future. By having a clear sense of direction and purpose, you can make intentional decisions that move you closer to your desired outcomes.

By consulting your future self in various time frames, you can ensure that your actions today align with your well-being and goals for tomorrow. While present pleasures come and go, the person you become over days, weeks, and years is shaped directly through the choices you make in the present moment. Taking into account the best interests of your future selves before succumbing to passing impulses alone is a wise approach.

For example, opting to indulge in a night of heavy drinking may leave your Next Morning Self feeling drained and burdened by the consequences. Choosing to stay in for a productive evening, however, will leave your Next Morning Self feeling accomplished and full of energy. It's important to consider the impact of your actions today on your future self in different time frames — whether it's in the next few hours, weeks, or even years — before engaging in behaviors that you may later regret.

Some benefits of considering your future self in habit decisions include:

- **Avoiding regret and negative outcomes.** Thinking about how your future self may feel based on your choices today helps ensure you act in ways align with your goals and values to prevent regret, wasted effort or lost opportunities. Your future self will appreciate optimal choices now.

- **Fostering accountability and integrity.** When you consider your future self, you recognize the responsibility you have to them based on choices made today. You feel compelled to act with integrity to your long-term priorities and values to avoid self-sabotage. Accountability to your future self motivates you to stay dedicated to meaningful habits and goals each day that accumulate greatly over time through consistency and practice.

It can help to actually have an imaginary conversation with your future self before making habit choices today. Ask your future self how you will feel about the options you are considering. Talk to the version of yourself that chooses to engage in a bad habit now. What implications and suffering does that version of yourself endure for your lack of discipline now? Do the same thing with the future you that chose well in this moment. What benefits and pleasures does that version of you experience because of your good decision now?

Choose the option your future self will appreciate and benefit from most based on your long-term goals and priorities. Make choices today your future self will thank you for through the progress and opportunities they enable by acting with your whole self — past, present and future — in mind.

Example:

As you contemplate having another glass of wine at dinner (or whether to order a bottle or just a glass), consult with your future self the next morning. Imagine waking up refreshed, alert, and ready for your important meeting, knowing that you made a responsible decision the night before. By visualizing the positive outcome of resisting immediate gratification, you can strengthen your resolve to prioritize your long-term well-being over short-term pleasure. This approach helps you develop self-control and discipline, enabling you to make better choices that align with your goals and values.

The Two Versions of Your Future Self

In life, we often face choices that can lead to two different versions of our future selves. One version experiences the deep fulfillment and pleasure that results from making decisions that prioritize long-term well-being and consult with the future self. The other version experiences the pain and suffering caused by the current self's choices that disregard the future self's needs and desires. For example, consider a scenario where you have the option to invest in your personal development by taking a course to learn new skills. By choosing to invest in yourself, you create a future self that benefits from the acquired knowledge, leading to better career opportunities and personal growth. This decision results in deep fulfillment and long-term satisfaction. On the other hand, if you choose to spend that money on short-term pleasures, such as an extravagant vacation, your future self might suffer from the lack of personal growth and missed opportunities. This decision could lead to feelings of regret and dissatisfaction in the long run.

Another example could be the choice to maintain a healthy lifestyle by exercising regularly and eating well. By prioritizing your health, you create a future self that enjoys the benefits of a strong, healthy body and a higher quality of life. This decision leads to long-term pleasure and fulfillment. However, if you choose to indulge in unhealthy habits, such as excessive eating and a sedentary lifestyle, your future self will suffer from health issues and a lower quality of life. This decision could result in pain, suffering, and a lack of fulfillment in the long run. Ultimately, the ability to consult with our future selves and make decisions that prioritize long-term well-being over short-term gratification can lead to a life filled with deep fulfillment, pleasure, and personal growth. By recognizing the potential consequences of our choices and considering the needs of our future selves, we can create a more satisfying and meaningful life.

Characteristics of Your Future Self

Some key attributes of your future self include:

A Sense of Purpose

Your future self pursues goals, causes, or contributions that provide you with a sense of meaning or purpose greater than instant rewards alone. Having purpose motivates you to sacrifice short-term pleasure for long-term fulfillment.

Growth Orientation

Your future self adopts a growth mindset by believing you can continuously expand your abilities, knowledge, skills, and potential through dedication, learning, and hard work. This makes you willing to step outside your comfort zone and see setbacks as temporary rather than permanent.

Value for Mastery

Your future self seeks mastery and excellence over time through deliberate practice and incremental progress. You value gaining wisdom, new capabilities, and achievements that come only from prolonged focus over years rather than days. Mastery takes precedence over instant success or validation.

Delayed Gratification

Your future self can envision rewards that may take months, years, or decades to achieve and finds motivation in advancing toward them rather than what can be gained in the present moment. You exhibit self-control and patience while building good habits and skills step by step.

Discipline & Habit

Your future self recognizes that real change and progress depends on consistent discipline and habit over willpower alone. You intentionally cultivate habits and routines that propel you forward each day however small your steps may be. Success comes through practice.

Flexible Optimism

Your future self maintains optimism and hope while also facing difficulties or setbacks with pragmatic flexibility. You expect challenges and see them as inevitable parts of progress rather than permanent impediments to your success. Flexible optimism leads you to try new strategies as needed to navigate obstacles, rather than attribute failure to what you might perceive in the short term as fixed inadequacies. To develop this mindset, you need a strong internal locus of control.

Examples:

Life: In envisioning your future self for life, you may see yourself as someone who lives with a strong sense of purpose. You prioritize meaningful goals that align with your core values, such as making a positive impact on others or contributing to a cause you deeply care about. Your future self seeks fulfillment and finds gratification in the long-term rewards that come from pursuing a purpose-driven life, even if it means sacrificing immediate pleasures for the sake of greater meaning.

Career: For your future self in your career, you envision continuous growth and development. You adopt a growth mindset, believing in your ability to learn and improve over time. Your future self embraces challenges, seeks out new opportunities, and remains resilient in the face of setbacks. Mastery is a driving force for your career aspirations, as you value honing your skills, acquiring knowledge, and achieving excellence through deliberate practice. Your focus is on long-term progress rather than seeking instant success or validation.

Business: In the context of business, your future self sees a vision of success built on discipline, habit, and flexibility. You recognize that sustainable progress in business requires consistent effort and the cultivation of effective habits. Your future self is committed to maintaining discipline, following through on tasks, and making daily progress, knowing that small steps add up to significant achievements over time. With a flexible and optimistic mindset, you embrace challenges as opportunities for growth and adaptation. Your future self is resilient, adapting strategies as needed to overcome obstacles and navigate the ever-changing business landscape.

Developing a Deeper Connection with Your Future Self

Here are some exercises to strengthen your connection with your future self:

- Find your "why" by connecting the meaningful habits and choices you perform and make today to the purpose, impact, or fulfillment they will provide your future self as well as those who celebrate those achievements with you. Remember your "why" whenever you're faced with options for instant gratification that conflict with your vision. Purpose fuels determination.

- Practice delayed gratification. Regularly choose longer-term rewards over instant pleasure or relief. Learn to appreciate waiting for more meaningful outcomes and gains that unfold over time through incremental and optimized habit building. Choose what your future self will appreciate most over what will only satisfy you in the moment. Delayed gratification connects your present to your future purpose.

- Visualize your future self. Spend time envisioning what you want to achieve 5, 10, or 20 years from now and who you aspire to become. Picture this future self in as much detail as possible, including how it feels to engage in key habits, relationships, and activities.

Visualization motivates us to bring our imagined selves to life.

- Journal to your future self. Write letters to your future self to give voice to your meaningful goals and priorities and clarify the vision that will motivate you to make good choices today that improve your tomorrow. Describe your purpose, values, and the rewards of delayed gratification in a personal journal. This reflection strengthens your reasoning for resisting fleeting pleasures that keep you from reaching your goals. Your thoughts become your actions.

- Review your progress regularly. Continually evaluate your growth and wins, large and small, to keep yourself motivated over time. Progress strengthens a growth mindset as we advance toward our best selves, so make adjustments to improve your chance of success and celebrate the progress you make as you advance toward your best self.

- Notice thoughts you use to justify instant gratification. Your present self may say things such as "I deserve this", "It won't matter in the long run", or "One time won't hurt." Challenge these thoughts by considering your future self's perspectives and needs. Which choice is more meaningful and which one will make your future self proud?

- Find balance through moderation. Rather than seeing choices as either/or battles between your present or future self, look for ways to meet your current desires strategically so they also support your progress and purpose over time. Moderation sustains motivation and helps you avoid burnout from feeling deprived in the present moment. Have your cake in moderation and eat it too, but on your own terms and in alignment with your own timeline, values, and aspirations.

- Watch for emotional reasoning that drives you to prioritize current feelings over future gains. Your present self may make choices to reduce discomfort, anxiety, restlessness, or other negative emotions in the moment without considering future consequences. Take a step back and reason through your choices to determine what your future self would prefer for optimal wellbeing and progress. Balance emotion with logic.

- Look for signs you are acting in your own self-interest. Choosing to engage in behaviors that build your skills, expand your mindset, strengthen your determination, or fulfill your sense of purpose and mastery serve your future self's interests. Giving in to instant pleasure alone often leaves you with feelings of guilt, regret, depletion, or meaninglessness that signal a misalignment with your deeper priorities or values. Progress, on the other hand, energizes you and deepens your self-trust.

- Review how you feel after making a choice. If you feel empowered, uplifted, and closer to your goals, that signifies that you are in alignment with your future self's needs. But if you feel emotionally drained, ashamed, or unsatisfied, you may have chosen to sacrifice self-mastery or purpose for immediate pleasure. Learn from your outcomes so that, next time, you make a choice better aligned with your vision of the future.

- Note that genetics influence your capacity for long-term thinking and delaying gratification. While everyone can improve these abilities through effort and practice, some people may require more conscious work to overcome or compensate for certain innate tendencies or temperaments. Understanding yourself motivates you to design strategies for meeting your goals that are tailored to your needs.

- Life experiences, trauma, adversity, or insecure attachments in childhood can impact your development of long-term thinking and your hope that your presents efforts will pay off in the future. Acknowledge that, while these early experiences can impact the present they need not define them. You can create new mindsets and expectations that fuel your progress with conscious work and time.

Signs Your Future Self is Guiding the Way

Here are some signs you are acting in your own best interest:

- You are engaging in behaviors that expand the boundaries of your comfort zone. Acting in your best interests means doing the things that challenge you, regardless of the discomfort you may experience in doing so. You seek new insights and capacities through experiences that push the envelope of what you once thought possible or easy to achieve. Growth comes from stepping out.

- You are strengthening your determination and self-discipline. Acting in your best interests builds your discipline and resilience. You value long term rewards over instant pleasure and gain freedom by dedicating yourself to life-changing habits. Discipline is the difference.

- You are improving your wellbeing and health. Living in service to your best interests means caring for yourself — body, mind, and relationships — in a balanced, sustainable way. You seek progress over perfection, rest when needed, build connection with others, and maintain resilience through self-care strategies tailored to your needs and values. Wellness supports growth.

- You learn and build wisdom. Acting in your own best interests means seeing each outcome as data that can guide you toward better choices and strategies in the future. You gain insight through both failures and wins, embracing opportunities to rethink and do differently. Judgment comes through experience and wisdom through reflection on it. Openness to learning propels you ahead.

- You serve the greater good. When you make choices that serve your best interests you consider the impact they have on those around you and on society in general. You seek purpose and meaning through your contributions to others as well as through personal gain. Improving the wellbeing of others and serving the common good expands your sense of purpose and personal fulfillment. We rise together.

Cognitive Dissonance

As you learn to make decisions based on your future self's goals, you may become more aware of — and uncomfortable with — the choices that keep you from meeting those goals. This can create what is known as cognitive dissonance — a misalignment of beliefs, values, or attitudes which causes you to experience discomfort. Experiencing cognitive dissonance can actually be a powerful motivator for change, because many people are uncomfortable holding contradictory beliefs about themselves. People will often change their behavior or beliefs to reduce the dissonance and better align their current self with their future self.

Here are some ways to promote alignment between your current and future self:

- Activities such as meditation, mindfulness, and brain exercises improve how well your prefrontal cortex works. A healthy prefrontal cortex helps you build good mental habits and self-control. While some people may need to work harder at delaying gratification due to their genes, anyone can get better at it with regular practice.

- Noticing your thoughts and behaviors helps you understand what motivates you and how to reframe your usual mindsets or responses. For example, ask yourself if wanting an instant reward conflicts with your bigger goals. Self-awareness is key to making choices that match your purpose and values. Your experiences, trauma, or childhood can impact how well you delay gratification or believe your efforts will pay off in the future. But you can choose new mindsets and expectations through work and time.

- Building one small habit or skill at a time, such as doing one push up or meditating one minute a day, helps you connect with your future self. Regular practice over time leads to amazing outcomes through steady progress, however small you start.

- Our culture and technology make it more difficult to delay gratification, but make the choice to limit distractions, build patience, and see technology as a tool to use when you want, rather than something that uses you. Stay focused on your purpose through the choices you make regardless of your schedule or external circumstances. Short-term rewards from clicks or entertainment will never fulfill you like achieving meaningful goals will.

Following through on choices that honor your future self helps you develop self-trust. As you learn to trust your own competence and follow-through, you gain confidence to take risks, adapt after failures, be creative, stay determined, and reach your full potential. Mastery comes from practicing your values each day through action, however small. When you believe that you can become whoever you aspire to be, you begin to act in accordance with that possibility. Let your vision for the future inspire you in the moments you feel like giving up or giving in to what's easy. In the meantime, celebrate your milestones and wins. You'll build motivation as you do.

Conclusion

The battle between our present and future selves is one we must participate in each and every day, but the choices we make from moment to moment can change our lives. As humans, our ancestors overvalued immediate rewards and discounted long-term consequences to ensure their own survival. Our primal brains' poor decision making and lack of follow through reaped outcomes far from optimal wellbeing or purpose. However, progress depends not on an unrealistic expectation of constant willpower or denial of present needs but on learning strategies to satisfy today's needs in ways that also move you ahead toward your most meaningful aspirations.

Understanding why you struggle at times to consider your future self during decision making leads to self-compassion and tailored strategies that strengthen the connection through practice. While the implementation of these strategies can be influenced by genetics, experiences, or environment, continuous practice and navigation of obstacles will help you build momentum. Don't wait for the perfect moment or solution to begin practicing. You can only turn your dreams into reality through consistent action now so start practicing now and course correct as you go. Ultimately, the actions you take will expand your capabilities and wisdom and lead you to self-mastery.

Progress over time depends on balancing your present and future goals through strategies tailored to your needs, values, and purpose. Make the means — the practices and habits — as engaging and meaningful as the ends. Design an environment to activate your optimal self, build accountability and determination through pre-commitment, adjusting expectations and confronting beliefs that may lead to excuses or akrasia. See each outcome as data you can use to guide yourself toward better choices instead of a reason to give up. With practice and patience, you gain competence and wisdom to achieve extraordinary goals through steady dedication alone. Remember to have patience, good things take time and effort. This is an ideal way for us to transition to our next principle where we discuss the most harmful iteration of our habits: addiction.

Summary Q & A

1. Why do our present selves often prioritize immediate rewards?
    Older, primal parts of our brain activate basic drives such as pleasure and avoidance of pain, making it easier to prioritize immediate rewards.

2. What are some key attributes of our future selves?
    Our future selves pursue goals that provide meaning and purpose. They adopt a growth mindset and believe in continuous improvement. They embrace delayed gratification for long-term meaning and rewards.

3. What is cognitive dissonance, and how can it motivate change?
    Cognitive dissonance refers to the discomfort we experience when holding contradictory beliefs, values, or attitudes about ourselves. Experiencing cognitive dissonance can motivate us to make changes in our lives to manage this discomfort.

4. How can we strengthen our prefrontal cortex for self-control?
    Activities such as meditation, mindfulness, and brain exercises can improve the functioning of our prefrontal cortex.

5. How does self-awareness contribute to making choices aligned with our purpose and values?
    By noticing our thoughts and behaviors, we can identify conflicts between our present circumstances and our future goals. Self-awareness enables us to make choices that align with our purpose and values.

6. How can building small habits connect us to our future selves?
    Building one small habit or skill at a time, even a small one, helps us connect our present and future selves. Regular practice and steady progress over time lead to significant outcomes.

7. How can we limit distractions and stay focused on our purpose in a culture that promotes instant gratification?
    Despite our busy schedules and external pressure, we can choose to prioritize progress over the fleeting pleasure of immediate rewards. By staying focused on our purpose and making choices aligned with it, we can resist the pull of instant gratification.

8. How does following through on choices that honor our future self create self-trust?

As we learn to trust in our own competence and reliability, we gain confidence to take risks, adapt after failures, and reach our full potential. By practicing our values through daily actions, we cultivate mastery and belief in our ability to become who we aspire to be.

9. What are some signs that indicate you are acting in your own best interest?

    Signs that indicate you are acting in your own best interest include feeling empowered and uplifted, building meaningful habits and skills, fulfilling your purpose or priorities, strengthening determination and self-discipline, improving well-being and health, and serving the greater good.

10. What strategies can be used to overcome akrasia and make choices aligned with your future self's priorities?

    Strategies to overcome akrasia include pre-commitment, designing your environment to activate your future self, building accountability with others who share your values, noticing and challenging limiting beliefs, and adopting empowering beliefs based on your progress.

Exercises

1. Reflect on a recent situation where you prioritized immediate gratification over long-term goals. How did it impact your progress? What steps can you take to align your present actions with your future aspirations?

2. Practice a mindfulness exercise for 10 minutes each day this week. Pay attention to your thoughts, emotions, and physical sensations. How does this increased self-awareness help you understand your motivations?

3. Choose one small habit that you can incorporate into your daily routine. It could be as simple as reading one page of a book, doing one push-up, or writing one sentence of gratitude. Commit to practicing this habit every day for the next month and observe how it connects you to your future self.

4. Identify one distraction or time-wasting activity that takes you away from your long-term goals. Develop a strategy to limit or minimize this distraction. Set specific boundaries and implement them over the next week. Reflect on how this change in behavior impacts your focus and progress.

5. Write a letter to your future self, describing the person you aspire to become and the goals you want to achieve. Outline the steps you plan to take to reach those goals. Keep this letter somewhere safe and revisit it periodically to keep yourself motivated.

6. Choose a challenging task or skill that aligns with your long-term goals. Break it down into small, manageable steps. Each day, focus on completing one of these steps. Observe how your discipline and commitment to sustained effort contribute to your progress over time.

7. Reflect on a time when you successfully delayed gratification to achieve a meaningful long-term reward. What strategies did you employ? How did it feel to overcome the temptation of instant gratification? Use this reflection to remind yourself of your capacity to make choices in service to your future self.

8. Celebrate a small milestone or win that you recently achieved, no matter how insignificant it may seem. Write down the accomplishment and take a moment to acknowledge your

progress. Share this celebration with a friend or family member to reinforce the positive impact of your efforts.

9. Spend dedicated time envisioning what you want to achieve 5, 10, or 20 years from now and who you aspire to become. Create a detailed mental picture of your future self, including the key habits, relationships, and activities you engage in. How does this visualization activate motivation and make your future self's priorities more emotionally compelling?

10. Write letters to your future self in a personal journal. Describe your purpose, values, and the rewards of delayed gratification. Use this reflection to strengthen your reasoning for resisting mere instant pleasure and make choices that align with your deeper priorities. How does journaling help give voice to your meaningful goals and priorities?

The materials and opinions in this book are for informational and educational purposes only, are not intended to take the place of any expert medical, physical, mental, or psychological health care, nor are they meant to diagnose, treat, prevent, or cure any physical, medical, mental, emotional, or psychological ailment, disease, or condition. The materials and opinions presented herein are not being offered by Arootah or its representatives, coaches, or employees in the capacity of a licensed therapist, health care professional, or mental health expert and should not be used as a substitute, replacement, alternative, or proxy for professional medical, physical, emotional, mental, or psychological health care treatment, counseling, therapy, psychoanalysis, substance abuse treatment, or any other mental or physical health advice, guidance, or counsel. You should maintain a relationship with a physician or other appropriate healthcare provider who is available to provide emergent and urgent care. If you encounter a medical emergency and are not able to obtain care from my primary care physician, contact 911 or report to a hospital emergency department.

Principle 8:
Differentiate Habits & Addictions

Recognizing the Characteristics & Impacts

"Addiction begins with the hope that something 'out there'
can instantly fill up the emptiness inside."
- Jean Kilbourne

What would your answer be if you asked yourself this question about a repetitive behavior of yours: If I were to stop this behavior right now for a month, could I do it without experiencing any discomfort, distress, or withdrawal symptoms? Would my quality of life, health, relationships, or productivity improve without it? In the realm of behavioral change, it is crucial to distinguish between habits and addictions, two distinct phenomena that can significantly impact our lives. While habits can be beneficial and contribute to positive routines, addictions represent complex and potentially harmful patterns of behavior. In this chapter, we will explore the unique characteristics of habits and addictions, shedding light on their fundamental differences and the implications they have on effective behavior change. By understanding these differences, we can navigate the challenges of addiction and cultivate healthy habits for long-lasting transformation.

Key Question:
What are the psychological and neurological aspects of addiction that set
it apart from habitual behavior?

While habits and addictions may share certain similarities, such as repetitive behaviors, it is essential to understand the underlying psychological and neurological factors at play and the potential risks and consequences of addictive behaviors.

Habits, in essence, are repetitive actions that have become automatic and ingrained in our lives through consistent practice. They often contribute to our overall well-being and productivity. Whether we maintain a daily exercise routine, a regular meditation practice, or a weekly cleaning schedule, habits can enhance our lives and fuel our personal growth. In general, we can control our habits and modify or eliminate them with relative ease when they no longer serve their intended purpose in our lives.

According to the Substance Abuse and Mental Health Services Administration (SAMHSA) in the United States, in 2019, approximately 20.4 million people aged 12 or older had a substance use disorder in the past year. This statistic includes both alcohol and illicit drug use disorders.[38]

On the other hand, addictions involve a loss of control and a compulsive engagement in behaviors despite negative consequences. Addictions are characterized by an intense craving and dependency on a substance, activity, or behavior. They hijack the brain's reward system, propelling some people into a destructive cycle in which they are compelled to seek and consume the addictive stimulus. Unlike habits, addictions are difficult to control, and individuals may experience significant negative impacts on their physical health, mental well-being, relationships, and overall functioning because of them.

Distinguishing between habits and addictions is crucial because addictive behaviors carry risks and consequences. While habits can be beneficial and contribute to personal growth, addictions

---

[38] Substance Abuse and Mental Health Services Administration. Results from the 2019 National Survey on Drug Use and Health: Detailed Tables. 2020, https://www.samhsa.gov/data/sites/default/files/reports/rpt29393/2019NSD UHFFRPDFWHTML/2019NSDUHFFR1PDFW090120.pdf.

can have severe detrimental effects on the lives of people suffering from addiction and the lives of those around them. By understanding the distinctions between the two, we can assess our own behaviors and seek appropriate support and intervention if necessary.

Throughout this chapter, we will explore the defining features of habits and addictions, delve into the psychological and neurological aspects underlying addictive behaviors, discuss the risk-reward dynamics in addiction, and highlight the importance of seeking professional help as appropriate. By gaining a deeper understanding of the nature of habits and addictions, we can make informed choices about our habits and cultivate healthier behaviors and lifestyles.

Defining Addiction & its Distinguishing Features

Addiction is a complex condition characterized by compulsive engagement in a substance, activity, or behavior despite negative consequences. The defining features of addiction include[39]:

- *Craving and Dependence:* Addiction is marked by an intense craving and a psychological or physical dependence on the addictive substance or behavior. Persons with addictions may experience a strong urge or desire to engage in the addictive behavior, often resulting in a loss of control.

- *Negative Consequences:* Unlike habits that can also have positive outcomes, addictions lead to negative consequences that affect various aspects of a person's life. These consequences can include physical health issues, strained relationships, financial difficulties, and a decline in overall well-being.

---

[39] Centers for Disease Control and Prevention. "Understanding Drug Use and Addiction." Centers for Disease Control and Prevention, 5 Aug. 2019,

- ***Tolerance & Withdrawal:*** Addictions are often accompanied by tolerance, where a person with an addiction requires larger doses or needs to engage in a behavior more frequently to achieve the desired effect. Additionally, they may experience withdrawal symptoms when they attempt to reduce or discontinue their use of the addictive substance or behavior, which further reinforces the addictive cycle.[40]

Types of Addictions

Addictions can take various forms, and distinguishing between them is crucial for recognizing and addressing these harmful behaviors. There are two primary categories of addictions: substance addiction and behavioral addiction.

Substance Addiction

Substance addiction is characterized by an excessive and uncontrolled use of drugs, including opioids, methamphetamines, alcohol, and cocaine. Individuals struggling with substance addiction continue to use these substances despite experiencing adverse effects on their physical health, relationships, and daily functioning.[41] Substance addiction often involves a physiological and psychological dependence on the substance, where the body becomes accustomed to its presence and experiences withdrawal symptoms when attempting to stop or reduce use. The effects of substance abusive can become pervasive.

The impact of substance addiction goes beyond the immediate physical effects. It can profoundly affect relationships, leading to strained familial and social dynamics, and it can have detrimental consequences in various areas of life, such as work,

---

[40] American Society of Addiction Medicine. "The ASAM Clinical Practice Guideline on Alcohol Withdrawal Management." ASAM, 2020, www.asam.org/docs/default-source/quality-science/the_asam_clinical_practice_guideline_on_alcohol-1.pdf?sfvrsn=ba255c2_2.

[41] Zou, Z., Wang, H., d'Oleire Uquillas, F., Wang, X., Ding, J., & Chen, H. (2017). Definition of Substance and Non-substance Addiction. *Advances in experimental medicine and biology, 1010*, 21–41. https://doi.org/10.1007/978-981-10-5562-1_2

education, and personal well-being. Substance addiction is often accompanied by tolerance, where larger amounts of the substance are required to achieve the desired effect, and withdrawal symptoms, which can be both physically and psychologically distressing.

Behavioral Addiction

Behavioral addiction, on the other hand, involves a compulsive engagement in activities that result in a loss of control and negative consequences. Examples of behavioral addictions include gambling, gaming, or shopping. Individuals with behavioral addictions develop a strong urge to engage in these activities, often experiencing a rush or high when doing so. They find it difficult to resist these urges, even when they interfere with their relationships, work or school responsibilities, and overall well-being.[42]

Similar to substance addiction, behavioral addiction can lead individuals to a cycle of negative consequences in which they may experience financial difficulties, strained relationships, poor academic or job performance, and a loss of interest in other aspects of life. Behavioral addictions can also have significant psychological impacts, such as feelings of guilt, shame, and a diminished sense of self-control.

Both substance addiction and behavioral addiction share common characteristics, such as the loss of control over the behavior, the compulsion to engage in the behavior despite negative consequences, and the potential for tolerance and withdrawal symptoms. However, they differ in the specific substances or activities involved. Recognizing and understanding these different types of addiction is essential in determining appropriate interventions and care for individuals struggling with addiction to facilitate their journey towards recovery.

---

[42] Zou, Z.; et al. (2017). Definition of Substance and Non-substance Addiction. Retrieved on October 2nd, 2018, from
https://www.ncbi.nlm.nih.gov/pubmed/29098666

Psychological & Neurological Aspects of Addiction

Addiction involves intricate psychological and neurological processes that lead people to begin and continue engaging with them despite negative consequences. Understanding these aspects can shed light on the underlying mechanisms of addiction. Key factors include:

Psychological Factors[43]

Psychological factors play a significant role in how and why some people may begin and continue to engage with addictive substances or behaviors. One important psychological factor in addiction is *emotional regulation*. Individuals may turn to addictive behaviors to cope with or regulate their emotions. For example, someone struggling with stress or anxiety may rely on substance use or compulsive behaviors to temporarily alleviate their negative emotions and experience a sense of relief or escape. Similarly, individuals may engage in addictive behaviors to *seek pleasure and reward*, as the addictive substance or activity can provide them with a temporary sense of gratification and enjoyment.

Stress management is another psychological factor that can influence addiction. Stressful life events, chronic stress, or difficulties in managing stress can leave people vulnerable to developing addictive behaviors. Individuals may use substances or engage in addictive behaviors as a maladaptive coping mechanism to cope with stress and alleviate its associated emotional and physiological burden.

Furthermore, underlying psychological factors such as *low self-esteem*, feelings of *loneliness* or social isolation, *trauma*, or untreated *mental health conditions* can contribute to the development and perpetuation of addiction. Some people

---

[43] Nutt, David J., and Fergus D. Law, 'Pharmacological and psychological aspects of drugs abuse', in Michael Gelder and others (eds), *New Oxford Textbook of Psychiatry*, 2 edn (Oxford, 2012; online edn, Oxford Academic, 1 Oct. 2012), https://doi.org/10.1093/med/9780199696758.003.0055, accessed 22 June 2023.

contending with these psychological factors use addictive substances or behaviors as a means of coping.

Examples:

- **Emotional Regulation:** An individual who struggles with social anxiety may find temporary relief from it by turning to alcohol to calm their nerves around other people. The act of drinking becomes a coping mechanism they use to regulate their emotions and alleviate distress.
- **Stress Management:** A person experiencing high levels of stress at work may turn to online gambling to escape their responsibilities and unwind. Engaging in gambling activities provides them temporary distraction from professional obligations and offers them a sense of excitement and relief from stress.
- **Pleasure & Reward:** Someone who feels lonely and lacks social connections may develop a shopping addiction. The act of shopping and acquiring new items may bring them a temporary sense of pleasure and fulfillment, helping them compensate for an emotional void and boost their mood.

Neurological Factors

Neurological factors also play a crucial role in addiction. As previously discussed, the brain's reward system involves the release of the neurotransmitter dopamine which is closely associated with addiction. Neurotransmitters serve as the communicative entities that traverse the space between two neurons. They enable the transmission of signals from the presynaptic neuron to the postsynaptic neuron, effectively facilitating neuronal communication. When individuals engage in addictive behaviors or consume addictive substances, dopamine is released, creating a pleasurable sensation and reinforcing the behavior.[44]

---

[44] Zhang, Y., Schlussman, S. D., Rabkin, J., Butelman, E. R., & Ho, A. (2019). The Neuroscience of Drug Reward and Addiction. Physiological Reviews, 99(4), 2115–

Dopamine Baseline

It is important to note that dopamine is released at a steady baseline rate and any deviation from this baseline can greatly influence our experiences. When the dopamine release surges beyond the baseline, we experience pleasure; a dip below it, on the other hand, can lead us to experience discomfort or pain. This constant release of dopamine, absent of external stimuli such as food or drugs, indicates an individual's baseline happiness or potential level of depression. Over time, this repeated exposure to addictive stimuli leads to changes in the brain's reward circuitry, including desensitization to natural rewards and an increased sensitivity to the addictive stimulus. As a result, the brain rewires itself to prioritize addictive behavior over other natural sources of pleasure and reward. Chronic exposure to substances or behaviors that trigger the release of large amounts of dopamine in the brain's reward pathway can eventually lower the baseline as the brain attempts to manage the surplus.[45]

The neurological changes that result from addiction can contribute to the development of tolerance, where larger amounts of the addictive substance or increased engagement in addictive behavior are required to achieve the same experience of reward. Additionally, withdrawal symptoms may occur when the addictive behavior is discontinued or reduced, reflecting the brain's adjustment to the absence of the addictive stimulus.

Understanding the psychological and neurological factors underlying addiction is crucial for effective treatment and intervention. By addressing these factors through therapies, counseling, and interventions aimed at enhancing emotional regulation, stress management, and coping skills, individuals can work towards breaking the cycle of addiction and establishing healthier habits.

2140. https://doi.org/10.1152/physrev.00014.2018

[45] Berke, Joshua D. "What does dopamine mean?." *Nature neuroscience* vol. 21,6 (2018): 787-793. doi:10.1038/s41593-018-0152-y

Examples:

- ***Substance Addiction:*** An individual regularly consumes cocaine, a powerful stimulant. Each time they use cocaine, the drug stimulates the release of dopamine in the brain's reward pathway, creating euphoria and reinforcing the behavior. Over time, the brain adapts to the presence of cocaine, leading the individual to experience cravings and the need for higher doses to achieve the same level of reward.

- ***Behavioral Addiction:*** A person heavily engages in online gaming. Each time they achieve a milestone or win a game, their brain releases dopamine, reinforcing the neurological value of the behavior and causing them to experience a sense of accomplishment and pleasure. As a result, they become increasingly dependent on gaming to experience that rewarding feeling, leading them to lose control over their behavior and suffer negative consequences in other areas of their life.

- ***Tolerance & Withdrawal:*** In the case of alcohol addiction, prolonged and excessive consumption of alcohol leads to tolerance, where larger amounts are needed to achieve the desired effects. When an individual attempts to reduce or stop drinking, they may experience withdrawal symptoms such as tremors, anxiety, and cravings, indicating the brain's adaptation to the presence of alcohol and the need for it to maintain normal functioning.

Addictive Cycle & the Role of Perpetuating Rewards

The addictive cycle encompasses the pattern of behavior that perpetuates addiction. It involves three main stages:

anticipation, engagement, and aftermath. Fundamental to this cycle is the role of rewards in sustaining addictive behaviors.[46]

1. **Anticipation:** This stage involves the anticipation of the rewarding experience the brain associates with the addictive behavior. It may include craving, preoccupation, and an intense desire to engage in the behavior.

Examples:

- *Craving:* A person with a nicotine addiction feels a powerful craving for a cigarette, especially in situations where they have developed a habit of smoking, such as after a meal or during a break.

- *Preoccupation:* An individual addicted to gambling constantly thinks about placing bets, researching strategies, or fantasizing about the potential winnings, even when engaged in other activities.

- *Intense desire:* Someone with a food addiction may constantly fantasize about their favorite high-calorie foods, yearning for the pleasure and satisfaction they bring.

2. **Engagement:** The engagement stage refers to an individual's actual participation in the addictive behavior, leading to the release of neurotransmitters such as dopamine, which provide a pleasurable or rewarding experience. This reinforces the behavior and strengthens the association between the behavior and the reward.

Examples:

- *Drug use:* A person addicted to opioids engages in the act of consuming a substance, which triggers the release of dopamine, producing feelings of euphoria and pain relief.

---

[46] Koob, G. F., & Volkow, N. D. (2016). Neurobiology of addiction: A neurocircuitry analysis. *The lancet. Psychiatry, 3(8), 760. https://doi.org/10.1016/S2215-0366(16)00104-8*

- *Gambling*: An individual with a gambling addiction actively participates in placing bets, experiencing the thrill and excitement of taking risks and anticipating winning a large sum of money.

- *Excessive shopping*: Someone with a shopping addiction engages in the act of shopping, experiencing a rush of pleasure and satisfaction from making purchases, whether online or in physical stores.

3. **Aftermath:** After engaging in the addictive behavior, individuals may experience a range of emotions, including guilt, shame, or regret, due to the negative consequences that follow. However, despite these negative emotions, the desire for the reward often overrides the negative consequences, perpetuating the addictive cycle.

Examples:

- *Substance abuse aftermath*: Following a drug binge, an individual may feel intense guilt and regret for the damage caused to their health and relationships. However, the desire for the pleasurable effects of the drug may overshadow these negative emotions, leading them to continue their use.

- *Gambling consequences*: After losing a significant amount of money due to gambling, an individual may experience feelings of shame and regret. Despite these negative emotions, the lure of potential winnings and the excitement of the gambling experience may compel them to continue engaging in the behavior.

- *Shopping addiction aftermath*: Someone with a shopping addiction may feel remorse and financial strain after accumulating excessive debt. However, the temporary pleasure and relief from emotional distress obtained through shopping may outweigh the negative consequences, leading them to repeat the behavior.

Understanding the addictive cycle and the role of rewards in sustaining addictive behaviors is crucial in addressing and transforming harmful habits. It highlights the powerful hold addictions can have over the lives of persons with an addiction and underscores the need for effective strategies that allow them to break free from them.

High-Risk, High-Reward Imbalance Phenomenon

Addiction is characterized by a significant risk-reward imbalance, where the immediate rewards of engaging in addictive behaviors outweigh the potential long-term consequences and risks. This imbalance results from how our brains are wired to prioritize immediate gratification over long-term outcomes.[47]

Immediate Rewards
The human brain has evolved to seek immediate rewards as a survival mechanism. The rewards associated with addictive behaviors, such as the euphoria induced by drugs or the excitement one experiences while gambling, are immediate, intense, highly potent, and habit-forming. They provide individuals with instant gratification that can temporarily alleviate their discomfort, stress, or negative emotions or temporarily lead to pleasure or euphoria. This immediate reward reinforces one's engagement with the behavior, making them more likely to repeat it in the future.

Long-Term Harm
In contrast, the potential negative consequences and risks of addictive behaviors often occur in the long term. The harmful effects of substance use disorder (SUD) on physical health, relationships, finances, and emotional health are gradual. As a result, the brain's reward system, which is wired to prioritize

---

[47] Volkow, Nora & Michaelides, Michael & Baler, Ruben. (2019). The Neuroscience of Drug Reward and Addiction. Physiological reviews. 99. 2115-2140. 10.1152/physrev.00014.2018.

immediate rewards, leads users to deny any potential of long-term risks.

This time difference between the immediate reward and the long-term consequences creates a significant imbalance. The allure of the immediate reward, especially in a person struggling with addiction, significantly outweighs any considerations of potential future harm, leading them to continue engaging in addictive behaviors despite the risks.

Understanding this risk-reward imbalance is crucial in comprehending the power of addiction and the challenges individuals face in breaking free from it. By recognizing our inherent bias toward immediate gratification, we can begin to develop strategies and interventions to address addictive behaviors and establish healthier habits through which we prioritize long-term well-being and fulfillment.

Impact of Addictive Rewards on the Brain & Behavior

Addictive rewards have a profound impact on the brain and behavior. The repeated exposure to rewarding stimuli leads to neuroadaptations in the brain's reward circuitry, resulting in tolerance, sensitization, and changes in motivation and decision-making processes.[48]

Tolerance refers to an individual's need to use more of a substance or engage in addictive behaviors more intensely and/or frequently to achieve the same "high" or level of satisfaction. Sensitization, on the other hand, is the heightened response to the rewarding stimuli, that makes the behavior even more alluring. These neuroadaptations can lead addiction sufferers to a shift in their priorities, where the pursuit of the addictive reward becomes their central focus, overriding other natural rewards and impairing their judgment and decision-making.

---

[48] Volkow, N. D., & Morales, M. (2019). The Neuroscience of Drug Reward and Addiction. Physiological Reviews, 99(4), 2115-2140. https://doi.org/10.1152/physrev.00014.2018

Bring the Risks Forward

Bringing the fear of the risks forward in time is indeed a powerful strategy to counteract the risk-reward imbalance in addiction. While these strategies cannot and should not replace professional care, they can make long-term consequences feel more immediate and real for individuals beginning recovery. Here are two strategies for forward thinking:

- **Speaking to the future self:** As discussed in Principle 7, one effective technique for forward-thinking is to encourage individuals to imagine having a conversation with their future selves. This involves envisioning the potential negative outcomes and consequences that could arise from continued engagement with their addictive behaviors. By vividly imagining the future self experiencing those consequences, individuals can establish a stronger emotional connection to the long-term risks. This exercise helps bridge the temporal gap between the immediate rewards and the delayed consequences, enabling individuals to make more informed decisions and prioritize their long-term well-being.[49]

- **Dickens Approach:** Inspired by Charles Dickens' story "A Christmas Carol," the Dickens Approach involves creating a tangible representation of the potential future consequences of addiction. Representations could include a detailed narrative, drawings, or collages depicting the negative outcomes that can result from addictive behaviors. By visually and emotionally engaging with these representations, individuals can experience a more immediate and visceral understanding of the long-term risks. This approach serves as a powerful reminder of the

---

[49] Everitt, Barry J. "Neural and psychological mechanisms underlying compulsive drug seeking habits and drug memories--indications for novel treatments of addiction." *The European journal of neuroscience* vol. 40,1 (2014): 2163-82. doi:10.1111/ejn.12644

potential harm that awaits if they continue down the path of addiction.

Both of these strategies aim to bring the potentially devastating consequences of the risks forward in time to give those suffering with addiction a sense of urgency in addressing their addictive behaviors. By emotionally connecting with the potential consequences, individuals can strengthen their resolve to overcome addiction and make choices that align with their long-term well-being. These approaches provide a way to counterbalance the immediate rewards of addictive behaviors and shift the focus toward the lasting impact of their choices.

Importance of Early Detection & Intervention

Early detection and intervention are paramount when it comes to addressing addiction. Recognizing the signs and symptoms of addiction in its early stages increases one's chances of successful treatment and recovery. It is crucial to be aware of the red flags that may indicate you or a loved one are developing an addiction. These signs and symptoms include a loss of control over the behavior, increased tolerance, withdrawal symptoms, neglect of responsibilities, and negative consequences in various areas of life.

The Signs, Symptoms, & Causes of Addiction

Addiction manifests in different ways, depending on the substance or behavior involved. It is important to understand the specific signs and symptoms of different types of addiction to facilitate early recognition and intervention. As discussed, there are two types of addiction, substance and behavioral with distinct symptoms and signs.

Substance Addiction

Many people suffering with substance addiction exhibit similar physical symptoms such as bloodshot eyes, changes in appetite and sleep patterns, and deterioration of physical appearance. Examples include:

Alcohol Addiction:

- Excessive consumption of alcohol despite negative consequences

- Frequent intoxication and impaired judgment

- Withdrawal symptoms such as tremors, sweating, and anxiety when attempting to quit or reduce use

Opioid Addiction:

- Increasing tolerance to opioids

- Withdrawal symptoms, including nausea, vomiting, muscle aches, and cravings

- Seeking multiple prescriptions (doctor shopping) to maintain drug supply

Cocaine Addiction:

- Restlessness, increased energy, and talkativeness

- Paranoia, anxiety, and irritability

- Financial difficulties due to spending large sums of money on cocaine

Behavioral Addiction

Signs that someone may be battling a behavioral addiction include a preoccupation with the behavior, unsuccessful attempts to quit or cut down, and an inability to manage personal and professional responsibilities. Examples include:

Gambling Addiction:

- Preoccupation with gambling, constantly thinking about past or future bets

- Failed attempts to stop or control gambling behavior

- Jeopardizing personal relationships, work, or education due to gambling activities

Gaming Addiction:

- Excessive gaming, often for extended periods, neglecting other responsibilities

- Irritability and mood swings when unable to play games

- Withdrawal from social interactions and loss of interest in other activities

Shopping Addiction:

- Compulsive and excessive shopping, often resulting in financial difficulties

- Feeling a rush or "high" while shopping

- Hiding purchases or lying about shopping habits to friends and family

High Risk Trait to Addiction: Impulsivity

Many people who are susceptible to addiction exhibit higher levels of impulsivity. Impulsivity is the inability to delay action following a thought or desire to do something. Those who act impulsively, in other words, struggle to create a buffer between their thoughts and their behaviors.[50]

In many contexts, impulsivity is positive. Impulsive individuals may speak more freely and may act on their ideas or desires without hesitation. In certain situations, such as crisis scenarios where rapid response is critical, impulsivity can be beneficial and life-saving.

---

[50] Ersche, K. D., & Sahakian, B. J. (2007). The neuropsychology of amphetamine and opiate dependence: Implications for treatment. Neuropsychology Review, 17(3), 317-336.

Pleasure vs. Escape from Pain

People generally think of addiction as solely a pleasure-seeking behavior. However, relief from pain is the other big draw. While pleasure and painlessness may seem similar, they are rooted in different motivations and experiences. When an individual develops pleasure-seeking behaviors, they are primarily driven by the positive reinforcement that the substance or activity provides them. This behavior is typically associated with the release of dopamine and other neurotransmitters in the brain that stimulate feelings of pleasure or reward. These individuals often start to use the substance or engage in the activity because it provides them with a sense of euphoria, joy, or satisfaction. As their brains adapt to the pleasurable experiences over time, they may develop a dependence, needing to increase their behavior or substance use to continue experiencing the level of pleasure that first drew them to it.

On the other hand, addictions that emerge from pain are more often related to negative reinforcement. In these scenarios, the person suffering with addiction uses the substance or behavior to cope with and numb physical or emotional discomfort, pain, or distress. The pain may emerge from anxiety, depression, trauma, stress, or physical pain. They are avoiding suffering more than they are seeking pleasure which motivates them to use the substance or engage in the activity again and again.

Both scenarios, in other words, ultimately lead to addiction, but an individual's journey to addiction and their underlying motivations can be quite different. It's worth noting that these two pathways are not mutually exclusive and can certainly overlap as some people may seek pleasure and relief from pain simultaneously.

Boredom

In today's hyper-connected, digital world, boredom has become a sort of rarity. As businesses have begun to recognize our cultural anxiety around boredom (or *horror vacui*), they have begun to provide a panoply of services, products, and platforms to keep us engaged. The barrage of potential distractions is virtually endless, from streaming services boasting thousands of hours of content to social media platforms designed to keep us scrolling endlessly to mobile games that engross us in virtual worlds. Even our pockets buzz with notifications, each one vying for our attention, keeping our minds continually stimulated.

In the context of addiction, however, this cultural aversion to boredom and the readily available distractions can become problematic. Boredom, a seemingly innocuous state of being, can in fact, play a significant role in the development of addictive behaviors. This role is rooted in our basic human drive for stimulation, novelty, and experiences beyond the mundane. If we do not find the world around us engaging, we may begin to experience a sense of emptiness, a vacuum that may tempt some of us to turn to substances or behaviors that provide us with immediate gratification.

The easy accessibility to addictive substances or behaviors becomes a shortcut to pleasure for many people struggling with emptiness. This reliance on external sources of pleasure for fulfillment can easily turn into a dependence, as the brain, ever adaptable, begins to require more of these substances or behaviors to achieve the same level of satisfaction.

In the absence of fulfilling and engaging tasks or pursuits, certain individuals can find themselves with a surplus of idle time. This surplus, coupled with the lack of fulfillment, can make them more vulnerable to addictive behaviors. Ironically, what may have begun as a quest for pleasure or an escape route from monotony can lead them to an even more confining state of addiction. The addiction then is no longer about seeking pleasure or avoiding boredom but about achieving a semblance of normality, as the brain adapts to the repeated stimulation. This scenario illustrates how essential it is to cultivate healthy and fulfilling hobbies, interests, and relationships that contribute to a meaningful life. By doing so, we can counter the void of boredom and reduce the risk of falling into the trap of addiction.

Balance & the Brain

The human brain, remarkably adaptive as it is, is perpetually striving for a state of balance or homeostasis. One of the areas this is most apparent is in our experiences of pleasure and pain, both of which are processed in the same regions of the brain. These two sensations function like a seesaw. When we experience pleasure, the seesaw goes up on one side; when we feel pain, it goes up on the other. The ultimate goal of the brain, however, is to maintain a level balance between these two extremes.

Imagine you are watching a delightful TV show. The enjoyment you derive from this activity raises the seesaw toward pleasure. However, as the show ends, you feel a sense of discontent, a subtle yearning for the pleasure to continue. This discontent indicates that the pleasure-pain seesaw is balancing toward pain, driven by the brain's search for homeostasis. As a result, you may feel inclined to watch another show in a bid to regain that momentary sense of enjoyment.

This balancing act is largely reflexive and often takes place beneath our conscious awareness. Yet, with heightened mindfulness, we can begin to perceive these shifts and discern the sensation of pleasure dipping toward the ground, the ensuing void, and the subsequent yearning for more pleasure.

Understanding the balancing act can also help us understand addiction. Highly pleasurable substances or behaviors often lead to a significant release of dopamine. However, the brain compensates for this dopamine surge by downregulating its own dopamine receptors, tipping the seesaw back towards neutrality. If an individual refrains from a substance or behavior long enough, dopamine levels become stabilized.

If they repeatedly give in to the cravings without allowing the dopamine levels to normalize, however, the seesaw will begin to tip in the direction of pain, eventually leading to a dopamine-deficit state or anhedonia. This state, characterized by a reduced capacity to experience pleasure, is akin to (and a symptom of) clinical depression; many people with anhedonia experience anxiety, irritability, insomnia, and a mental preoccupation with using again. The substance or behavior that once brought them immense pleasure now becomes a tool they need to feel "normal," as the brain strives to maintain homeostasis.

Exploring Treatment Options & Support Resources

Various treatment options and support resources are available to individuals recovering from addiction. One's choice of treatment depends on several factors, including the type and severity of addiction, individual preferences, and the presence of any co-occurring mental health disorders. Treatment options may include:

Inpatient or residential treatment programs: These programs provide intensive and structured treatment in a residential setting, offering a supportive environment and access to various therapeutic interventions. Examples include:

- The Betty Ford Center (substance addiction)

- The Meadows (substance addiction and behavioral addictions)

Outpatient treatment programs: Outpatient programs allow individuals to receive treatment while living at home and continuing with their daily responsibilities. They offer flexibility and access to counseling, therapy, and support groups. Examples include:

- Hazelden Betty Ford Foundation (substance addiction)

- SMART Recovery (substance addiction and behavioral addictions)

Individual therapy: One-on-one therapy sessions with addiction counselors or therapists can help individuals explore underlying issues, develop coping strategies, and address the psychological aspects of addiction. Examples of therapy modalities include:

- Cognitive Behavioral Therapy (CBT)

- Motivational Interviewing (MI)

- Dialectical Behavior Therapy (DBT)

Group therapy and support groups: Group therapy provides opportunities for individuals to share their experiences with others facing similar challenges so they can learn from one another. Support groups structured on 12-step programs offer participants ongoing support and a sense of community in recovery. Examples include:

- Alcoholics Anonymous (AA) and Narcotics Anonymous (NA) (substance addiction)

- Gamblers Anonymous (behavioral addiction)

Medication-assisted treatment: Certain medications, combined with counseling or behavioral therapies, can be effective in helping those in recovery manage cravings, reduce withdrawal symptoms, and prevent a return to use (sometimes known as a relapse) for specific substance addictions. Examples include:

- Methadone or buprenorphine for opioid addiction

- Naltrexone for alcohol or opioid addiction

- Acamprosate for alcohol addiction

It is important to note that recovery from addiction is a journey that requires ongoing commitment, support, and effort. Engaging in aftercare programs, participating in individual therapy, attending support group meetings, and maintaining a healthy lifestyle are crucial elements of long-term recovery.

By recognizing the signs of addiction, seeking professional help, and exploring the treatment options and support resources available to them, individuals can take significant steps toward addressing addiction.

Overcome Addiction: Rewire Reward Pathways

If you suspect that you may be battling an addiction, you should first seek out the aforementioned professional help. As you begin the recovery process, you will learn to rewire the reward pathways in your brain. There are a few ways to accomplish this.

Breaking the Addictive Cycle by Establishing New Habits

To overcome addiction, you must break the addictive cycle. This involves disrupting the pattern of seeking the addictive substance or engaging in the addictive behavior and replacing it with healthier alternatives.

Breaking the addictive cycle requires a combination of self-awareness, determination, and support. Recognizing triggers and avoiding high-risk situations is an essential first step. Identifying the underlying reasons for the addiction, such as stress, trauma, or emotional pain, can also help in developing healthier coping mechanisms.

Creating new habits to replace the addictive behavior is another key strategy in recovery. Engaging in activities that promote physical and emotional well-being, such as exercise, hobbies, or mindfulness practices, can provide a sense of fulfillment and help fill the void left by the addiction. Establishing a daily routine that includes healthy habits and positive rituals can help the brain repair itself. By establishing new habits that are "healthy", individuals can rewire their reward pathway and create a positive, fulfilling life with no need for addictive substances or behaviors.

Evidence-Based Strategies to Rewire the Reward Pathway
Numerous evidence-based strategies have been developed to
help individuals rewire their reward pathways and overcome
addiction. Those in recovery can use these strategies to modify
the brain's response to rewards and reinforce healthier
behaviors. Some examples of these strategies include:

> *Cognitive Behavioral Therapy (CBT)*: CBT focuses
> on identifying and modifying negative thought
> patterns and behaviors an individual may associate
> with their addiction. Doing so helps them develop
> effective coping strategies, manage cravings, and
> improve their problem-solving skills.[51]

> *Contingency Management*: In this approach, the
> person in recovery uses tangible rewards or incentives
> for maintaining abstinence or achieving treatment
> goals. Positive reinforcement encourages them to
> make healthier choices and reinforces the connection
> between positive behaviors and rewards.[52]

> *Mindfulness-Based Interventions*: Mindfulness
> practices, such as meditation and mindfulness-based
> stress reduction, can help individuals develop an
> awareness of their cravings, emotions, and triggers
> without judgment. This increased self-awareness
> improves their self-regulation and helps them break
> the automatic response to addictive stimuli.

---

[51] "American Addiction Centers." Cognitive Behavioral Therapy (CBT) for Addiction & Substance Abuse. American Addiction Centers, 13 Mar. 2023, https://americanaddictioncenters.org/therapy-treatment/cognitive-behavioral-therapy.

[52] National Institute on Drug Abuse. "The Science of Addiction Treatment and Recovery." Drugs, Brains, and Behavior: The Science of Addiction, 10 July 2020, https://nida.nih.gov/publications/drugs-brains-behavior-science-addiction/treatment-recovery.

The Power of Support: Build a Recovery Network

Significance of a Support System in Addiction Recovery

Building a strong support system is a crucial component of addiction recovery. Addiction can be an isolating and overwhelming journey, and having a network of people who understand, support, and encourage others in their recovery can make a significant difference. A support system provides emotional support, accountability, and guidance throughout the recovery process.

When facing the complex and often overwhelming challenges of addiction, individuals need a safe space to share their experiences, fears, and triumphs. The support system can include friends, family members, peers in recovery, and addiction support groups. Each member of the support system plays a unique role in providing different forms of support, creating a web of interconnected relationships that foster resilience and growth.

The Benefits of Peer, Family, & Community Support

Peer Support: Peer support is an essential element of addiction recovery. Connecting with others who have experienced similar challenges can provide those in recovery with a sense of validation, understanding, and shared wisdom.

Family Involvement: Involving family members in the rehabilitation process can significantly impact an individual's recovery. Family support and understanding create a healthier home environment and improve communication among members of the family unit. Family therapy sessions can help families repair relationships, rebuild trust, and address any enabling behaviors or codependency issues that may have contributed to the addiction. Family involvement creates a network of support that extends beyond formal treatment settings, providing individuals ongoing encouragement and accountability.

Community Resources: Communities often offer valuable resources to individuals in addiction recovery. Local organizations, faith-based groups, and/or community centers may provide support groups, sliding scale fee counseling services, and educational programs. Community resources foster a sense of belonging, increase access to additional support services, and drive one's engagement in sober activities and events.

The Role of Therapy, Counseling, & Support Groups

Therapy, counseling, and support groups play a crucial role in addiction rehabilitation. These resources provide individuals with professional guidance, emotional support, and a sense of community during the recovery journey.

Therapy and counseling sessions offer individuals a safe space to explore the underlying factors contributing to their addiction and develop strategies to prevent returning to use. Therapists can provide personalized treatment plans, address co-occurring mental health conditions, and help their clients navigate challenges during recovery.

Support groups based on 12-step programs, such as Alcoholics Anonymous (AA) or Narcotics Anonymous (NA), offer those suffering with addiction peer support and a sense of belonging. Sharing experiences, insights, and challenges with others who have faced similar struggles can empower these individuals and provide them with a network of understanding and encouragement. We will elaborate further on the importance of a strong support network in the next section.

In addiction rehabilitation, a comprehensive approach that combines therapy, counseling, and support groups is often most effective for healing. This multidimensional support system provides individuals with the tools, resources, and encouragement they need to rewire their reward pathways, build resilience, and embark on a transformative journey toward a healthier and more fulfilling life free from addiction.

The Role of Aftercare Programs & Ongoing Support

Aftercare programs and ongoing support are essential for maintaining long-term recovery. Completing a treatment program is just the beginning of the journey, and individuals need continued support to navigate the challenges and temptations that may arise post-treatment. Aftercare programs offer structured support and guidance, helping individuals transition back into daily life while maintaining their sobriety.

Examples of aftercare programs include:

Sober Living Homes: Sober living homes provide a structured and supportive environment for individuals in early recovery. Residents have access to a drug-free living space, peer support, and accountability measures. Sober living homes bridge the gap between intensive treatment and independent living, allowing individuals to practice relapse prevention skills in a supportive community.

Alumni Programs: Many treatment centers offer alumni programs that allow individuals to stay connected to the treatment community even after completing the program. These programs may include ongoing support groups, educational workshops, and social activities. Alumni programs provide a sense of continuity, connection, and ongoing learning for individuals in recovery.

Ongoing Counseling & Therapy: Ongoing therapy and counseling sessions are vital in helping individuals address underlying issues, manage triggers, and maintain their emotional well-being. Regular therapy sessions provide a safe space in which those in recovery can process challenges, develop coping skills, and receive guidance from a trained professional.

By developing a strong system of peer, family, therapeutic, and community support, individuals in recovery can navigate the challenges of addiction and sustain long-term recovery.

The Environment

Environmental factors play a critical role in both how individuals develop and subsequently manage addictions. It can influence one's susceptibility to addiction, act as a trigger for addictive behaviors, and significantly impact the likelihood of relapse.

A person's environment encompasses many elements that may influence their behavior: their physical surroundings, the cultural and societal norms they're immersed in, their living situation, the people they interact with, and their accessibility to substances or addictive behaviors. Together, these factors can either accelerate or mitigate addiction.

One aspect of environment involves immediate triggers—that is, the locations, people, objects, or emotions linked to addictive behavior. For those in recovery, these cues can spark cravings even after a period of abstinence, which often leads to relapse. This is why one critical aspect of addiction recovery often is making significant changes to one's environment to reduce these triggers such as moving to a new place, severing ties with certain individuals, or avoiding specific locations associated with past usage.

The phenomenon that Vietnam War veterans experienced surrounding heroin use is a classic example of how environment can impact addiction. Known as the "Vietnam Effect,"[53] researchers regularly reference it in studies on addiction. Many soldiers who used heroin while overseas ceased usage upon returning to the United States. This

---

[53] Robins, L. N., Davis, D. H., & Nurco, D. N. (2010). Vietnam Veterans Three Years after Vietnam: How Our Study Changed Our View of Heroin. American Journal on Addictions, 19(3), 203-211. doi:10.1111/j.1521-0391.2010.00046.x

cessation indicates that the stress and trauma of war and the environmental cues were significant factors in their drug use. When they returned to their homes, away from the environment of war, their addictions often subsided without medical intervention.

In contrast, individuals treated in clinical settings who returned to the same environment that fostered their addiction often relapsed. This discrepancy illustrates the importance of addressing environmental factors in addiction treatment. By modifying or completely changing one's environment, it's possible to remove many of the cues that trigger addictive behavior.

However, environmental changes alone may not be sufficient for everyone to overcome addiction. Personal factors, including genetics, personality traits, and co-existing mental health conditions, also play a vital role. Recovery is often most successful when those healing from addiction employ a combination of strategies — including individual therapy, group support, medication, lifestyle changes, and, crucially, changes in environment.

The Recovery Process

How Long Does It Take to Reset the Dopamine System?

So, let's break this down into simple terms. If you want to reset your brain's reward system, you must completely disconnect from whatever is causing your addiction for around 30 days, as suggested by Dr. Anna Lembke, author of *Dopamine Nation*.[54][55] This can be a substance, a person, a behavior — anything that's feeding the addictive loop. As a reminder, please speak with

---

[54] Lembke, Anna. Dopamine Nation: Finding Balance in the Age of Indulgence. Dutton, an imprint of Penguin Random House, 2021.
[55] "The Art of Manliness." How to Do a Dopamine Reset, 28 Feb. 2023, https://www.artofmanliness.com/character/habits/how-to-do-a-dopamine-reset/.

your doctor or medical professional before undergoing this experiment.

What happens during this 30-day period? Well, your brain is like a complex highway system with thousands of roads that have been forged over time. When you're addicted to a substance or behavior, your brain has learned to use the same highway route over and over. It's laid more asphalt, created more lanes, and made that route highly accessible. This is your dopamine system at work, rewarding you each time you take that familiar route.

But when you stop taking that route cold turkey for 30 days, something interesting happens. Your brain goes, "Hey, we're not using this highway anymore, let's start dismantling it." Those that have the misfortune of falling into the addiction trap describe the first 10 days as misery. You're basically in construction zone hell. All the feel-good stuff is gone, you're left with the pain and discomfort, and you've got no easy detour around it. You may have anxiety, trouble sleeping, trouble controlling your emotions because your brain misses its favorite highway.

However, according to Dr. Lembke, if you can push through these difficult two weeks, something wonderful begins to happen around week three. It's like the sun starts to shine again. By the fourth week, most people start feeling significantly better. Our brains can bounce back once we cut off an addictive behavior or substance.

Frame it as a 30-day experiment with a potentially huge reward: a better life. While it's a challenging experiment, remember, most significant change happens when you move out of your comfort zone. If you're willing to try it, you might find that you start noticing and appreciating other pleasures in life that you'd forgotten or overlooked.

Why Relapses Occur & How to Prevent Them

Think of a person fighting addiction as being in an ongoing tug-of-war. This person is constantly working against a persistent, invisible adversary: their cravings. For those who have been battling addiction for a long time, this opponent won't be retiring after they make it through a few weeks of sobriety. It lurks, awaiting the opportunity to strike when the person's attention is diverted.

Many people can reach a point where they can lay the rope down, no longer needing to participate in the tug-of-war. This usually occurs about a month into sobriety. However, for others, especially those wrestling with severe addiction, the game never ends. The moment they turn away or get distracted, they find themselves drawn back into the struggle. The pathway is still open and there are triggers everywhere — usually triggers that they haven't had to deal with during the first 30 days. While they may not make a deliberate decision to return to using addictive behaviors or substances to cope, they may have an unconscious, knee-jerk reaction to these triggers and then BANG! Right back to where they started. As with habits, they MUST get right back on the horse immediately without succumbing to the "What the Hell Effect"!

Why does this happen? An unexpected trigger can lead to substance use again and bring a quick rush of excitement causing dopamine levels to spike. However, the subsequent calm isn't a return to normalcy; it's a plunge into a deficit. This leaves the person feeling a powerful desire to get back to normal. The plummet in dopamine levels fuels them to seek the substance or behavior.

Interestingly, relapses aren't just triggered by negative events or stress. For some people struggling with addiction, positive milestones and achievements can cause them to lose focus and accidentally set the loop in motion. Recognizing that success and happiness can make them vulnerable is a critical part of self-realization and it allows them to set up safeguards when things are going well.

Vigilance: The Antidote for Stubborn Addictions

Consider a car journey on a winding mountain road. As a driver, you're always on alert to avoid crossing the yellow line or steering off the road into a ditch. Even if you've traveled miles and miles, the hazards are always just as close to you. For individuals with a very powerful addiction, recovery is like this treacherous car journey.

While this may seem like a challenging way to live, for someone suffering with serious addiction, adopting this mindset can bring them deep comfort. It is a solid reminder that if they keep your eyes on the road, they will not only arrive safely at their destination, but they will enjoy the ride as well. Unwavering vigilance is critical in the journey towards sobriety.

In fact, many 12-step programs teach participants to focus on the "one day at a time" principle. By dividing the overwhelming task of lifelong sobriety into manageable daily goals, those in recovery can avoid complacency and prepare themselves for potential triggers. As with any long ride, the journey may be challenging at times, but with constant vigilance, they can navigate the road safely.

Honesty

Consider honesty as the light that illuminates a path in a dark forest. For those wrestling with addiction, this path symbolizes their recovery journey.

When we commit to truthfulness, we stimulate certain neural pathways in our brain, particularly the ones connecting our prefrontal cortex (responsible for decision-making and foreseeing consequences) and our limbic system (the center of our emotions and rewards).

These pathways often become disoriented when we're in the grip of addiction, with the prefrontal cortex losing control as the limbic system reacts reflexively to the cravings. By engaging in honesty, we're essentially empowering the prefrontal cortex to regain its rightful control over our decision making. This is analogous to looking before we leap, considering not just the immediate relief from use but the long-term consequences of relapse.

Besides its neurological benefits, honesty also promotes deep and genuine human interactions, which, in themselves, can be sources of dopamine, the brain's reward chemical. Some people are drawn to these profound connections and find casual, surface-level interactions less satisfying. It's these intimate bonds, enriched by honest exchanges, that help satisfy our brain's craving for dopamine, effectively rendering harmful substance use unnecessary for the reward.

Thus, by fostering honesty, we can cultivate a powerful tool in our arsenal against addiction, helping restore brain balance and building meaningful relationships that can support recovery.

Clinical Experiments: Pharmaceuticals & Psychedelics

It's an exciting time in the world of addiction treatment as researchers explore various experimental approaches to recovery, including the use of pharmaceutical drugs and psychedelics. These researchers strive to open new possibilities that could radically change the traditional therapeutic landscape for people struggling with addiction.

Pharmaceutical interventions often aim to target specific pathways in the brain that contribute to addictive behaviors. Medical professionals employ medications such as naltrexone and buprenorphine, for instance, in the treatment of opioid addiction. These substances work by either blocking the opioid receptors in the brain or by providing a controlled substitute, which helps users manage withdrawal symptoms and cravings.[56]

Psychedelics, on the other hand, offer a different approach. Researchers are studying substances such as psilocybin, LSD, and MDMA for their potential therapeutic uses. The theory behind this approach is that these substances can facilitate deep emotional and psychological insights during guided therapy sessions, helping individuals to confront and overcome their addictions.[57]

For instance, early research into psilocybin-assisted therapy for nicotine addiction has shown promising results, with participants reporting significant reductions in craving and increased abstinence rates. Similarly, studies involving MDMA-assisted therapy for alcohol addiction have demonstrated encouraging outcomes.

However, it's crucial to note that these approaches are still in their experimental stages. While initial findings are promising, we lack comprehensive long-term data to fully understand their effectiveness and potential side effects. Moreover, the use of these substances requires professional supervision and appropriate therapeutic settings to ensure safety and efficacy. While these new frontiers in addiction treatment are indeed thrilling and hold much potential, they also underline the importance of rigorous, ongoing study before researchers can fully grasp their long-term impacts and applications in the field of addiction recovery.

---

[56] "Pharmaceutical Interventions Often Aim to Target Specific Pathways in the Brain That Contribute to Addictive Behaviors." Neuroscience of Behavioral and Pharmacological Treatments for Addictions, National Center for Biotechnology Information, 2011, https://www.ncbi.nlm.nih.gov/pmc/articles/PMC3063555/.

[57] Johnson, M.W. (2022). Classic Psychedelics in Addiction Treatment: The Case for Psilocybin in Tobacco Smoking Cessation. In: Barrett, F.S., Preller, K.H. (eds) Disruptive Psychopharmacology . Current Topics in Behavioral Neurosciences, vol 56. Springer, Cham. https://doi.org/10.1007/7854_2022_327

Conclusion

Throughout this chapter, we have explored the nature of habits and addictions, shedding light on their distinct characteristics. Habits are behaviors that are automatic and often beneficial that we can consciously control. On the other hand, addictions involve a loss of control that drives individuals to compulsively engage in addictive behaviors despite negative consequences. It is essential to *differentiate between habits and addictions* to ensure individuals struggling with addiction-related concerns receive appropriate interventions and support.

One of the key factors driving addictive behaviors is the *power of rewards*. Addictive substances or behaviors trigger the release of neurotransmitters, such as dopamine, in the brain's reward system, creating a pleasurable and reinforcing experience. This association between the addictive stimulus and the rewarding response strengthens the addictive cycle and makes it difficult to break free from addictive patterns. Understanding the role of rewards in addictive behaviors helps us comprehend the allure and challenge of overcoming addiction.

Early detection and intervention are **_absolutely vital_** when it comes to addressing addictions. Recognizing the signs and symptoms of addiction allows individuals and their loved ones to take proactive steps towards seeking help. It is important to emphasize that addiction is a complex condition that often requires professional assistance. Seeking the expertise of addiction specialists, therapists, and counselors can provide sufferers with the necessary guidance and support for recovery.

Furthermore, fostering a *supportive environment* is crucial for individuals struggling with addiction. Creating a non-judgmental and compassionate environment that allows individuals to feel safe and supported as they heal is fundamental to recovery. Encouraging open conversations, promoting understanding, and offering unconditional support to sufferers can make a significant difference in their recovery process.

In conclusion, unraveling the power of rewards is crucial in understanding addictions and facilitating habit transformation. This understanding of rewards will also be crucial in our next chapter on momentum. Like recovery, momentum is built one moment, one day, and one reward at a time and is often contingent on the people and environments that surround us.

Summary Q & A

1. What are the defining features of addiction?
    The defining features of addiction include intense craving, dependence, negative consequences, tolerance and withdrawal symptoms.

2. How do habits differ from addictions?
    Habits are repetitive actions that have become automatic and ingrained, serving as useful routines. Addictions involve a loss of control, intense craving, and compulsive engagement in behaviors despite negative consequences.

3. What are the two primary categories of addictions?
    The two primary categories of addictions are substance addiction, which involves the excessive and uncontrolled use of drugs, and behavioral addiction, which involves compulsive engagement in activities such as gambling or gaming.

4. What are some psychological factors that contribute to addiction?
    Psychological factors such as emotional regulation, stress management, and underlying issues like low self-esteem or untreated mental health conditions can contribute to the development and perpetuation of addiction.

5. What are the three stages of the addictive cycle?
    The three stages of the addictive cycle are anticipation, engagement, and aftermath. Anticipation involves craving, preoccupation, and an intense desire for the addictive behavior. Engagement refers to an individual's actual participation in the behavior, leading to the release of dopamine and reinforcing the behavior. Aftermath involves experiencing negative emotions but still desiring the reward, perpetuating the addictive cycle.

6. How do addictive rewards affect the brain and behavior?
    Addictive rewards lead to neuroadaptations in the brain's reward circuitry, resulting in tolerance and sensitization. Tolerance refers to the need for higher doses or more intense behaviors to achieve the same level of reward. Sensitization is the heightened response to the rewarding stimuli that makes

the behavior more alluring. These adaptations can shift priorities, impair judgment, and reinforce the cycle of addiction.

7. Why is early detection and intervention crucial for addiction?
Early detection and intervention increase the chances of successful treatment and recovery. Recognizing the signs and symptoms of addiction allows for timely support and prevents the escalation of negative consequences. Early intervention can address the issue before it becomes more severe and ingrained.

8. How can bringing the fear of risks forward help counteract the risk-reward imbalance in addiction?
Bringing the fear of risks forward involves strategies such as imagining a conversation with the future self or creating tangible representations of potential future consequences. By emotionally connecting with the long-term risks, individuals can gain a clearer perspective on the potential harm associated with their addictive behaviors and make more informed decisions. These approaches counterbalance the immediate rewards and help prioritize long-term well-being.

9. What are some evidence-based strategies for rewiring the reward pathway in addiction recovery?
Some evidence-based strategies include cognitive behavioral therapy (CBT), contingency management, and mindfulness-based interventions.

10. Why is building a strong support system important in addiction recovery?
Building a strong support system provides those in recovery with emotional support, accountability, and guidance, making a significant difference in the healing process.

Exercises

1. Think about a habit you have and analyze its impact on your life. Is it a beneficial habit that contributes to your well-being, or is it potentially harmful?

2. Identify a behavior in your life that you suspect may be turning into an addiction. Describe the signs and symptoms that make you believe it is becoming problematic. Consider the negative consequences you have experienced because of this behavior.

3. Research and choose one substance addiction and one behavioral addiction to further explore. Write a short essay comparing the two types of addictions, considering factors such as the specific substances or activities involved, the impact on physical health and relationships, and the potential for tolerance and withdrawal.

4. Identify one addictive behavior or substance in your life and brainstorm three healthier alternatives or habits that can replace it. Write a short essay describing how these new habits can contribute to rewiring the reward pathway and create a more fulfilling life without addiction.

5. With your doctor's approval, take on the 30-day challenge of disconnecting from a specific addictive behavior or substance. Keep a daily journal documenting your experiences, including the difficulties, improvements, and any observations of other pleasures in life. Reflect on your progress and insights at the end of the challenge.

6. Develop a relapse prevention plan for a hypothetical scenario. Identify potential triggers, both negative and positive, and outline strategies to prevent return to use. Include specific actions, coping mechanisms, and supportive resources that can be utilized in times of vulnerability.

7. Take some time to imagine yourself in the future, living with the consequences of your addictive behaviors. Write a letter or have a conversation with your future self, discussing the negative outcomes and potential harm your addiction has caused. Reflect on how it would feel to experience those

consequences and use this exercise to strengthen your motivation for change.

8. Make a list of common signs and symptoms of addiction discussed in the book. Reflect on your own behaviors and identify any red flags that may indicate a problem with addiction. This exercise will help you increase self-awareness and recognize when intervention may be necessary.

9. Behavioral Addiction Inventory: Select one behavioral addiction mentioned in the book (e.g., gambling, gaming, shopping) and create an inventory of behaviors associated with that addiction. Assess your own engagement in these behaviors and reflect on whether they may be indicative of a potential addiction.

10. Make a list of activities, hobbies, or interests that you find fulfilling and engaging. Reflect on how these pursuits contribute to a meaningful life and provide you with a sense of purpose and satisfaction. Consider incorporating more of these activities into your daily life to counteract boredom and reduce your risk for addiction.

Principle 9:

Embrace the Power of Momentum

Maintaining Consistent Habit Improvement

*"The key to success is to start before you are ready and
keep going even when you don't feel like it."*
- Marie Forleo

Have you ever put off doing the dishes for days, only to find
yourself cleaning your entire kitchen once you finally get
started? This kind of momentum is a powerful force when it
comes to habit change. It is the driving energy that propels you
forward and makes sticking to your habits and goals easier.
When you have momentum on your side, you strengthen the
neural pathways in your brain every time you successfully
repeat a habit; over time, this repetition makes the behavior
more automatic and ingrained. As you witness the positive
effects of your habits, your motivation and confidence grow.
Moreover, momentum shapes your identity by helping you
believe that you are the type of person who can achieve your
goals.

Key Question:
*How does momentum play a crucial role in habit formation, and what
strategies can individuals employ to build and maintain momentum to
support the development of sustainable habits?*

However, you can lose momentum with even the smallest of
slip-ups or deviations in your routine. In this chapter, we will
explore the importance of momentum in habit change and
discuss strategies we can use to build and maintain it. By

understanding the role of momentum and learning how to protect it, we can create lasting change and achieve mastery in any area of our lives.

According to a survey conducted by the American Psychological Association, 75% of respondents reported that once they started making progress toward a goal, they were motivated to continue and build on that momentum. Seeing progress can significantly increase motivation and drive further action.[58]

Success is rarely linear, so we will also explore what happens when you inevitably stumble, and how to get back on track quickly before you lose momentum completely. We will discuss how to deal with obstacles, learn from your mistakes, and continue making progress even when the path forward is unclear.

Powerful momentum and an unbroken chain of habits are what ultimately lead to mastery and success. By focusing on continuity and consistency over time, we can reshape or replace any habit and achieve any habit goal. Momentum is the key to unlocking long-term progress and long-lasting change.

Barriers to Momentum

In the pursuit of building and maintaining momentum, it is important to recognize and address the potential barriers that can hinder our progress. Despite our best intentions and efforts, slip-ups and challenges can emerge in the habit change process, threatening to disrupt the flow of momentum we have worked hard to establish. In this section, we explore some common speed bumps along the way to building momentum and provide insights into how we can navigate and overcome them. By understanding these challenges and implementing effective strategies, we can build resilience, stay on track, and continue moving forward toward our goals and aspirations.

[58] Pappas, S. (2021, October 1). Rousing our motivation. *Monitor on Psychology, 52*(7). https://www.apa.org/monitor/2021/10/feature-workers-motivation

Let's delve into the barriers that can impede momentum and discover the ways to overcome them.

Why One Slip-up Can Ruin Momentum

Momentum is powerful but elusive. One small mistake or break in your routine can disrupt your momentum and undo days or even weeks of progress. This is because habits are very path-dependent — you strengthen (build new habits) and weaken (eradicate old habits) based on the frequency and consistency with which you perform them. Each repetition of a habit deepens the groove in your mind and makes that behavior more automatic. Let's look at examples of these types of slip-ups:

Life: Missing a day of your daily exercise routine. This break disrupts your momentum, lowering your motivation and eventually derailing your fitness goals.

Career: Failing to meet a crucial deadline. This break in consistent performance undermines your motivation, making it easier for you to justify slacking off or procrastinating on other tasks, resulting in a decline in overall productivity.

Business: Deviating from a disciplined investment strategy during market volatility. This break in your approach can lead to subpar performance, eroding client trust and damaging your reputation. You will need to make significant efforts to regain momentum and rebuild trust.

When you skip a habit once, you start to move away from that well-worn groove. Your mind begins to forget the trigger and reward associated with that habit loop. One slip-up weakens the connection between the trigger, craving, behavior, and reward in your mind. Now, the next time you face that same trigger, your mind won't automatically pull you into action. You've disrupted your rhythm and given yourself an opportunity to get off track.

Worse yet, when you miss a habit once, you're likely to miss it again. When you break your momentum, your motivation declines and it's easier to give yourself excuses that make it OK to skip the habit again. Your identity also starts to weaken as you question whether you are really the "type of person" who can commit to a habit every day.

The more often you break the chain of repetition, the less momentum and motivation you have. Your habit begins to weaken until eventually you have to exert a huge amount of willpower to get started again. This is why it is critical to never miss practicing the habit twice. One slip-up is inevitable, but it's important that you get right back on track immediately before you lose momentum completely. Consistency over perfection is the key to building strong habits and long-term success.

The WTH Effect

The *What the Hell Effect* ("WTH") occurs when you give up on a goal or habit completely after making one small mistake or slip-up. It's the feeling you have when you think, "Oh WTH, I've already ruined my perfect streak, I might as well give up now." The WTH Effect can also occur when you tell yourself you'll "start again on Monday" rather than abandoning your goal completely. Like abandoning your goals, delaying action can also be a mistake because the longer you wait, the harder it becomes to regain momentum. The WTH Effect illustrates how easily you can lose momentum, and while it's common to justify continued failure after an initial stumble, it poses one of the biggest threats to building long-term habits and success. Here are some examples:

> **Life:** Trying to maintain a daily meditation practice. After missing a day due to a busy schedule, you feel discouraged and decide to abandon the practice altogether, assuming that one missed session has rendered all your previous efforts useless.

Career: Setting a goal to read professional development books regularly. When you fail to finish a book on time, you become frustrated and give up on the habit of reading altogether, missing out on valuable knowledge and growth opportunities.

Business: Implementing a disciplined investment strategy. After experiencing a small loss on one trade, you start questioning your strategy and abandon it completely, potentially missing out on profitable opportunities in the future and hindering your long-term investment performance.

When a habit or goal goes awry, don't let one small mistake turn into an avalanche of self-sabotage. If you notice yourself slipping into "WTH" thoughts, take a moment to reconnect with your motivation and remind yourself why your habit or goal is important. Then simply get back to business with the very next task, rather than starting over or planning a "fresh start next week". By focusing on progress over perfection, you can endure obstacles, slip-ups, and plateaus and still achieve amazing results through persistence and consistency over time.

Creating Momentum

Creating momentum is a vital component of achieving lasting success in our endeavors. It involves building and sustaining habits that propel us forward, step by step, toward our goals. In this section, we will explore the power of starting small as we build momentum and delve into the strategies that enable us to make consistent and gradual progress. By understanding the significance of small changes, the mindset required for long-term habit building, and how to bounce back from setbacks, we can harness the power of consistency and propel ourselves toward remarkable results.

Starting Small to Support Momentum

It is important to start small when building or breaking habits because small changes are more sustainable and help you build momentum over time. When you start small, your habits are:

- *Easy to accomplish.* Small habit changes require little willpower or motivation to get started. They don't feel overwhelming or impossible, so you have no excuse not to get started right away. Success is as simple as doing one push-up or reading one page in a book per day.

- *Gradual.* Small habits allow you to build up your progress in a gradual, step-by-step fashion. You start with one push-up and add one more each week. You read one page today and two pages tomorrow. This gradual progression makes habits much more manageable and is less shocking to your system. Momentum builds up slowly but surely through small increases over time.

- *Flexible.* Small habits can be easily adjusted up or down depending on your needs or circumstances. If you start to struggle, just cut back to the previous level. This flexibility makes the habit very sustainable, since you can respond and adapt to challenges. There is no sense of "all or nothing" perfection that many people experience when they make more extreme habit changes.

- *Easy to track.* When you start small, progress is clearly visible and measurable, which helps you stay motivated. You can see your habit becoming more and more regular through simple progress.

Let's look at some straightforward examples of starting small.

Life: To begin developing a meditation practice, start with five minutes of daily meditation and gradually increase the duration for long-term benefits.

Career: To build a new career skill, practice public speaking by recording short videos of yourself and gradually challenging yourself in small increments.

Business: To devise a new investment strategy, begin with a small portion of capital, diversify investments, and gradually scale positions based on performance and experience.

Starting small when building habits is the secret to long-term success and progress. Big changes are rarely sustainable, but small steps will get you where you want to go by helping you make incremental improvements and build daily momentum. Focus on gradual progress, not radical transformation. Start small and build up from there.

What it Takes

To build long-term habits, you need focus, diligence, and persistence. However, you also need patience and self-compassion. If you want to make ongoing progress, you must establish the right mindset and principles to overcome obstacles in your path and stay motivated. The habits that stick are the ones that become a seamless part of your daily rhythm and routine. To build habits that last, keep the following tips in mind:

Never miss twice: One slip-up is inevitable in the habit-building process. What matters most is getting back on track immediately after. Missing one day makes it easier to miss again, which allows momentum to fade and your habit to weaken. Never miss two days in a row. Get right back to your routine as if nothing happened. Consistency is key.

Done is better than perfect: Forget "I'll start over on Monday" or "I give up;" that's perfectionistic thinking. Building habits should be flexible, not an all or nothing endeavor. Focus on consistency and just keep moving forward one day at a time. A messy job done well is better than a perfect job not done at all. Do your habit and move on.

Don't break the chain: Each day, write an X on your calendar every time you stick to your new habit. This visual chain will keep your progress going and motivation levels high. Don't break the chain. Keep it going day after day, and eventually, the chain of Xs will trigger your habit by default. Build the chain through consistency.

Progress over perfection: Remind yourself that success is in the practice, not perfection. Building habits is a long journey with many ups and downs, twists and turns. Judge your progress based on consistency over weeks and months, not short-term success or failure. Practice daily and focus on progress, not perfection. Habits strengthen over time with each small win.

The Power of Consistency

Radical transformation cannot be achieved overnight. Rather, it is the result of small habits practiced daily over a long period of time. Consistency and persistence are the keys to remarkable results.

Here are examples of the power of never breaking the chain:

Jerry Seinfeld's Productive Habit

The comedian Jerry Seinfeld reveals that the secret to his success was developing the habit of writing new jokes every day. He kept a big year-long wall calendar and every day that he sat down to write, he would mark an X on that day. "After a few days you'll have a chain. Just keep at it and the chain will grow longer every day. You'll like seeing that chain, especially when you get a few weeks under your belt. Your only job next is to not break the chain." Seinfeld's habit of daily practice led to remarkable results in his career over the long run.

Stephen King's Daily Writing Habit

The prolific author Stephen King writes for at least three to four hours every morning of the year, including holidays and weekends. This habit of daily writing has led him to publish 54 books over 46 years. King believes that inspiration is for amateurs; "professional writers just get up and put one word after another." His habit of consistent daily practice has fueled his remarkable creative output.

Serena Williams' Habit of Extreme Dedication

The tennis champion Serena Williams is known for her extreme dedication and habit of hard work and practice. She spends up to five hours on the court each day, in addition to constant strength and conditioning training. Her daily commitment to deliberate practice has made her the most accomplished female tennis player in history. Williams attributes her success to building the habit of pushing through challenges and fatigue through sheer determination and force of will. Her habit of continuous dedication and perseverance has been the foundation of her success.

Kobe Bryant's Tireless Work Ethic

The NBA legend Kobe Bryant was known for his tireless work ethic and habit of continuous practice. He would show up to practice hours before his teammates to work on skills and conditioning. After team practices ended, he would continue practicing for hours on end. His habit of deliberate practice and dedication made him one of the greatest basketball players of all time. Bryant said, "Success is no accident. It is hard work, perseverance, learning, studying, sacrifice and most of all, love of what you are doing." His habit of continual hard work and perfection of his craft led to his remarkable success and achievements.

Jerry Rice's Habit of Daily Sprints

The NFL wide receiver Jerry Rice is considered by many to be the greatest football player of all time. His success was built on the habit of daily conditioning, especially running intense wind sprints. Even after practice ended, Rice would continue running 40 and 50-yard sprints to build his endurance and stamina. Over his 20-year career, his habit of daily sprint work made him an exceptionally durable and consistent player. Rice said, "Today I will do what others won't, so tomorrow I can accomplish what others can't." His habit of going above and beyond through daily practice and conditioning fueled his success.

The common thread between these stories is the power of habit through consistency. The habits of consistency and continuous self-improvement enable us to accomplish great things, regardless of our field or profession. While talent plays some role, remarkable mastery is developed primarily through dedication and practice. Success is built incrementally through small, repeated actions we practice each and every day over the long run. Choose your habits and practice them daily. Start today, start small, but never quit, never break the chain. Mastery will follow.

What to Do Once You've Broken the Chain

Slip-ups happen. You will inevitably stumble at some point in the habit-building process. The key is how you respond after missing a day or break in your routine. Here are a few steps you can take to get back on track:

Start again immediately: The sooner you get back to your habit, the less momentum you will lose. Don't wait until next week or the start of the month. Just take the next physical step to restart your routine, even if you're not motivated. This is by far the most important recovery strategy to remember after you've broken the chain. If one missed day turns into two, it can easily turn into months from there.

Don't dwell on your mistake: Avoid judging yourself harshly or spiraling into feelings of guilt or shame. Learn from your mistake and move on quickly.

Reconnect with your motivation: Remember why you started practicing this habit in the first place. Review your original motivations and goals to renew your commitment. Success is a marathon, not a sprint. Refocus on the bigger picture.

Start small if needed: If it feels overwhelming to dive back in where you left off, cut back to an earlier stage of your habit. Make it as easy as possible to get restarted. You can build back up to your previous level over time as your consistency and motivation improve.

With the right mindset, mistakes become opportunities for growth rather than reasons to quit. Get curious about your slip-ups instead of judging yourself for them. Learn from your failures and come back stronger by renewing your motivation, starting again immediately, and building your consistency over time. Success is a journey, not a destination. Stay focused on progress, not perfection. You've got this!

Post Situation Analysis

Building better habits requires continuous learning and adjustment. Reviewing your behavior, either positive or negative, is a powerful learning tool you can use to optimize the changes you are making. If you are working to build a habit and you've overcome some challenges, taking stock to learn from how you've overcome those challenges can keep your momentum going so that, when you face those challenges again, you are able to repeat productive behaviors and stop yourself from engaging in negative behaviors. This is basically a post-mortem review, often referred to as a "Post Situation Analysis," and it allows you to reflect on your behaviors and decision-making.

Post Situation Analysis reviews are even more valuable when things do not go as intended or when you faced a challenge and broke the chain. It is an opportunity to gain valuable insights. By carefully examining ineffective strategies or failed attempts, you can identify obstacles and make better choices in the future. What may initially appear as a failure or setback can actually lead to the discovery of new paths and solutions. It can also shed light on external influences that need modification to overcome bad habits.

To maximize the benefits of post-situation analysis, approach your experiences objectively with a desire to learn rather than with harsh self-judgment. Seek out constructive options and strategies to try in the future. Each small adjustment contributes to your wisdom and effectiveness, as you commit to continuous improvement over the years.

Here are some useful questions to ask yourself during this period of reflection:

- What worked well? Identify specific choices or strategies you made or used to successfully execute your habit goal. Look for wins to build upon.

- What didn't work well? Notice any triggers, obstacles, or behaviors that undermined your habit. Consider alternative options to try next time. View setbacks as learning opportunities rather than failures.

- What unexpected challenges arose? Review any surprises you encountered so you can prepare yourself for the next habit loop. Expect ups and downs.

- What could I have done differently? Look for options you didn't choose that may work better next time. Be willing to experiment with new solutions. Continuous improvement requires flexibility.

- What did I learn? Key insights and lessons gained through experience build wisdom over time. Look beyond outcomes alone to gain awareness of your tendencies, strengths you can to advance your goals, and limitations you must learn to navigate. Reflection fuels progress.

- How did I feel during/after? Review the emotions you felt before, during, and after you engaged in a habit as cues for what motivates or drains you. Notice when patterns of thoughts are tied to different emotions. Make choices next time to activate positive motivation and a constructive mindset. Your psychology influences outcomes.

- What external factors influenced me? Consider environmental or social triggers, time pressures, lack of accountability or support, resource constraints or any outside influences that impacted your behavior. While you can't control everything, you can make adjustments to optimize selected factors within your control and use them for motivation or demotivation.

- How can I stay accountable and motivated? Look at options for building in more accountability or motivation through your environment, relationships, pre-commitments, or habits to strengthen your follow-through next time.

- What small improvements can I make? Don't aim for an unrealistic overhaul of all your behaviors after you've successfully implemented or failed to implement a habit into your routine. Look for minimum effective doses, small tweaks to your plan or environment that can significantly boost your success and motivate you to move forward. Lasting change happens gradually. Celebrate small wins.

- Am I being too self-critical? Review how you speak to yourself throughout your reflection. Identify the beliefs you hold that discourage you as well as the beliefs that motivate you. Develop a balanced and compassionate perspective to build confidence in your ability through continuous progress over perfection. Learn from your experiences but don't dwell in regret.

Momentum & Bad Habits: Two Methods

People generally think about momentum when they are trying to instill new habits in their lives but the same principle applies to breaking bad habits. That said, you need more than momentum to deal with bad habits. Bad habits are hard to break because they are often the result of underlying triggers, cravings, and rewards we have not fully addressed.

Simply stopping a bad habit is not a one-and-done decision. It often requires ongoing work and commitment to avoid relapse. Even years after quitting, the temptation may arise during times of stress or weakness. This is especially true of addictions where the memory of the substance will try to find an opening back in. Grief for instance is a frequent trigger that causes those suffering from addiction to relapse because it isn't a trigger they face during their every day lives. The roots of old habits run deep and we must continually manage them.

Overcoming a habit, especially a deeply ingrained one, can be quite challenging, but there are two common approaches that many people have used for success: Replacement and Cold Turkey.

Replacement: When tackling habits, the Replacement Method involves identifying the triggers and rewards associated with an undesired behavior and then substituting it with a healthier behavior that yields a similar reward. As an example, let's consider a common habit: excessive social media use.

1. *Identify the Trigger:* What usually prompts you to check your social media? It could be boredom, a notification on your phone, or a desire to procrastinate. Identifying the trigger is the first crucial step to substituting the undesired habit.

2. *Identify the Reward:* What gratification do you derive from scrolling through your social media feed? Is it the need to stay updated, a sense of connection with others, or simply a way to pass time? Understanding the perceived reward helps you to create an effective substitution.

3. *Find a Substitute Habit:* Now, find a healthier habit that addresses the same need as the unwanted habit. If

social media use is a response to boredom, you could substitute it with reading a book or pursuing a hobby. If it's a means of procrastination, replace it with a five-minute meditation or planning your tasks for the day.

4. *Gradual Replacement:* Remember that change is a process, not an event. Start by consciously practicing the substitute habit each time you feel the urge to check social media. With time, this new behavior will become your automatic response to the trigger.

Cold Turkey: Going "Cold Turkey" refers to stopping an unwanted habit abruptly and entirely. This method requires a great deal of willpower and is often used when moderate changes are ineffective or when the habit is harmful, such as substance addiction.

Let's consider vaping in the context of the Cold Turkey approach. Many people believe they derive rewards like relaxation or improved concentration from vaping. However, these are limiting beliefs. In reality, nicotine in vape devices causes addiction, and any perceived 'benefits' are merely the temporary relief from nicotine withdrawal symptoms, such as restlessness or mood changes. In reality, the constant anticipation of the next 'hit' disrupts a user's concentration and increases stress levels.

So, when you quit vaping cold turkey, you're removing the detrimental habit entirely without a need to replace it because there are no real rewards from it, only consequences — likely an early, and very painful, death. In the initial phase, withdrawal symptoms may increase, and this is where resilience and possibly professional help become vital. It's crucial to assess your situation honestly and consider seeking professional advice when dealing with addictions.

Over time, the cravings become less powerful, and your brain, which was previously manipulated by nicotine, begins to regulate its dopamine levels. As a result, you reduce your baseline stress, recover your concentration, and improve your overall health. The triggers, over time, will fail to induce any craving as your brain eliminates the neural pathways. Like a well-worn black asphalt pathway covered in beautiful grass, the neural pathway is a thing of the past.

Both strategies have their place and can be effective depending on the habit in question and an individual's personality and lifestyle.

Why Habit Change is Slow & Difficult

We have reinforced our existing habit loops over days, months, even years of practice. The neural connections between the triggers and rewards of a bad habit are like two-lane highways compared to the dirt roads of a new, good habit. We need to make a conscious and consistent effort to wear those dirt roads into highways. Success requires patience and persistence.

Simply being aware of your habit and wanting to change is not enough. Knowledge does not equal change. Your bad habit continues bringing you back to the same place through nearly automatic reactions and ingrained impulses in your brain. You must actively practice and strengthen your new habit to overwrite the old one. Mere repetition, however, is insufficient.

Practice does not make perfect; practice makes permanent. Mindless repetition of a bad habit will only make this habit stronger. You must practice intentionally, focusing on the new rewards and neural connections you aim to develop. Stay motivated by tracking your progress and rewards.

Success requires diligence and dedication. Do not become discouraged if progress feels slow. Your new habit is fighting an uphill battle against your old way of reacting and responding. But have hope — with consistency and persistence, your new habit will become second nature to you. Stay committed to continuous improvement and patient practice. Track rewards and progress to stay motivated for the long haul. You can achieve victory over your bad habit by starting today, starting small but never stopping. Your brain will adapt and old habits will fade through conscious new behaviors made permanent over time. Progress, not perfection.

The Comfort Trap: Why Familiarity Feels Easier

Our brains are wired to seek comfort and familiarity. What is familiar requires less effort and is more automatic, while new habits demand conscious work. This preference for the familiar is a benefit when it comes to useful habits and behaviors. Brushing your teeth, making coffee in the morning, and driving to work barely require any thought because you've repeated them over time. These familiar habits boost your productivity and wellbeing through routine.

However, the comfort of familiarity also makes bad habits difficult to break. Unhealthy behaviors provide temporary relief through the familiar, even when they are harmful in the long run. Your brain would rather follow its worn path than expend the effort to forge a new trail. This is how addictions and self-sabotage take hold through the comfort trap of familiar routines.

To build better habits, you must be willing to endure discomfort for greater gain. Success requires leaving the familiar behind in pursuit of the unfamiliar territory of growth and progress. The path is difficult, especially at first, but the rewards are worth the effort.

Conclusion

In the end, building better habits comes down to dedication and consistency over time. Momentum is built gradually through small wins and a refusal to quit. While the path is challenging, have hope. With daily practice, continual improvement, and a growth mindset, you can overcome old habits and achieve lasting change.

Remember why you started and stay focused on progress, not perfection. Learn from your mistakes and never stop moving forward. Success is earned through persistence and patience, one habit at a time.

Forget comfort; seek growth. The unfamiliar becomes familiar with practice. Leave the familiar behind for rewards beyond what you've known. Keep your goals in sight and practice daily. The roots of old habits will begin to die as you strengthen new connections through repetition.

Stay dedicated and never miss twice. Track rewards and renew your motivation daily. Keep your habit chain unbroken. Done is better than perfect; just start and keep going. Progress daily and never stop improving. Victory comes with time and repetition.

You have everything within you already to achieve remarkable change. Knowledge is useless without action. Start now, start small, but start building momentum. Practice, learn, grow and become through consistency over time. Develop persistence and patience, and you'll get there. Just keep going! Growth and mastery will follow.

Summary Q & A

1. What is momentum in the context of habit change?
   Momentum refers to the powerful force generated by consistently repeating successful habit behaviors, which leads to increased motivation, confidence, and a shift in identity toward the new habit.

2. How does one small slip-up affect momentum?
   A single slip-up or break in a habit can disrupt momentum and undo days or even weeks of progress. It weakens the connection between the trigger, craving, behavior, and reward in the mind, making it harder to automatically engage in the habit in the future.

3. What is the "What the Hell Effect"?
   The "What the Hell Effect" describes the tendency we have to give up on a goal or habit completely after making one small mistake or slip-up. It's the feeling we have when we think, "Since I've already ruined it, I might as well give up entirely."

4. Why is it important to start small when building habits?
   Starting small makes it easier to accomplish habits, make gradual changes, respond to challenges with flexibility, and visualize and measure our progress. Small steps help us build momentum and increase the likelihood of our long-term success.

5. What are some principles to keep in mind when building long-term habits?
   Never miss twice, prioritize consistency over perfection, don't break the chain of habit repetitions, and focus on progress rather than perfection. These principles help us build sustainable habits and maintain momentum.

6. What should you do once you've broken the chain of your habit?
   After a slip-up, it's important to avoid self-judgment and quickly move on. Reconnect with your motivation, start again immediately, and consider starting small if needed. Learn from your mistakes to strengthen your habit loop.

7. What is the key to building strong habits and achieving lasting change?
    The key is to focus on continuity, consistency, and gradual progress over time. By prioritizing progress over perfection and maintaining momentum, you can reshape or replace any habit and unlock long-term success.

8. To what habit did Jerry Seinfeld credit his success?
    Jerry Seinfeld credited his success to the habit of writing new jokes every day.

9. Why are bad habits hard to break?
    Bad habits are hard to break because they often have underlying triggers and rewards that we need to address before we can stop engaging in them.

10. How can bad habits be permanently eliminated?
    To permanently eliminate a bad habit, you need to uncover the deeper motivations behind it and substitute it with new rewards and routines.

Exercises

1. Recall a recent slip-up or break in one of your habits. Write down the specific trigger that led to the slip-up and reflect on how it affected your momentum. What thoughts or rationalizations did you have that made it easier to skip the habit again? Analyze the impact of the slip-up on your motivation and identity. What lessons can you learn from this experience to prevent future disruptions in your habit momentum?

2. Imagine a scenario where you have made a small mistake that tempts you to give up on a habit completely. Write a short motivational speech to yourself, reminding yourself of your initial motivations and goals. Emphasize the importance of staying focused and resilient, even in the face of setbacks. Use empowering language to combat the "What the Hell Effect" and encourage yourself to continue with your habit despite any slip-ups.

3. Choose a new habit you want to develop or an existing habit you want to strengthen. Break down that habit into smaller, manageable steps. Write down the smallest possible action you can take to initiate the habit. Then, outline a gradual progression of steps, adding a little more difficulty or intensity over time. This exercise will help you create a roadmap of small actions that will support momentum and sustainable habit building.

4. Create a habit tracker for one of your habits. Use a simple calendar or a habit-tracking app to mark an "X" or checkmark for each day you successfully perform the habit. Display the tracker in a visible location, such as your refrigerator or bathroom mirror. Commit to not breaking the chain of habit repetitions. Track your progress daily for at least one month and observe how the visual representation of your consistency impacts your motivation and momentum.

5. Think of a habit that you recently missed for a day or more. Set a specific date and time to restart that habit. Create a plan

for how you will get back on track and outline the first action you will take. On the chosen day and time, immediately perform the habit without hesitation. Take note of how quickly you regained momentum and how this restart positively impacted your habit journey.

6. Identify a bad habit that you want to eliminate and choose a healthier habit to replace it with. Write a step-by-step plan outlining how you will transition from the old habit to the new one. Consider the triggers and rewards associated with both habits and devise strategies to address them. Track your progress and reflect on the positive changes you experience.

7. Create a set of positive affirmations related to the habit you want to develop. Write them down and repeat them to yourself every day, preferably in the morning. Reflect on how affirmations can reinforce your commitment to consistency and help rewire your mindset to support the desired habit.

8. Close your eyes and visualize yourself successfully performing the desired habit with ease and confidence. Imagine the positive outcomes and benefits associated with the habit. Engage your senses and emotions in the visualization to make it more impactful. Reflect on the feelings and motivation the exercise generates.

9. Find a friend or family member who is also working on developing a habit. Become each other's accountability partners, checking in regularly to share progress, provide support, and hold each other accountable. Reflect on the value of having a partner in consistency and how it contributes to your motivation and success.

10. Design a reward system to reinforce your commitment to consistency in developing a habit. Identify specific milestones or targets, and assign rewards for reaching them. Consider both intrinsic and extrinsic rewards that align with your values and preferences. Track your progress and celebrate each milestone you achieve.

Principle 10:
Activate Conscious Intervention

Choosing Behaviors with Intention

"Between stimulus and response there is a space.
In that space is our power to choose our response.
In our response lies our growth and our freedom."
— Viktor Frankl

Have you ever paused for a moment when you felt a habitual urge surfacing and asked yourself: Is this behavior truly serving me, or am I about to mindlessly engage in a habitual behavior that could hinder my growth, health, or happiness? In the realm of habit formation, we often find ourselves caught in a loop of automatic behavior, repeating patterns that may not align with our desires and goals. But within this loop, there is a powerful opportunity for change — an opportunity for conscious intervention and deliberate intention. By bringing awareness to our habits, we unlock our potential to break free from negative patterns and cultivate positive change. In this chapter, we explore the transformative power of conscious intervention in breaking bad habits and the intentional mindset we need to instill and nurture positive habits. By embracing the space between stimulus and response, we tap into our inherent capacity to choose, to shape our own behaviors, and ultimately, to pave the way for growth, freedom, and the realization of our fullest potential.

Key Question:
How can we intervene to break automatic patterns of behavior that result in bad habits, and be intentional with conscious decision making to cultivate positive habits?

259

In this chapter, we embark on a profound exploration of conscious intervention, aiming to answer the fundamental question of whether we possess the capacity to truly decide our habits.

It takes an average of 66 days to form a new habit. This number emphasizes the importance of conscious intervention and persistence in altering one's behavior to establish new habits. It also highlights the fact that habit formation is not an overnight process, and individuals need to consistently practice and reinforce new behaviors to make them automatic and long-lasting.[59]

Furthermore, we will delve into the realm of conscious intention, understanding how we can purposefully instill and cultivate positive habits that align with our values and aspirations. By harnessing the transformative power of intention, we can proactively shape our lives, nurture positive behaviors, and pave the way for personal growth and success.

Mindfulness & Habits

Amidst the pervasive discussions about mindfulness and its benefits, many people may wonder: what is the practical value of incorporating mindfulness into our lives? How does it relate to conscious intervention and intention, and how can it empower us to transform our habits?

Mindfulness, at its core, is the practice of being fully present and aware of our thoughts, emotions, and actions in the present moment, without judgment or attachment. While it is often associated with stress reduction and enhanced well-being, its practical benefits extend far beyond that.[60]

[59] Lally, P., van Jaarsveld, C. H. M., Potts, H. W. W., & Wardle, J. (2010). How are habits formed: Modelling habit formation in the real world. European Journal of Social Psychology, 40(6), 998-1009. doi:10.1002/ejsp.674

[60] Davis, D. M., & Hayes, J. A. (2012, July 1). What are the benefits of mindfulness? *Monitor on Psychology, 43*(7). https://www.apa.org/monitor/2012/07-08/ce-corner

In the realm of conscious intervention, mindfulness serves as a powerful tool for self-awareness. By cultivating mindfulness, we develop the ability to observe our habits and automatic behaviors with clarity and non-judgment. We become attuned to the triggers, cues, and patterns that shape our actions, allowing us to redirect our behavior towards more desirable outcomes.

Moreover, mindfulness enhances our capacity for intentional decision-making. When we approach each moment with mindfulness, we create a space for conscious choice. We can pause and reflect before acting, allowing us to align our intentions with our values and make decisions that support our long-term goals and well-being.

Examples:

> **Life**: Mindful eating is a practice that involves bringing full awareness to the experience of eating. It involves paying attention to the flavors, textures, and sensations of each bite, as well as recognizing feelings of hunger and satiety. By practicing mindful eating, individuals can become more conscious of their eating habits, make healthier food choices, and develop a healthier relationship with food.

> **Career**: By practicing mindfulness, individuals can cultivate the ability to step back and observe their thoughts, emotions, and biases when faced with important career decisions. This awareness can help reduce impulsive reactions and allow for more deliberate, intentional decision-making that aligns with long-term career goals.

> **Business**: In the fast-paced and high-stakes world of high finance, mindful risk management can be crucial. Professionals can use mindfulness to enhance their awareness of market conditions, potential risks, and personal biases that may impact investment decisions. By practicing mindfulness, finance professionals can make

more informed and calculated decisions, managing risk with greater clarity and composure.

Respond Consciously, Not Impulsively

Practicing mindfulness also fosters self-regulation and emotional intelligence. By cultivating awareness of our emotions, we gain the ability to respond rather than react impulsively. This emotional resilience enables us to navigate challenges, stressors, and triggers with greater composure, making conscious decisions that lead to positive habit transformation.

In essence, mindfulness provides the practical bridge between conscious intervention, intention, and habit transformation. It equips us with the tools we need to break free from automatic behavior, to consciously decide our habits, and to align our actions with our deepest aspirations.

Break Bad Habits: Conscious Intervention Strategies

Conscious intervention is a powerful approach to breaking bad habits and taking control of our behavior. It involves being fully present and actively engaging in the process of habit transformation.[61] By bringing conscious awareness to our automatic patterns, we can disrupt any of the four components of the habit loop (trigger, craving, behavior, or reward) and make intentional choices that align with our desired outcomes.

Breaking bad habits is crucial for personal growth, professional success, and our overall well-being. Conscious intervention allows us to break free from negative habits that may hinder our productivity, decision-making, and relationships. It empowers us to reclaim control over our actions and create positive change.

---

[61] "Changing Habits." UNC Learning Center, 21 Nov. 2016, learningcenter.unc.edu/tips-and-tools/changing-habits/.

At its core, conscious intervention begins with developing self-awareness. It involves recognizing the triggers, rewards and environmental factors that contribute to our undesired habits. By understanding these influences, we can gain insight into the underlying motivations and emotional states that drive our behaviors. Self-awareness allows us to recognize the moments when our automatic patterns are activated and provides us with an opportunity to intervene consciously.

Mindfulness Practices

Mindfulness practices play a vital role in conscious intervention. Mindfulness cultivates a non-judgmental awareness of the present moment, enabling us to observe our thoughts, emotions, and physical sensations without getting caught up in them. By practicing mindfulness, we *create a space* between our triggers and our responses, allowing us to pause and make more conscious choices. This heightened awareness helps us break free from habitual reactions and respond in ways that align with our values and goals.

Examples:

Life: Dedicate a few minutes each morning to practice mindful breathing or meditation. During challenging moments, such as when facing a difficult conversation or a high-pressure situation, you can pause, take a deep breath, and bring your attention to the present moment. By cultivating mindfulness, you can develop greater self-awareness and consciously choose responses that are aligned with your values and nurture your personal growth.

Career: You can integrate short mindfulness breaks throughout the day, where you step away from your desk, take a few mindful breaths, and bring your attention back to the task at hand. By incorporating mindfulness into your work routine, you can improve productivity and make more intentional choices in managing investments.

Business: When faced with important business decisions, you can engage in mindful reflection by creating a quiet space, clearing your mind, and focusing on the present moment. This practice allows you to observe thoughts and emotions without judgment, facilitating a clearer understanding of the situation. By incorporating mindfulness into your decision-making process, you can cultivate a more holistic perspective, consider long-term implications, and make choices that align with your business goals and values.

Cognitive Restructuring

Another essential aspect of conscious intervention is cognitive restructuring. This technique involves challenging and reframing negative thoughts associated with our bad habits.[62] This is similar to the limiting and empowering beliefs discussion in Principle 5. By examining the underlying assumptions and changing our perspective, we can shift our mindset and create new narratives that support positive change. Cognitive restructuring empowers us to replace self-limiting beliefs with empowering ones and opens up new possibilities for behavior.

Examples:

Life: Suppose you have a tendency to engage in negative self-talk that undermines your self-confidence and hinders personal growth. Through cognitive restructuring, you can identify these negative thoughts and replace them with positive affirmations and realistic perspectives. For example, if you catch yourself thinking, "I always fail at new challenges," you can reframe your perspective as, "Every challenge is an opportunity for growth and learning." By consciously restructuring your thoughts, you cultivate a more empowering mindset that supports positive habits and personal development.

---

[62] "Changing Habits." UNC Learning Center, 21 Nov. 2016, learningcenter.unc.edu/tips-and-tools/changing-habits/.

Career: You may encounter setbacks or market downturns in your career that trigger feelings of self-doubt and fear. By applying cognitive restructuring techniques, you can challenge the negative beliefs and focus on realistic perspectives. For instance, instead of catastrophizing market fluctuations and thinking, "I'm a failure if I make a wrong investment decision," you can reframe it as, "Every investment carries inherent risks, and I am constantly learning and adapting to navigate changing market conditions." By consciously reshaping your thoughts, you build resilience and maintain confidence in your investment decisions.

Business: Cognitive restructuring can help you reframe setbacks in your business as opportunities for growth and innovation. For instance, instead of perceiving a failed product launch as a personal failure, you can view it as valuable feedback for refining your strategies and improving future outcomes. By consciously reframing your thoughts and beliefs, you cultivate a mindset that empowers you to embrace challenges, adapt to change, and foster a culture of continuous improvement.

Alternative Behaviors

Alternative behaviors are new and healthier actions or activities you engage in as substitutes for your undesired habits. These behaviors are consciously chosen to replace the old habits and serve as positive alternatives for them. For example, if you want to break the habit of excessive screen time, you might choose to engage in physical exercise, spend time outdoors, or pursue a hobby instead. By consciously selecting alternative behaviors, individuals create new pathways in their brain and reinforce positive actions.

Examples:

Life: Imagine you want to break the habit of excessive social media usage that consumes a significant portion of your free time. As an alternative behavior, you can replace scrolling through social media with engaging in physical exercise, such as going for a walk or practicing yoga. By consciously choosing to engage in these activities whenever the urge to use social media arises, you not only create healthier habits but also experience the benefits of physical activity and improved well-being.

Career: In your career, you may want to establish a habit of proactive networking to expand your professional connections. Instead of waiting to receive invitations to networking events, you can consciously choose to reach out to industry professionals through email or schedule virtual coffee meetings to discuss industry trends. By proactively initiating these interactions, you establish relationships that can lead to valuable insights, collaboration opportunities, and career advancement.

Business: Suppose you aim to instill a habit of continuous improvement within your business operations as there currently isn't any program at the moment. An alternative behavior could be to allocate a specific time each week for team brainstorming sessions or conducting regular performance reviews. By consciously prioritizing these activities and incorporating them into your business routine, you create a culture of continuous learning and innovation, driving your business's success.

Coping Mechanisms

Coping mechanisms are specific strategies or techniques you can use to manage and deal with stress, emotions, or difficult situations. These situations can act as triggers which can set off unwanted behavior (the bad habit). Examples of coping mechanisms include deep breathing exercises, journaling, practicing mindfulness, seeking social support, or engaging in relaxation techniques.

Examples:

Life: During a particularly stressful day, you can take a few moments to sit quietly, close your eyes, and focus on your breath. By consciously engaging in these coping mechanisms, you can regulate your emotions, reduce stress levels, and respond more calmly and effectively to challenging situations.

Career: Employing coping mechanisms such as taking short breaks to stretch or practicing visualization exercises can help you regulate your stress response and enhance your focus. For instance, before an important presentation, you can take a few minutes to visualize yourself delivering a successful and impactful speech. By consciously utilizing these coping mechanisms, you can manage stress levels and maintain a composed and confident demeanor in professional settings.

Business: Coping mechanisms such as seeking social support from mentors or peers, participating in business-related forums or communities, or engaging in relaxation techniques such as guided imagery or progressive muscle relaxation can help you navigate these situations. By consciously utilizing these coping mechanisms, you can access valuable advice, gain perspective, and recharge your energy, enabling you to make sound decisions and lead your business effectively.

Supportive Environments

Creating a supportive environment is essential for implementing alternative behaviors. Surrounding ourselves with individuals who encourage and reinforce our positive habits can greatly enhance our chances of success. Seeking support from friends, family, or joining support groups can provide the necessary accountability and motivation we need to sustain the desired changes.

Examples:

Life: Suppose you want to create a supportive environment to develop a habit of daily exercise. You can seek out a workout buddy or join a fitness class where you can connect with like-minded individuals who share similar health goals. By surrounding yourself with people who prioritize physical activity, you receive encouragement, motivation, and a sense of camaraderie that strengthens your commitment to regular exercise.

Career: Building a supportive environment can involve networking with colleagues or industry professionals who share your passion for financial markets. By engaging in professional organizations, attending industry conferences, or participating in online forums, you can connect with individuals who offer you valuable insights, support, and guidance in navigating the complexities of the financial industry. This supportive network provides you with opportunities for collaboration, learning, and career advancement.

Business: Creating a supportive environment within your business involves fostering a culture that values growth, teamwork, and open communication. For instance, you can establish regular team meetings or brainstorming sessions in which employees are encouraged to share ideas, provide feedback, and support each other's professional development. By fostering an inclusive and collaborative atmosphere, you cultivate an environment that promotes innovation, boosts employee morale, and drives the success of your business.

Build Good Habits: Conscious Intention Strategies

Understanding Conscious Intention

Conscious intention is a powerful force that empowers us to shape our habits and transform our lives. It involves the deliberate and mindful decision to take control of our actions, thoughts, and behaviors. By harnessing conscious intention, we can break free from the grip of automaticity and actively choose the habits that align with our values and goals. Conscious intention brings awareness and purpose to our actions, allowing us to make intentional choices that lead to positive outcomes. In this section, we will explore strategies for cultivating conscious intention in habit formation. By developing self-awareness, designing effective cues, setting clear intentions, and utilizing implementation intentions, we can harness the power of conscious intention to create lasting change and lead a more intentional and fulfilling life.

Setting Clear Intentions & Goals

Setting clear intentions and goals is a fundamental step in cultivating positive habits. By defining what we want to achieve and the habits we want to develop, we provide ourselves with a sense of direction and purpose. Clear intentions help us align our actions with our desired outcomes and provide a roadmap for habit formation. Whether it's improving our health, enhancing our productivity, or fostering personal growth, setting clear intentions empowers us to focus our efforts on the habits that will lead us to success.

Examples:

Life: If we've committed to improving physical fitness, we might set a clear intention by establishing a goal to exercise for at least 30 minutes every day. By clearly defining this intention, it becomes easier to prioritize physical activity and make it a non-negotiable part of our daily routine.

Career: If a portfolio manager is committed to deepening their knowledge of financial markets, they might set a clear intention to dedicate a specific amount of time each week to read research reports, analyze market trends, and attend relevant industry events. This intention helps cultivate the habit of continuous learning and professional development, which can lead to better investment decisions and career growth.

Business: Setting clear intentions in a business may involve establishing goals for team collaboration and innovation. For example, a business may set an intention to create an environment of open communication and idea-sharing by implementing regular team brainstorming sessions and fostering a culture that values diverse perspectives. By setting this intention, the habit of collaboration and innovation becomes ingrained in the team's work processes, driving creativity and improving outcomes.

Designing Effective Triggers to Initiate Desired Habits

Designing effective triggers (i.e., cues) is an essential strategy for initiating and reinforcing positive habits. Triggers serve as reminders and signals that prompt us to engage in the desired behavior. By creating specific cues and triggers associated with the habit we want to cultivate, we can prime ourselves for action and make it easier to initiate the habit consistently.

Examples:

Life: Suppose we've set a goal to establish a daily meditation practice. We might design an effective cue by placing a meditation cushion or a reminder note in a visible location, such as near the bedside table. This visual cue serves as a trigger that prompts us to engage in the habit of meditation as soon as we wake up, increasing the likelihood of follow-through.

Career: If a portfolio manager wants to improve their decision-making process by considering a broader range of perspectives, they might design schedule regular meetings with colleagues from different departments or teams to discuss investment ideas. The scheduled meetings serve as triggers that remind them to actively seek diverse viewpoints, fostering a habit of inclusive decision-making.

Business: Suppose a business sets a goal to enhance their risk management practices. Designing an effective cue could involve implementing a daily risk assessment meeting where team members discuss potential risks, review mitigation strategies, and share insights. This scheduled meeting acts as a trigger that prompts the team to focus on risk management consistently, helping them to establish a habit of proactive risk assessment and mitigation.

Implementation Intentions to Reinforce New Habits

Utilizing implementation intentions is a powerful technique to reinforce the development of positive habits. Implementation intentions involve specifying the exact time, place, and action associated with the desired habit. By clearly defining the when, where, and how of habit execution, we increase our likelihood of following through and create a stronger association between the cue and the behavior.

Examples:

Life: Let's say you want to develop a daily exercise habit. You can create an implementation intention by specifying the exact details of when and where you will exercise. For instance, you might say, "When I wake up in the morning, I will put on my workout clothes and go for a run in the nearby park." By clearly defining the time and location for your exercise routine, you are more likely to follow through with your intention and reinforce the habit. This approach can help you proactively prioritize your health and well-being.

Career: Suppose you aim to improve your analytical skills in your career to make better investment decisions. You can create an implementation intention by stating, "Before I start analyzing any investment opportunity, I will spend 30 minutes reviewing relevant financial statements and industry reports." By setting this intention and linking it to a specific action, you create a structured approach to reinforce the habit of thorough analysis. This proactive approach can contribute to your professional growth and success in making informed investment choices.

Business: Imagine you want to improve your networking skills to expand your professional connections and grow your business. You can create an implementation intention by stating, "Whenever I attend a business event, I will introduce myself to at least three new people and exchange contact information." By setting this intention, you proactively plan how you will engage with others and create opportunities for meaningful connections. This intentional networking approach can help you broaden your network, foster collaborations, and open doors to new possibilities in your career, without requiring you to specifically mention the hedge fund industry.

Leveraging the Power of Repetition & Reinforcement

One of the key "intention" strategies in cultivating positive habits is harnessing the power of repetition and reinforcement. By consistently repeating a behavior and reinforcing it with positive outcomes, we can strengthen the neural pathways associated with that habit and make it more automatic.

Examples:

Life: Suppose you want to develop a habit of practicing gratitude daily. You can leverage the power of repetition by setting aside a specific time each day, such as before bed or during breakfast, to reflect on and write down three things you are grateful for. By consistently engaging in this practice and reinforcing it with positive emotions, you reinforce the habit of gratitude and gradually make it a natural part of your daily routine.

Career: Imagine that you want to cultivate a habit of effective networking to expand your professional connections and opportunities. You can leverage the power of repetition by committing to attend networking events or industry conferences regularly. Set a goal to attend at least one networking event per month, such as industry conferences, meetups, or online networking sessions.

Business: Let's say you want to establish a habit of conducting regular performance reviews where you and your team can provide constructive feedback that improves your business's operation. You can leverage the power of repetition by scheduling monthly or quarterly review meetings and consistently engaging in the process. By repeating this practice and reinforcing positive behaviors and achievements, you create a culture of continuous improvement and growth within your team or organization.

Habit Stacking & Keystone Habits

Both habit stacking and instilling keystone habits are intentional strategies you can use to reinforce positive behaviors and facilitate habit formation. They provide practical ways for you to align new habits with existing routines and leverage the power of interconnected habits for sustained change.

As we discussed during Principle 4, habit stacking is a strategy that involves linking a new habit you want to establish with an existing habit that is already a part of your daily routine. By stacking the new habit onto an existing one, you create a trigger that reminds you to engage in the desired behavior. For example, if you want to develop a habit of daily meditation, you can stack it onto your existing habit of brushing your teeth. After brushing your teeth, you can make it a routine to sit quietly for a few minutes and meditate. The existing habit of brushing your teeth acts as a cue or trigger for the new habit of meditation, making it easier to integrate into your daily routine.

Keystone habits — also discussed under Principle 4 — are powerful habits that have a ripple effect on other areas of your life. They are habits that, when cultivated, tend to create positive changes and inspire you to develop other beneficial habits. For instance, regular exercise is often considered a keystone habit because it has been shown to have positive effects on physical health, mental well-being, and productivity. By establishing a habit of regular exercise, you may find that it influences other areas of your life, such as improved sleep, increased energy levels, and enhanced focus. Instilling keystone habits can be an effective way to initiate positive change and create a domino effect in transforming other aspects of your life.

Proactive vs. Reactive: Prevention vs. Treatment

When it comes to our health, we often recognize the importance of being proactive (i.e., intentional) rather than reactive (i.e., interventional). Intervention is a lot more painful to deal with than intention. Prevention is the key to avoiding potential health issues and maintaining overall well-being. We exercise, eat nutritious food, and prioritize self-care to prevent the onset of diseases and ailments. Similarly, the concept of intentional (i.e., proactive) habit cultivation aligns with the idea of prevention. Reactive behavior align with intervention.

Being proactive with our habits means taking conscious and intentional actions to shape our behaviors before they become problematic or detrimental. It involves recognizing the power of habits in influencing our lives and actively choosing to cultivate positive habits that contribute to our well-being and success. Intention, and thus prevention, is a much better use of our precious resources of time and energy.

In contrast, being reactive with our habits is akin to dealing with a disease that could have been prevented. It often involves trying to break bad habits or addressing the negative consequences of our actions after they have already occurred. Reactive habits can lead to detrimental outcomes and may require significant effort and resources to rectify.

By adopting a proactive approach to habit cultivation, we prioritize prevention and invest in our personal growth and development. We recognize that habits play a vital role in shaping our lives and that consciously instilling positive habits can help us avoid pitfalls, enhance our well-being, and achieve our goals.

In the context of health, being proactive means exercising regularly, eating a balanced diet, and practicing self-care to prevent potential health issues. Similarly, proactive habit cultivation involves setting clear intentions, designing effective cues, utilizing implementation intentions, and leveraging repetition and reinforcement to establish positive behaviors and prevent the negative consequences of unhealthy habits.

By taking a proactive stance towards our habits, we empower ourselves to shape our lives and create a foundation for long-term success and fulfillment. It allows us to be intentional, purposeful, and mindful in our actions, cultivating habits that support our values, goals, and overall well-being.

Mindful Decision-Making

In the realm of habit transformation lies a powerful tool we can use to shape our behaviors and reshape our lives: mindful decision-making. While our habits often seem automatic and ingrained, there exists a space between stimulus and response where we have the ability to make conscious choices. This space is a realm of empowerment, where we can pause, reflect, and intentionally decide how we want to act. Mindful decision-making involves cultivating self-awareness, aligning our choices with our values, and practicing self-regulation. By harnessing the power of this space, we can break free from automatic patterns, align our actions with our conscious intentions, and embark on a transformative journey of positive habit change.

Exploring the Space Between Stimulus & Response

In the realm of habit transformation, the space between stimulus and response holds immense power. It is within this space that we have the opportunity to make mindful decisions that can shape our habits and ultimately transform our lives. By recognizing and expanding this space, we can break free from the grip of automaticity and exercise conscious control over our actions. Instead of succumbing to impulsive reactions, we can pause, reflect, and respond in a way that aligns with our desired habits.

Cultivating Self-Awareness & Self-Reflection

Self-awareness and self-reflection are essential tools we can use to make intentional choices that support habit transformation. By cultivating an understanding of our thoughts, emotions, and triggers, we can develop a heightened sense of awareness in the decision-making process. This awareness allows us to pause and evaluate whether our choices align with our desired habits and long-term goals. Through self-reflection, we gain insights into the underlying motivations and beliefs driving our behaviors, empowering us to make conscious decisions that contribute to positive habit change.

Applying Values-Based Decision-Making

Values-based decision-making serves as a guiding compass in habit transformation. By aligning our choices with our core values, we ensure that our habits are in harmony with what truly matters to us. When faced with decisions that impact our habits, we can ask ourselves: Does this choice reflect my values? Does it help me become the person I want to become? By answering these questions, we can make conscious decisions that reinforce positive habits and propel us toward our desired self.

Practicing Self-Regulation & Self-Control

Self-regulation and self-control are essential skills for aligning our actions with conscious intentions and breaking free from automatic patterns. It involves managing impulses, resisting temptation, and exerting control over our behavior. By practicing self-regulation, we can override the allure of instant gratification and make choices that support our long-term goals and desired habits. It allows us to resist the pull of automatic, ingrained behaviors and consciously choose actions that lead to positive habit transformation.

Suppose, for example, you have a habit of mindlessly snacking on unhealthy foods during stressful moments. Through practicing self-regulation and self-control, you develop the ability to recognize the trigger of stress and the automatic response of reaching for unhealthy snacks. In the space between stimulus and response, you consciously choose to engage in a healthier coping mechanism, such as taking a few deep breaths, going for a short walk, or having a healthy snack instead. By practicing self-regulation, you break free from the automatic pattern and align your actions with your conscious intention of nourishing your body and maintaining a healthy lifestyle.

By exploring the space between stimulus and response, cultivating self-awareness and self-reflection, applying values-based decision-making, and practicing self-regulation and self-control, we empower ourselves to make mindful decisions that support habit transformation. Through these intentional choices, we can break free from automatic patterns, align our behaviors with our conscious intentions, and embark on a transformative journey of positive habit change.

Conclusion

In this chapter, we have used Principle 10 to explore how conscious intervention and intention can reshape the journey of habit transformation. By embracing the space between stimulus and response, we unlock the power to choose our actions consciously and deliberately to shape our habits. In doing so, we are able to break free from automatic patterns and cultivate positive change through proactive and intentional decision-making.

Throughout this chapter, we have delved into various strategies and techniques that empower us to break bad habits and establish positive ones. We have explored the importance of self-awareness, mindfulness practices, cognitive restructuring, alternative behaviors, coping mechanisms, and supportive environments. Each of these elements plays a crucial role in our ability to intervene consciously and reshape our habits.

By setting clear intentions and goals, designing effective cues and triggers, utilizing implementation intentions, and leveraging the power of repetition and reinforcement, we lay the foundation for cultivating positive habits. Additionally, we have examined the role of mindful decision-making in empowering our choices and explored the significance of self-awareness, values-based decision-making, self-regulation, and self-control in aligning our actions with conscious intentions.

Moreover, we have acknowledged the challenges that arise in breaking bad habits and maintaining positive ones. Through strategies such as overcoming temptation, creating supportive environments, practicing self-compassion, resilience, and self-reflection, we strengthen our ability to navigate setbacks and sustain progress.

Ultimately, the conscious intervention and intention principles discussed in this chapter offer us a powerful framework for taking ownership of our habits and transforming our lives. By becoming more aware of our triggers, actively engaging in decision-making, and intentionally shaping our behaviors, we step into a realm of personal empowerment and growth. As we embrace the space between stimulus and response, we tap into our innate ability to choose, evolve, and forge a path of freedom and fulfillment.

In the wise words of Viktor Frankl, "Between stimulus and response there is a space. In that space is our power to choose our response. In our response lies our growth and our freedom." This principle reminds us of the tremendous potential within that space, the power to pause, reflect, and make conscious decisions that align with our values and aspirations.

As we conclude our exploration of Principle 10, we invite you to embrace conscious intervention and intention as transformative tools in your journey of habit transformation. By applying these principles, you unlock the power to break free from the constraints of automaticity, cultivate positive habits, and pave the way for personal growth, fulfillment, and the realization of your true potential. May you harness the power of conscious intervention and intention to create the life you envision, one intentional choice at a time.

Summary Q & A

1. What is conscious intervention and why is it important in shaping our habits?

    Conscious intervention is important because it allows us to break free from negative habits, regain control over our behavior, and create positive change in our lives.

2. What is cognitive restructuring and how does it support conscious intervention?

    Cognitive restructuring involves challenging and reframing the negative thoughts and beliefs we associate with our bad habits. By changing our perspective and replacing self-limiting beliefs with empowering ones, cognitive restructuring supports conscious intervention by shifting our mindset and allowing us to create new narratives that support positive behavior change.

3. What are alternative behaviors, and how can they help in breaking unwanted habits?

    Alternative behaviors are consciously chosen actions or activities that serve as positive substitutes for undesired habits. By engaging in alternative behaviors, individuals create new pathways in their brain and reinforce positive actions, effectively breaking free from old habits and establishing healthier ones.

4. Why is setting clear intentions and goals important in cultivating positive habits?

    Setting clear intentions and goals provides a sense of direction and purpose in habit formation. It helps us align our actions with our desired outcomes and create a roadmap for success. Clear intentions enable us to focus our efforts on the habits that will lead us to personal growth, productivity, and fulfillment.

5. What is the purpose of designing effective triggers (cues) in habit formation?

    Designing effective triggers allows us to surround ourselves with reminders and signals that prompt us to engage in behaviors we desire, making it easier for us to initiate the habit consistently.

6. What is the difference between habit stacking and keystone habits?

   Habit stacking involves linking a new habit with an existing one to create a trigger for the desired behavior. Keystone habits are powerful habits that have a ripple effect on other areas of life, inspiring us to develop other beneficial habits.

7. Why is honesty important in recovery and habit transformation?

   Honesty is important in recovery because it helps individuals break free from a pattern of habitual deception and fosters personal growth and sustained healing.

8. How can mindful decision-making empower choices for habit transformation?

   Mindful decision-making allows us to make conscious choices in the space between stimulus and response, aligning our actions with our values and breaking free from automatic patterns. It empowers us to reshape our habits and embark on a transformative journey.

9. What role does self-awareness play in making intentional choices for habit transformation?

   Self-awareness helps us understand our thoughts, emotions, and triggers, enabling us to evaluate whether our choices align with our desired habits and goals. It empowers us to make conscious decisions that contribute to positive habit change.

10. How does self-regulation and self-control support habit transformation?

    They help in breaking free from ingrained habits and fostering positive change.

Exercises

1. Take a moment to reflect on your current habits. Write down three habits that you would like to change or improve. For each habit, identify the triggers, behaviors, and rewards associated with it. This exercise will help you develop self-awareness and lay the foundation for conscious intervention.

2. Choose one undesired habit that you want to replace with a healthier alternative behavior. Create an action plan outlining specific steps you will take to engage in the alternative behavior consciously. Set a realistic timeline and establish accountability measures, such as sharing your action plan with a supportive friend or family member. Implement the action plan and track your progress regularly.

3. Select one positive habit that you want to cultivate. Write a clear and specific intention statement that reflects your commitment to this habit. Include why this habit is important to you and how it aligns with your values and aspirations. Place your intention statement somewhere visible, such as on your desk or as a screensaver, to serve as a reminder and reinforcement of your conscious intention.

4. Identify three examples of effective triggers (cues) from life, career, or business contexts that can initiate positive habits.

5. Think about a habit you want to break and design a habit stacking strategy by linking it with an existing habit in your daily routine.

6. Identify a habit you want to reinforce or strengthen in a business setting. Leverage the power of repetition by scheduling regular meetings or check-ins related to that habit. Write down a plan for how often and when these meetings will occur, and outline the purpose and desired outcomes of each meeting.

7. Reflect on a keystone habit that you believe could have a positive ripple effect on other areas of your life. Describe the specific benefits and changes you expect to see in other aspects of your life once you've established this habit. Write down a plan for how you will initiate and maintain this keystone habit.

8. Think about a habit you want to proactively prevent or avoid. Identify potential triggers or situations that may lead you to engage in the undesired behavior. Develop a plan for how you will actively intervene and replace the undesired habit with a more positive alternative when faced with those triggers.

9. Choose a habit related to your health and well-being that you want to be more proactive about. Create a daily or weekly routine that includes specific actions or practices you can perform to prevent potential health issues and promote overall well-being. Write down the details of your proactive routine and commit to following it for a specified period.

10. Consider a situation in which you have been reactive rather than proactive with a habit. Reflect on the negative consequences of being reactive and the effort required to rectify the situation. Write down strategies and action steps you can take to shift from reactive to proactive behavior and prevent similar situations in the future.

Conclusion

As we end our exploration into the transformative power of habits, we have reached a pivotal moment: the crossroads of change. Behind us lies the familiar and comfortable, our habitual ways of being. Ahead lies the unfamiliar path of progress, growth, and impact. While this path may be challenging, it can lead us to a life of meaning and fulfilment. The decision is yours: remain as you are or choose growth.

Principle 1, *Master the Art and Science of Habits*, lays the foundation. Understanding the architecture of habits is essential for mastery, as we can modify the loop to cultivate positive habits and eliminate negative ones. The brain's involvement in habit formation and modification, with various regions and chemicals playing crucial roles, offers opportunities for optimization. Balancing factors such as stress, willpower, and activation energy is vital in establishing and maintaining habits. Our habits reflect our self-awareness, values, and identity, and although they may feel automatic, they originate as conscious decisions that we can reshape through continuous choices. By harnessing this power and understanding habit architecture, we can unlock the potential for personal development and transformation.

Principle 2, *Design Your Habit Plan*, emphasizes the importance of habit analysis and planning in achieving successful habit change. By setting measurable criteria, clear objectives, and selecting appropriate strategies, we lay the foundation for transformation. Integrating intrinsic and extrinsic resources into our plans enhances our chances of success. Understanding the distinction between the plan and the process is vital—the plan provides a roadmap while the process encompasses the broader journey of habit change. By following the principles outlined in this book, we engage in a comprehensive process that enables us to cultivate positive habits and eliminate negative ones, leading to personal growth, career advancement, and business success.

Principle 3, *Embrace Accountability*, teaches us that accountability and support are indispensable elements in achieving habit mastery, providing the motivation, reinforcement, and consequences necessary for consistent progress. By anchoring our habits to external sources of accountability and surrounding ourselves with a supportive environment, we create a strong foundation for sustained habit change. Technology platforms and habit trackers offer additional tools to enhance awareness and reinforce our commitment. Through the power of accountability and support, we gain the strength to overcome obstacles and achieve lasting results. As we transition to exploring the influence of triggers on our behavior, we continue our journey towards unlocking the full potential of habit transformation.

Principle 4, *Harness the Power of Triggers*, affirms that triggers hold significant influence over our habits and the potential for lasting behavioral change. Throughout this chapter, we explored the intricacies of triggers, from understanding their types to harnessing their power for habit change. Recognizing their role as catalysts for habits, we empower ourselves to maintain long-term transformation. Triggers shape our routines, form new habits, and eliminate old ones. By intentionally managing triggers, designing cue-action associations, and creating trigger-rich environments, we solidify new habits and replace unwanted ones. Armed with this knowledge, it is now your turn to apply these strategies in your life, career, and business. By customizing triggers to your preferences and utilizing their power, you can establish a trigger system that supports and sustains your desired habits. Remember, habit change is a process, and consistency is key. Through deliberate choices and conscious actions, you are on the path to manifesting the life you envision.

Principle 5, *Rewire Your Mind*, emphasizes the profound influence of beliefs, mindset, and thought patterns on our habits and potential for growth. By recognizing the power of limiting beliefs and cognitive biases, we gain the freedom to challenge and replace unhelpful thought patterns with empowering alternatives. Nurturing an optimistic mindset and staying properly nourished provide vital support for strengthening habits and routines that propel us towards our goals. As we break free from unhelpful beliefs and cultivate a mindset of possibility, we unlock our true capacity for change and open ourselves to outcomes beyond our previous limitations. By taking command of our thoughts and aligning them with purpose, we shape our habits and transform our reality.

Principle 6, *Unlock Rewards & Consequences*, sheds light on the pivotal role that rewards and consequences play in the process of habit formation and transformation. Understanding their power empowers us to make informed decisions, sustain motivation, and reinforce positive behavior change. By recognizing the rewards associated with our habits and leveraging them strategically, we create a strong system of reinforcement that aligns with our values and goals. Simultaneously, consequences serve as effective motivators, emphasizing the impact our habits have on our well-being and overall success. By unlocking the potential of rewards and consequences, we pave the way for lasting habit transformation and personal growth.

Principle 7, *Consult Your Future Self*, brings attention to the ongoing battle between our present and future selves, emphasizing that the choices we make in each moment can shape our lives. While our primal brains tend to prioritize immediate rewards over long-term consequences, progress relies on strategies that satisfy present needs while aligning with our meaningful aspirations. Understanding why we sometimes struggle to consider our future selves leads to self-compassion and the development of tailored strategies to strengthen that connection through practice. Balancing present and future goals, building accountability, adjusting expectations, and confronting limiting beliefs contribute to steady progress. By embracing imperfect action, consistency, and dedication, we expand our capabilities and wisdom, transforming dreams into reality. With patience and effort, we navigate the journey of habit change and unlock our potential for self-mastery.

Principle 8, *Differentiate Habits & Addictions*, explores the distinction between habits and addictions, highlighting their unique characteristics. Habits are consciously controlled automatic behaviors that can be beneficial, while addictions involve a loss of control and compulsive engagement in behaviors despite negative consequences. Understanding the role of rewards in addictive behaviors helps us comprehend the allure and challenges of overcoming addiction. Early detection, intervention, and a supportive environment are crucial for addressing addictions and facilitating recovery. Differentiating between habits and addictions ensures appropriate interventions and support are provided to individuals in need.

Principle 9, *Embrace the Power of Momentum*, teaches us that building better habits requires dedication, consistency, and a refusal to quit. Through daily practice, continual improvement, and a growth mindset, we can overcome old habits and achieve lasting change. Progress is made through persistence, patience, and a focus on progress rather than perfection. By embracing discomfort and seeking growth, we leave behind familiar patterns and open ourselves up to rewards beyond what we have known. Dedication, daily practice, and tracking our progress help us strengthen new connections and weaken old habits. With persistence, patience, and unwavering commitment, we have the power within us to achieve remarkable change and unlock growth and mastery. The key is to start now, start small, and build momentum through consistent action. Keep going, never stop learning, and success will follow.

Principle 10, *Activate Conscious Intervention*, highlights the significance of conscious decision-making and intentional actions in the process of habit transformation. Through self-awareness, mindfulness practices, and cognitive restructuring, we can break free from automatic patterns and actively shape our habits. By setting clear intentions, utilizing effective cues, and reinforcing positive behaviors, we lay the groundwork for cultivating lasting habits. Challenges and setbacks are addressed through strategies such as creating supportive environments and practicing self-compassion. Embracing conscious intervention empowers us to take ownership of our habits and live a life aligned with our values and aspirations. Embracing conscious intervention and intention as transformative tools allows you to unlock your true potential one intentional choice at a time.

In conclusion, our exploration of the transformative power of habits has led us to a pivotal moment—a crossroads where we must choose between the familiar comfort of old habits and the uncharted path of progress and growth. Throughout the book, we have delved into ten principles that serve as guideposts on this transformative journey. We have learned that habits can be consciously mastered, plans can be designed, accountability can be embraced, triggers can be harnessed, minds can be rewired, rewards and consequences can shape our behavior, future selves can be consulted, momentum can be built, differentiation between habits and addictions is crucial, and conscious intervention can activate lasting change.

It is important to recognize that knowledge alone is not enough; it is the application of this knowledge that truly empowers us. The principles and strategies presented in this book provide the framework for habit transformation, but it is up to each individual to take action and implement them in their lives. The decision to embark on the path of growth and change lies within you.

Remember, progress is a journey that requires dedication, consistency, and a refusal to quit. It is about embracing discomfort, seeking growth, and staying focused on progress rather than perfection. By nurturing self-awareness, cultivating a growth mindset, and intentionally designing our environments and actions, we have the power to reshape our habits and unlock our true potential.

As you move forward, may you find the courage to leave behind old patterns, to persist in the face of challenges, and to embrace the transformative power of habits. Success lies in the small steps taken each day, the deliberate choices made in alignment with your values and aspirations. So, go forth with determination and patience, for good things take time and effort. Your journey of habit transformation awaits, and the potential for a life of meaning, fulfillment, and impact lies within your reach.

About Arootah

Arootah is a coaching and advisory business serving financial services executives who want to unlock potential in their companies and lives. We devise pragmatic strategies that stimulate growth, inspire peak performance, and strengthen accountability. We've identified and distilled proven behaviors at the intersection of finance, technology, and wellness. Our clients are empowered to raise their standards, overcome their challenges, and achieve results.

AROOTAH

Resources

Habit Coach to Instill & Eradicate Habits

Transform your life, achieve peak performance with Habit Coach, and leverage proven methods from successful hedge fund professionals.

Discover firsthand why some of the most successful individuals rely on habit training to help them break negative habits and build positive ones.

Winner of the 2022 Crowdbotics Innovator Award
Discover at Arootah.com/HabitCoach

Proactively Create Your Ultimate Day and Stick to It

The app guides you to prioritize what matters
most, track your progress, and elevate your growth.

Habit Coach helps you:
- Increase MINDFULNESS
- Bring POSITIVE BEHAVIOR CHANGE
- Eliminate BAD HABITS
- Create LIFE-CHANGING routines

Customize your habit transformation journey and choose
from various categories   to tailor your experience to   your
unique needs. Achieve holistic fulfillment across financial
security, career, family, relationships, health, philanthropy,
and more!
Get straight to the point of creating better habits or
breaking bad ones with a simple scoring list. Not all habits
are   equal— that's why the   app's weighing   mechanism
rewards you with higher scores for performing priority
habits.

Achieve Your Habits Faster
Optimize the app by using it in
conjunction with Arootah Coaching and Advisory.

Why don't you always do what is in your best interests? Need help prioritizing what matters most in your life, career, or business?

Maximize Your Impact with Coaching

Building new habits or breaking counterproductive ones can be challenging. Collaborate with world-class life, health, executive, and career coaches and maximize your results. Habit Coach provides a platform for coaches to hold you accountable and ensure you stay on track to achieve your goals. Harness the power of the app for an optimal return by leveraging the apps in combination with an Arootah coach or advisor.

Decision Manager App
Leverage technology with a tool that provides a process to analyze your options, ensuring that any major decision you're facing is made with confidence.

- Eliminate biases that cloud judgment
- Develop conviction in your decisiveness
- Become informed to achieve better outcomes

Learn More: https://arootah.com/apps/

Software and Apps
Arootah Software and Apps allow you to leverage technology to optimize your most precious resource: time. Our apps help you gain clarity in chaos, improve your judgment in decision-making, and accomplish the goals to elevate your life.

Learn More: https://arootah.com/apps/

Speaking Engagements
Arootah Speaking Engagements offers actionable leadership, work culture, goal setting, and energy optimization to motivate teams to achieve greater success. Whether your team wants to earn more business, accomplish work/life goals, or adopt healthier habits, we provide the roadmap.

Learn More: https://arootah.com/about/speaking-engagements/

Executive Coaching
Arootah Executive Coaching gives corporate leaders and other financial executives an edge by infusing technology into coaching to elevate clarity, strategy, and accountability. Our coaches can empower you to harness opportunities, overcome institutional challenges, and lead with a roadmap.

Learn More: https://arootah.com/executive-coaching/

Leadership Training
Arootah Leadership Training is designed by executives for executives as drawn from Rich Bello's impactful career. Learn to maximize your influence and create a positive ripple effect throughout the organization.
Peak Performance topics include, but are not limited to:

- Mindset

- Time Management
- Decision-making
- Goal Setting
- Energy, Discipline, & Focus
- Procrastination

Learn More: https://arootah.com/leadership-development-trainings/

Team Coaching

To transform your business, invest in your people. Arootah Team Coaching helps teams discover their most innovative strategies for working together propel the firm forward. Teams will leave with heightened collaboration and decision-making skills, self-leadership, and collective productivity.

Learn More: https://arootah.com/team-coaching/

Business Consulting

Arootah Business Consulting advises hedge fund executives, single-family offices, and multi-family offices on how to maximize performance across Investments and Operations, leveraging the expertise of advisors from some of the world's most prestigious firms.

Learn More: https://arootah.com/business-consulting/

Hedge Fund Advisory

Arootah Hedge Fund Advisory propels your business forward by leveraging our experience across the key areas of a firm: investments and operations. Our industry veterans will support you throughout the entire life cycle: from startup to raising capital to ongoing operations and beyond.

Learn More:
https://arootah.com/business-consulting/hedge-fund/

Family Office Advisory

Arootah Family Office Advisory supports the unsung heroes who drive the engine of all aspects of a family office, including philanthropy, business ventures, wealth preservation, and more. Our experience managing family offices helps your clients navigate the three most valuable assets: time, money, and family.

Learn More: https://arootah.com/business-consulting/family-offices/

Remote Work Advisory
Arootah Remote Work Advisory offers strategies to leverage global opportunities and manage resources. We've led through the most unforeseen events of the last 25 years, minimizing disruption and maximizing opportunity.

Learn More: https://arootah.com/remote-work-advisory/

Corporate Wellness
Arootah Corporate Wellness is a comprehensive well-being solution that brings greater productivity, improves employee engagement, and strengthens workplace culture. Our comprehensive program leverages health coaching, nutrition, fitness, and stress management from a Chief Wellness Officer.

Learn More: https://arootah.com/corporate-wellness/

Talent Acquisition
From attracting top talent to creating fair, consistent recruiting processes, Arootah Talent Acquisition services support HR leaders to thrive at every stage of the employee lifecycle.

Learn More: https://arootah.com/talent-acquisition/

Health Coaching
Arootah Health Coaching supports wellness that combines expertise in overall well-being with accountability strategies to keep you on track. Leverage technology to create impactful habits and control over your energy.

Learn More: https://arootah.com/personal/health-coaching/

Life Coaching
Arootah Life Coaching supports you in creating a life aligned with your highest priorities. We enhance coaching with technology while our coaches motivate you to bridge the gap between where you are and where you want to be, to lead a life that supports what matters most to you.

Learn More: https://arootah.com/personal/life-coaching/

Career Coaching
Arootah Career Coaching illuminates the career that will link your talents to your desired professional trajectory. We can help you navigate transitions, explore new career paths, and advance in your industry.
Learn More: https://arootah.com/career-coaching/

Remote Work Coaching
Arootah Remote Work Coaching infuses technology in coaching to combat proximity bias. Empowering you to lead your business with frictionless progress, autonomy, and liberation.

Learn More: https://arootah.com/remote-work-coaching/

Appendix

Case Studies
Life:

Title: Breaking Free: Sarah's Journey to Conquer the Sugar Habit

Introduction: In this case study, we follow Sarah's transformative journey as she confronts her unhealthy sugar habit. Through the lens of the ten principles of habit change, we witness how Sarah's conscious intervention and intentional decision-making enable her to break free from the clutches of her habitual behavior about sugar and establish a positive relationship with food.

Principle 1: Awareness and Understanding:

Sarah begins her journey by deepening her awareness and understanding of the adverse effects of excessive sugar consumption on her health. She educates herself about the risks of high sugar intake, including weight gain, increased risk of chronic diseases, and energy crashes. This newfound knowledge is a powerful motivator for Sarah to take control of her sugar habit. She learns that sugar activates the brain's reward system, releasing dopamine and creating feelings of pleasure. The dopamine release can lead to cravings and addiction-like behaviors. Sugar provides a quick energy boost by converting into glucose, the brain's primary energy source. Large amounts of sugar can cause blood sugar spikes and fluctuations, affecting brain function and mood. High sugar intake can contribute to inflammation and oxidative stress in the brain, potentially impacting cognitive function and increasing the risk of neurological diseases. Sugar consumption can disrupt neurotransmitter balance, affecting mood and well-being. Excessive sugar intake can disrupt the gut-brain axis, influencing communication between the gut and the brain and potentially contributing to mental health issues.

Principle 2: Design your Habit Plan:

Having learned about the harmful effects of sugar, Sarah sets clear goals for reducing her sugar intake. She defines specific limits for daily sugar consumption by establishing metrics, and in this case, it is straightforward as she can easily count the grams of sugar she consumes per day using nutritional labels. She sets milestones to track her progress, reducing her daily limit until she reaches her goal. She brainstorms using mind mapping and follows her course to success. She uses her resources of a nutritionist, health coach, and curated books on nutrition to guide her, as well as her inner compass. By setting achievable and measurable goals, Sarah sets herself up for success in breaking her sugar habit.

Principle 3: Embrace Accountability:

To fortify her commitment, Sarah creates implementation intentions that guide her food choices. She plans her meals, consciously opting for whole foods and alternatives to sugary snacks. By pre-determining her responses to sugar cravings and having a plan, Sarah empowers herself to make intentional choices. Sarah consults with a health coach and nutritionist for advice regarding healthful lifestyle choices and diet. She also makes her inner circle of family, friends, and coworkers aware of her choice to commit publicly and enlist their support for her goal. She also finds a habit-tracking app to help her account for and see her progress daily.

Principle 4: Harness the Power of Triggers:

Sarah identifies triggers to her habit of sugar intake – the bakery, birthday parties, and even her morning coffee. Sarah redesigns her environment to minimize temptation and support her goal of reducing sugar intake. She removes sugary snacks from her pantry and replaces them with healthier options. Sarah also surrounds herself with supportive individuals who encourage her to conquer the sugar habit.

Principle 5: Rewiring your Mind:

Sarah integrates healthier habits into her routine, effectively replacing her sugar-laden snacks with nutritious alternatives. For example, she pairs her morning coffee with a piece of fruit instead of a sugary pastry. She disables her limiting beliefs about needing sugar and replaces them with empowering beliefs about living healthfully. By habit stacking, Sarah reinforces positive food choices and creates new associations that support her quest for a healthier lifestyle.

Principle 6: Rewards and Consequences:

Sarah asks herself, what rewards did I get for eating sugar? She ascertained that the rewards were temporary because they only included it tasting good and giving her the occasional sugar high. She then thought of the consequences, which had many health risks and detriment to her physical body. When she weighs the rewards and consequences, she finds that the consequences far outweigh the rewards. She decides to cut sugar from her diet and celebrates her achievements, acknowledging her progress and rewarding herself with non-food incentives. She treats herself to activities she enjoys, such as a relaxing spa day or a day out in nature. By focusing on the positive aspects of her journey, Sarah strengthens her motivation and builds a positive mindset.

Principle 7: Consult Your Future Self:

Sarah's present self asks her future self, what will happen if I continue this habit of eating sugar? The long-term consequences include weight gain, obesity, an increased risk of heart disease and certain cancers, a higher likelihood of developing type 2 diabetes and insulin resistance, dental problems such as tooth decay and cavities, potential cognitive decline, and increased risk of conditions like dementia, and nutritional deficiencies due to displacement of healthier foods.

These are not very appealing. Then she asks her future self, what will happen if I break my bad habit of eating sugar? And, with that, all the consequences disappeared and were replaced with health and vitality, a better mood, and even clearer skin.

Principle 8: Differentiate Habits and Addictions:

Sarah asks herself, am I addicted to consuming sugar? She asks herself, if I were to stop this behavior right now for a month, could I do it without experiencing any discomfort, distress, or withdrawal symptoms, and would my quality of life, health, relationships, or productivity improve without it? She works through the addiction quiz and finds that she is not leaning towards an addiction but instead has a negative habit. She determines that her case does not need a medical professional. However, she is inclined to work with a health coach and nutritionist and rely on the tools she has gained. Sarah develops healthy coping mechanisms to deal with cravings and emotional triggers. She engages in stress-reducing activities like meditation, yoga, or journaling to manage her emotions without resorting to sugar. Sarah also seeks professional help or guidance to navigate emotional challenges and develop healthier coping strategies.

Principle 9: Embrace the Power of Momentum:

Sarah understands that slip-ups may occur during her journey, but she approaches them with resilience and adaptability. She views setbacks as learning opportunities and reframes them as opportunities to grow stronger. Sarah learns from her mistakes, adjusts her strategies, and bounces back with renewed determination. She maintains her momentum by using a calendar or habit tracker and rewarding herself for a certain number of days without sugar.

Principle 10: Activate Conscious Intervention:

Sarah embraces the power of conscious intervention in her relationship with sugar. She recognizes the space between craving and indulging, allowing herself to pause and consciously choose healthier options. By bringing intention to her food choices and actively participating in decision-making, Sarah takes control of her sugar habit and transforms her relationship with food.

Conclusion: Through Sarah's inspiring journey, we witness the transformative power of applying the ten principles of habit change to conquer the sugar habit. Sarah breaks free from her sugar addiction with heightened awareness, clear goals, strategic planning, environmental modifications, habit stacking, positive reinforcement, supportive accountability, coping mechanisms, resilience, and conscious intervention. She embraces a healthier, more balanced lifestyle.

Hopefully, Sarah's story inspires and empowers you on your journey to conquer unhealthy habits and cultivate positive change. Remember, with determination, self-awareness, and conscious decision-making, you, too, can rewrite your relationship with habits and pave the way for a healthier, more fulfilling life.

Title: The Power of Rest: A Journey to Optimal Sleep

Introduction: In this case study, we delve into the realm of proper sleep and explore the transformative power of cultivating this essential habit. Sleep is vital to our overall well-being, affecting our physical health, cognitive function, emotional balance, and productivity. By applying the ten principles of habit change, we will follow the journey of Mark, a working professional struggling with sleep deprivation. Together, we will witness how conscious intervention and intentional decision-making can help Mark break free from unhealthy sleep patterns and establish a positive sleep routine that nurtures his well-being.

Principle 1: Awareness and Understanding:

Mark begins his journey by increasing his awareness and understanding of the importance of proper sleep. He learns about the recommended sleep duration for adults, the benefits of quality sleep, and the negative consequences of sleep deprivation. Mark learns that proper sleep improves cognitive function, memory, and concentration, enhances mood and emotional well-being, strengthens the immune system and reduces illness risk, increases energy, productivity, and physical performance, helps stress management and mental health, supports healing, muscle growth, and weight regulation, reduces the risk of cardiovascular disease and improved heart health, enhances beauty and appearance, and improves athletic performance and reduced injury risk. By understanding the significance of sleep, Mark is motivated to make it a priority in his life.

Principle 2: Design Your Habit Plan:

Mark determines his objective to be eight quality hours of sleep per night. He sets clear goals for his sleep routine. Once he determines the ideal amount of sleep he needs and establishes a consistent sleep schedule, he assigns those metrics to his habit-tracking app. Mark understands that having specific goals will help him stay committed and accountable for his sleep habits. He brainstorms the best ways to accomplish his sleep goals and whom he might reference for support. Mark decides to consult with a sleep coach to help him with tips on maintaining his sleep schedule and practices to incorporate into his day for a better night's rest. He uses this information and couples coaching with his habit tracker to hold himself accountable to his new goals.

Principle 3: Embrace Accountability:

Mark creates implementation intentions to reinforce his commitment related to his sleep routine. He establishes a pre-sleep routine, including dimming the lights, reading a book, and disconnecting from electronic devices. By linking specific cues to his desired actions, Mark automates his sleep routine and increases the likelihood of success. Mark also embraces the support of a health coach specializing in sleep and informs those close to him of his goals. Mark seeks help and accountability from his partner, family, or friends. He shares his sleep goals and progress with them, allowing them to provide encouragement and gentle reminders. This support system helps Mark stay accountable and committed to his sleep routine.

Principle 4: Harness the Power of Triggers:

Mark identifies his triggers to poor sleep: late night use of his iPhone, caffeine after 2 pm and eating a late dinner. He holds himself accountable for changing these behaviors to achieve optimal sleep. Mark optimizes his sleep environment to promote better sleep quality. He ensures his bedroom is dark, quiet, and at a comfortable temperature. Mark also invests in a comfortable mattress and pillows, creating a sleep sanctuary that supports his restorative sleep.

Principle 5: Rewire Your Mind:

To anchor his sleep routine, Mark incorporates sleep-related activities into existing habits. For example, he associates brushing his teeth with preparing for bed and practicing relaxation techniques before sleep. Mark seamlessly integrates positive sleep habits into his daily routine by habit stacking. He replaces thoughts of late-night work, scrolling, or eating with positive thoughts of well-being and healthy sleep choices.

Principle 6: Unlock the Impact of Rewards and Consequences:

Marks asks himself what the rewards are for getting proper sleep. Mark identifies his top motivating rewards for getting adequate sleep as improved athletic performance, improved cognitive performance, and increased energy. He uses these rewards as motivation and the inverse results as consequences. He also asks himself, what are the consequences of not having a healthy sleep habit? He finds through research that they include impaired cognitive function, reduced productivity and performance, mood disturbances, poor judgment and decision-making, and increased risk for mental and physical long-term health disorders. Weighing these potential rewards and consequences only strengthens his resolve for habitual good sleep habits. Mark reinforces his commitment to proper sleep by celebrating small victories and milestones along the way. He rewards himself with non-material incentives, such as a relaxing bath or a morning walk in nature. Mark strengthens his motivation and establishes a positive association with his sleep habits by acknowledging his progress.

Principle 7: Consult Your Future Self:

Mark asks his future self what will happen if he continues the practice of adequate sleep. He is pleased to see that his quality of life will improve. He identifies the top benefits of adequate sleep to be:

- Enhanced cognitive function, including concentration and memory
- Improved mood and emotional well-being
- Increased creativity and innovation
- Higher productivity and performance
- Strengthened immune system
- Improved physical health and reduced risk of chronic conditions
- Better memory consolidation and learning
- Reduced stress and anxiety
- Enhanced physical coordination and performance
- Overall well-being and improved quality of life

This list is enough for his complete buy-in to committing to better sleep. If he does not get adequate sleep, then he expects the inverse results.

Principle 8: Differentiate Habits and Addictions:

Mark asks himself, if I were to stop this behavior right now for a month, could I do it without experiencing any discomfort, distress, or withdrawal symptoms, and would my quality of life, health, relationships, or productivity improve without it? If he stopped sleeping well for a month, he would certainly experience discomfort and distress and decreased quality of life. He doesn't feel a healthy sleep schedule would be considered an addiction. To keep himself on track with this excellent habit, Mark develops coping mechanisms to manage stress and minimize sleep disruptions. He practices stress-reducing techniques, such as deep breathing exercises and journaling, before bed. Mark also establishes a worry journal, allowing him to unload his thoughts and concerns before sleep, promoting a more peaceful state of mind.

Principle 9: Embrace the Power of Momentum:

Mark uses his good track record on his calendar and habit tracker to keep the momentum going. He also checks in with his sleep coach for added personal accountability. Mark acknowledges that challenges may arise during his sleep journey. He develops resilience and adaptability by viewing setbacks as learning opportunities rather than failures. If he encounters a night of poor sleep, Mark reframes it as a chance to identify potential triggers and adjust his strategies accordingly. Mark utilizes his habit tracker app to note his daily sleep schedule and regularly consults with his health coach.

Principle 10: Activate Conscious Intervention:

Mark embraces the space between stimulus and response in his sleep routine. He pauses and reflects on his choices, consciously prioritizing his sleep over other activities that may interfere with his rest. When he notices he might be sabotaging a good night's rest, he intervenes and redirects his behavior. By bringing conscious awareness and intention to his sleep habits,

Mark takes control of his actions and empowers himself to make choices that promote optimal sleep.

Conclusion:

Through applying the ten principles of habit change, Mark embarks on a transformative journey toward proper sleep. With increased awareness, clear goals, implementation intentions, an optimized sleep environment, habit stacking, positive reinforcement, supportive accountability, coping mechanisms, resilience, and conscious intervention, Mark establishes a positive sleep routine that enhances his overall well-being.

By prioritizing sleep and making intentional decisions, Mark experiences improved sleep quality, enhanced cognitive function, increased energy levels, and a greater sense of well-being. He becomes an active participant in his sleep journey, harnessing the power of conscious intervention to shape his habits and transform his life.

Hopefully, Mark's story inspires you to embark on your journey of proper sleep and embrace the ten principles of habit change to create a sleep routine that nurtures your well-being. Remember, by cultivating the habit of adequate sleep, you lay the foundation for a healthier, more vibrant life.

Career:

Title: Unleashing Potential: Emma's Quest to Overcome Procrastination and Propel Her Career

Introduction:

In this case study, we follow Emma's journey as she confronts her procrastination habit and its impact on her career growth. By applying the ten principles of habit change, we witness how Emma's conscious intervention and intentional decision-making empower her to break free from the grip of procrastination and unlock her true professional potential.

Principle 1: Awareness and Understanding:

Emma begins her transformation by becoming aware of the detrimental effects of procrastination on her career. She educates herself about the consequences, such as missed deadlines, diminished productivity, and limited growth opportunities. This newfound understanding fuels her desire to take charge of her habit and strive for excellence in her professional endeavors.

Principle 2: Design Your Habit Plan:

Emma determines her objective to eradicate procrastination from her professional life. She sets clear and ambitious career goals, both short-term and long-term. She defines specific milestones and establishes a timeline to track her progress. By forming meaningful goals, Emma creates a sense of purpose and direction, inspiring her to overcome procrastination and propel her career forward. She brainstorms how to avoid procrastination and embraces operational productivity with ease. She taps into her intrinsic and extrinsic resources to support her goal with solid facts and determination. She finds a career coach to further her understanding and development and starts creating timelines for her projects, including deadlines and start lines. She uses the combination of coaching and her habit tracker to maintain organization and accountability.

Principle 3: Embrace Accountability:

To combat her tendency to procrastinate, Emma creates implementation intentions. She breaks her goals into actionable steps and plans specific times to work on them. By visualizing herself completing tasks and committing to a structured schedule, Emma fosters a proactive mindset and ensures she follows through with her commitments. Emma seeks the guidance of a career coach to help her be accountable for her goals and eliminate procrastination. She focuses on time management as a key strategy to combat procrastination and uses her habit tracker to ensure she makes the best use of her time. Emma seeks support from mentors, colleagues, or a career accountability partner who shares her aspirations. She engages in regular check-ins and progress discussions, allowing others to hold her accountable for her actions. This supportive network provides guidance, encouragement, and constructive feedback, fostering her professional growth and combating the allure of procrastination.

Principle 4: Harness the Power of Triggers:

Emma identifies her triggers: scrolling on social media and overscheduling herself. Emma optimizes her work environment to minimize distractions and boost productivity. She declutters her workspace, eliminates unnecessary digital temptations, and creates a dedicated area solely for work-related tasks. By designing an environment conducive to focus and concentration, Emma enhances her ability to stay on track and overcome the urge to procrastinate.

Principle 5: Rewire Your Mind:

Emma intentionally transforms her limiting beliefs around time management to pursue her goal. Emma incorporates productive habits into her daily routine to counteract procrastination. For example, she establishes a morning ritual that includes reviewing her tasks, prioritizing them, and dedicating focused time to important projects. By habit stacking, Emma establishes a positive momentum that helps her overcome resistance and maintain consistent progress in her career.

Principle 6: Unlock the Impact of Rewards and Consequences:

Emma asks herself, what are the consequences of procrastination? Emma finds them and deters these consequences, including increased stress and anxiety, decreased productivity and efficiency, missed opportunities and deadlines, negative impact on reputation and perceived reliability, more errors and mistakes, a decline in motivation and self-esteem, strained relationships, time pressure and reduced enjoyment, and stagnation and unfulfilled goals. She asks what are the rewards for procrastination. She finds none. With this information, Emma strengthens her commitment to her goal. She celebrates her accomplishments along the way, acknowledging her milestones and rewarding herself for achieving her goals. She acknowledges her progress and treats herself to meaningful rewards, such as a day off or a personal indulgence. She appreciates seeing firsthand that effective time management affords her more time for enjoyment rather than less. By cultivating a sense of achievement and self-reward, Emma reinforces her motivation to overcome procrastination and excel in her career.

Principle 7: Consult Your Future Self:

Emma asks her future self what will happen if she continues to procrastinate. The answer is dismal and includes all the negatives she acknowledges as consequences. She then asks what will happen if she does not continue to procrastinate. The answer is much brighter. A life free of procrastination includes increased free time and leisure, enhanced quality of work, increased productivity, and personal growth and self-confidence.

Principle 8: Differentiate Habits and Addictions:

Emma asks herself, if I were to continue this behavior right now for a month, could I do it without experiencing any discomfort, distress, or withdrawal symptoms, and would my quality of life, health, relationships, or productivity improve without it? The answer she found was that it would affect her life negatively, but not in such a dire way that she should consider her procrastination an addiction. She feels confident in eradicating this bad habit without professional intervention. Emma develops effective coping mechanisms to manage stress and overcome procrastination triggers. She practices stress-relieving techniques such as deep breathing exercises, mindfulness, and regular physical activity. Emma also cultivates a growth mindset, reframing challenges as opportunities for learning and growth. Emma strengthens her resilience and combats the urge to procrastinate by embracing healthy coping mechanisms.

Principle 9: Embrace the Power of Momentum:

Emma keeps a detailed calendar and habit tracker to manage her time effectively. Every day she crosses off for not procrastinating motivates her to keep going. She is also inspired by meeting her deadlines. Emma acknowledges that setbacks are part of the journey and approaches them with resilience and adaptability. She learns from her mistakes, analyzes the underlying causes of procrastination, and adjusts her strategies accordingly. Emma embraces a growth mindset, recognizing that each setback is an opportunity to learn, improve, and forge ahead in her career.

Principle 10: Activate Conscious Intervention:

Emma harnesses the power of conscious intervention to combat procrastination. She embraces the pause between intention and action, consciously choosing productive behaviors over procrastination. If she finds herself slipping into her old habit, she has the tools to reroute herself and continue to manage her time efficiently. Emma cultivates an intentional mindset, recognizing that her career success depends on her ability to make deliberate decisions and take consistent action.

Conclusion:

By applying the ten principles of habit change, Emma transforms her career trajectory by overcoming procrastination. Emma unleashes her true professional potential with heightened self-awareness, clear goals, structured planning, an optimized environment, productive habits, positive reinforcement, supportive accountability, effective coping mechanisms, resilience, and conscious intervention.

Hopefully, Emma's story will inspire and motivate anyone seeking to break free from the chains of procrastination and propel their career forward. By embracing these principles, you, too, can conquer procrastination, unlock your professional potential, and achieve lasting success in your chosen field. Remember, the power to transform your career lies within your hands. Start today, and the possibilities are limitless.

Title: Embracing Growth: Alex's Journey of Professional Development

Introduction:

In this case study, we follow Alex's path of embracing professional development as a positive habit in his career. By applying the ten principles of habit change, we witness Alex's conscious intervention and intentional decision-making empower him to cultivate a lifelong commitment to growth and achieve remarkable success in his professional endeavors.

Principle 1: Awareness and Understanding:

Alex begins his journey by developing awareness of the importance of continuous professional development. He understands that staying relevant, acquiring new skills, and expanding knowledge is essential in today's rapidly evolving work landscape. By recognizing the value of professional growth, Alex becomes motivated to pursue development opportunities actively.

Principle 2: Design Your Habit Plan:

Alex sets specific and meaningful professional development goals aligned with his career aspirations. He identifies areas for improvement, outlines the skills they wish to acquire or enhance, and sets measurable milestones to track progress. By establishing clear objectives, Alex creates a roadmap that guides his learning journey and fuels his ambition. He brainstorms ways to achieve his professional development goals through mind mapping and creating a visual. He uses resources from books written about professional development to guide his efforts. He also consults with a career coach to gain more ideas and tools for professional development. He learns how to use his calendar and habit tracking app to outline his yearly professional development goal and marks them down to make sure he is making progress, both in the short-term and long term.

Principle 3: Embrace Accountability:

Alex creates implementation intentions for his professional development activities to ensure consistent progress. He devises actionable plans, schedules dedicated time for learning, and integrates development tasks into his routine. Alex establishes a disciplined approach to professional growth by planning and committing to specific actions. Alex seeks support from mentors, colleagues, or a professional development accountability partner who shares his drive for growth. They engage in regular check-ins, progress discussions, and knowledge-sharing sessions. This supportive network provides guidance, encouragement, and constructive feedback, fostering Alex's professional growth and propelling his development forward. Alex utilizes a habit-tracking app to ensure he is on target with his professional development goals.

Principle 4: Harness the Power of Triggers:

Alex takes inventory of triggers that may deter him from or propel him toward his goals. He notes limiting beliefs about success as a deterrent and aspirations for success to be a propellant. Alex optimizes his environment to support his professional development endeavors. He creates a designated workspace conducive to focused learning, free from distractions. He curates a collection of relevant resources, such as books, online courses, or industry events, to facilitate continuous learning. Alex cultivates an atmosphere that fosters growth and learning by intentionally shaping his environment.

Principle 5: Rewire Your Mind:

Alex writes down all his potential limiting beliefs to face and eradicate them. He then writes his empowering beliefs and sets them in plain sight around his workspace for motivation. Alex leverages habit stacking to incorporate professional development into his daily routine. He links his learning activities with existing habits, such as listening to educational podcasts during his daily commute or allocating specific time slots for reading industry-related articles. By habit stacking, Alex seamlessly integrates professional development into his life, making it a natural and consistent part of their routine.

Principle 6: Unlock the Impact of Rewards and Consequences:

Alex sees that professional development offers several rewards, including knowledge and skill enhancement, career advancement, increased productivity, networking opportunities, boosted confidence and motivation, adaptability, a continuous learning culture, and personal and professional fulfillment. Alex acknowledges and celebrates his achievements throughout his professional development journey. He recognizes milestones reached, skills acquired, and personal growth attained. Alex rewards himself with meaningful incentives, such as attending a professional conference or treating himself to a professional development-related purchase. By reinforcing his progress, Alex fuels his motivation and sustains his commitment to growth. He also sees the consequences of not committing to professional development as stagnation, lack of upward career trajectory, less income, and less professional regard from peers.

Principle 7: Consult Your Future Self:

Alex asks his future self, what will my life look like if I pursue professional development? He sees the many benefits ahead of him in this endeavor, including personal and professional fulfillment, enhanced confidence and motivation, networking, collaboration, and career advancement. He is determined to take this path instead of the other path of not pursuing professional development, which would leave him stagnant and unfulfilled.

Principle 8: Differentiate Habits and Addictions:

Alex asks himself, if I were to stop this behavior right now for a month, could I do it without experiencing any discomfort, distress, or withdrawal symptoms, and would my quality of life, health, relationships, or productivity improve without it? Alex determines that his professional development habit is not an addiction, but he is cognizant of overworking and stress levels. Alex develops effective coping mechanisms to manage challenges and overcome obstacles encountered on his professional development journey. He practices stress management techniques, such as meditation or journaling, to maintain balance and resilience. Alex also embraces a growth mindset, reframing setbacks as opportunities for learning and improvement. By developing healthy coping mechanisms, Alex remains adaptable and perseveres through challenges.

Principle 9: Embrace the Power of Momentum:

Alex loves meeting his professional development goals. He considers them important milestones in his overall career. Alex also understands that setbacks and changes are inevitable but approaches them with resilience and adaptability. He views unexpected shifts as opportunities to learn and pivot his professional development strategies accordingly. Alex uses his small wins in professional development to motivate himself to keep going. He also tracks his yearly progress. By staying flexible and embracing change, Alex continues to evolve, adjust, and thrive in his pursuit of professional growth.

Principle 10: Activate Conscious Intervention:

Alex harnesses the power of conscious intervention in his professional development journey. He actively pauses to reflect, evaluates his progress, and makes intentional decisions regarding his learning priorities. If he notices himself demotivated or not taking action, he knows how to check himself through his personal tools and support system. By taking deliberate steps, Alex ensures his professional development aligns with his evolving goals and aspirations, leading to purposeful and impactful growth.

Conclusion:

Alex transforms his approach to professional development by applying the ten principles of habit change. Alex embarks on a lifelong journey of growth and achievement with heightened awareness, goal setting, implementation intentions, optimized environment, habit stacking, positive reinforcement, supportive accountability, effective coping mechanisms, resilience, and conscious intervention.

Hopefully, Alex's story inspires and empowers you to embrace professional development as a positive habit in your career. By adopting these principles, you, too, can unlock your potential, remain relevant, and experience continuous growth in your professional endeavors. Pursuing professional development is a lifelong journey, and the rewards are immeasurable. Start today, embrace change, and shape your career destiny.

Business:

Title: Breaking the Chains of Inefficiency: Emily's Journey of Overcoming the Lack of Process in Business Finance

Introduction:

In this case study, we delve into Emily's transformative journey as she tackles the bad habit of lacking process in business finance. Through applying the ten principles of habit change, we witness how Emily consciously intervenes and embraces intentional decision-making to establish effective processes that drive efficiency, accuracy, and success in the financial operations of her business.

Principle 1: Awareness and Understanding:

Emily becomes aware of the detrimental effects of lacking process in her business's finance department. She understands that financial operations become disorganized without established procedures, prone to errors, and hinder overall productivity. This realization motivates Emily to address and rectify this issue.

Principle 2: Design Your Habit Plan:

Emily sets clear goals to establish efficient processes in her business's finance department. She aims to streamline workflows, implement standardized procedures, and enhance the accuracy and timeliness of financial reporting. By defining these goals, Emily creates a roadmap that guides her efforts and provides a sense of direction. Emily utilizes habit trackers and time management software in this endeavor.

Principle 3: Embrace Accountability:

Emily creates detailed implementation intentions to ensure the successful implementation of new processes. She breaks down the necessary steps, assigns responsibilities, and establishes timelines for each process improvement initiative. By outlining specific actions and committing to them, Emily ensures that the transition to efficient processes is well-organized and actionable. Emily establishes a system of supportive accountability within the finance department. She fosters open communication, encourages feedback, and conducts regular check-ins to implement efficient processes successfully. Emily promotes a culture of transparency, collaboration, and continuous improvement, empowering the team to take ownership of their responsibilities. Emily confers with a business coach to learn effective methods of implementing processes. She uses her habit tracker app to note progress and see when processes have derailed.

Principle 4: Harness the Power of Triggers:

Emily identifies her triggers that lead to disorganization and procrastination, getting in the way of her process. Emily optimizes the work environment to support the establishment of efficient processes. She organizes workstations, implements software and tools that automate repetitive tasks and ensures access to necessary resources and documentation. By designing a conducive environment, Emily fosters productivity and enables her team to execute the new processes seamlessly.

Principle 5: Rewire Your Mind:

Emily disables any limiting beliefs she has around productivity and success. She empowers herself with positive statements about achievement. Emily leverages the habit stacking technique to integrate new processes into the daily routines of her finance team. She identifies and aligns existing tasks with the latest procedures, creating a natural integration of efficient processes into their workflow. By incorporating these processes as habitual components, Emily ensures consistency and sustainability.

Principle 6: Unlock the Impact of Rewards and Consequences:

Emily asks herself what the rewards are. Through research, she finds them to be increased efficiency, cost savings, adaptability, improved decision-making, scalability and growth, and competitive advantage. The consequences of ineffective processes are the inverse of the rewards and include decreased productivity, loss of money and time, and competitive disadvantage. Emily acknowledges and celebrates the successful implementation of efficient processes. She recognizes individual and team achievements, highlighting improved accuracy, time savings, and increased productivity. Emily provides positive reinforcement through verbal recognition, rewards, and incentives, fostering motivation and encouraging continued adherence to the established processes.

Principle 7: Consult Your Future Self:

Emily conferences with her future self. She asks herself, what will happen if I employ efficient processes in this business? What will happen if I don't? The answer is clear: success and growth if she does, and stagnation and even failure if she doesn't.

Principle 8: Differentiate Habits and Addiction:

Emily asks herself, if I were to stop this behavior of ineffective processes right now for a month, could I do it without experiencing any discomfort, distress, or withdrawal symptoms, and would my quality of life, health, relationships, or productivity improve without it? The answer is no; if she stops this inefficient habit, she has everything to gain and nothing to lose. Emily equips her team with effective coping mechanisms to manage challenges and overcome obstacles encountered during the process improvement journey. She provides training and resources to enhance their skills, encourages knowledge sharing, and supports their professional development. By equipping the team with the necessary tools, Emily strengthens their ability to adapt and overcome hurdles.

Principle 9: Embrace the Power of Momentum:

Emily fosters resilience and adaptability within the finance team. She encourages them to embrace change, view setbacks as learning opportunities, and approach challenges with a growth mindset. By fostering a culture of resilience and adaptability, Emily ensures the team can navigate any unexpected circumstances and continue to evolve and improve its processes. Emily reinforces her team's victories and ensures they are acknowledged and celebrated.

Principle 10: Activate Conscious Intervention:

Emily practices conscious intervention in her business's finance operations. She regularly evaluates the effectiveness of the established processes, identifies areas for further improvement, and makes intentional decisions to refine and optimize the workflows. By actively intervening and making deliberate choices, Emily ensures that the financial processes continuously evolve and align with the company's objectives.

Conclusion:

Emily's transformative journey showcases the power of conscious intervention and intentional decision-making in overcoming the lack of process in business finance. Through her dedicated efforts and adherence to the ten principles of habit change, Emily establishes efficient processes that drive efficiency, accuracy, and success in her business's financial operations. As she continues to refine and optimize these processes, Emily sets a powerful example for fostering growth, productivity, and continuous improvement in business finance.

Good & Bad Habits in Life, Career, & Business

Bad Habits

Life:

1. Procrastination: Delaying personal tasks and responsibilities, leading to increased stress and a sense of being overwhelmed.

2. Unhealthy eating habits: Consistently consuming excessive amounts of unhealthy foods, leading to weight gain, poor nutrition, and potential health issues.

3. Sedentary lifestyle: Lack of regular physical activity or exercise, which can contribute to a decline in overall fitness and well-being.

4. Excessive screen time: Spending excessive time on electronic devices, such as smartphones, tablets, and computers, which can lead to reduced productivity and decreased social interactions.

5. Poor sleep habits: Consistently getting insufficient sleep or having irregular sleep patterns, resulting in fatigue, decreased cognitive function, and potential health issues.

6. Lack of financial discipline: Impulsive spending, failure to budget, and accumulating debt, which can lead to financial stress and instability.

7. Negative self-talk: Engaging in self-deprecating thoughts or negative self-talk, which can impact self-esteem, confidence, and overall mental well-being.

8. Procrastination in personal goals: Putting off personal aspirations or goals, leading to a lack of personal growth and fulfillment.

9. Excessive multitasking: Trying to juggle multiple tasks simultaneously, resulting in decreased focus, reduced efficiency, and potential errors.

10. Isolation and social withdrawal: Avoiding social interactions and isolating oneself, which can lead to feelings of loneliness, lack of support, and decreased overall happiness.

These habits can have a significant impact on personal well-being and overall quality of life. Recognizing and actively working to address these habits is crucial for personal growth and a more fulfilling lifestyle.

Career:

1. Procrastination: Delaying important tasks and deadlines, leading to decreased productivity and increased stress.

2. Poor time management: Failing to prioritize tasks effectively, resulting in missed deadlines and a lack of work-life balance.

3. Lack of goal setting: Not setting clear and achievable goals, leading to a lack of direction and motivation in the workplace.

4. Lack of communication: Failing to communicate effectively with colleagues, superiors, or clients, which can lead to misunderstandings and conflicts.

5. Resistance to change: Being resistant to new technologies, processes, or ideas, hindering personal and professional growth.

6. Negativity and complaining: Adopting a negative attitude, complaining about work or colleagues, which can impact morale and hinder team dynamics.

7. Poor work-life balance: Neglecting personal well-being and spending excessive time at work, leading to burnout and decreased overall satisfaction.

8. Failure to take initiative: Waiting for instructions instead of taking proactive steps to contribute to the organization's success.

9. Lack of self-care: Ignoring physical and mental health needs, which can negatively impact job performance and overall well-being.

10. Inadequate networking: Failing to build and maintain professional relationships, limiting opportunities for career growth and advancement.

These habits can significantly impact one's career progression and overall satisfaction. Recognizing and addressing these habits is an important step towards personal and professional development.

Business:

1. Overtrading: Engaging in excessive buying and selling of securities, leading to increased transaction costs and potential portfolio underperformance.

2. Chasing trends: Succumbing to the temptation of investing in the latest market trends without proper research or analysis, potentially leading to poor investment decisions.

3. Lack of risk management: Failing to adequately assess and manage risks associated with investments, exposing the fund to significant losses.

4. Insider trading: Engaging in illegal activities by trading securities based on non-public, material information, which can lead to severe legal and reputational consequences.

5. Inadequate due diligence: Failing to conduct thorough research and analysis before making investment decisions, potentially resulting in poor investment performance.

6. Lack of transparency: Not providing clear and timely information to investors about the fund's strategies, positions, and performance, which can erode investor trust.

7. Herd mentality: Blindly following the investment decisions of others without independent thinking, potentially leading to suboptimal investment choices.

8. Failure to adapt: Resisting or being slow to adopt new technologies, strategies, or market dynamics, potentially missing out on opportunities for growth and profitability.

9. Overconfidence: Having an excessively positive view of one's own abilities and underestimating risks, leading to imprudent investment decisions.

10. Inadequate compliance and ethics: Ignoring or circumventing regulatory requirements and ethical standards, exposing the fund to legal and reputational risks.

These habits can significantly impact the success and reputation of hedge funds. Cultivating a culture of discipline, rigorous research, risk management, compliance, and ethical conduct is essential for sustainable growth and investor confidence.

Good Habits

Life:

1. Regular Exercise: Engaging in physical activity on a consistent basis to improve fitness, boost energy levels, and maintain overall health.

2. Healthy Eating: Nourishing the body with a balanced diet that includes fruits, vegetables, whole grains, and lean proteins, promoting optimal nutrition and well-being.

3. Mindfulness and Meditation: Practicing mindfulness and meditation techniques to reduce stress, increase self-awareness, and cultivate a sense of calm and clarity.

4. Adequate Sleep: Prioritizing quality sleep by establishing a consistent sleep routine and ensuring sufficient rest to support physical and mental well-being.

5. Personal Growth and Learning: Actively pursuing personal growth through reading, learning new skills,

attending workshops, or engaging in hobbies and creative pursuits.

6. Gratitude Practice: Cultivating a habit of expressing gratitude daily, focusing on the positives in life and appreciating the present moment.

7. Financial Planning: Practicing responsible financial habits such as budgeting, saving, and investing wisely to achieve financial stability and future goals.

8. Social Connections: Nurturing relationships with family, friends, and community, fostering a sense of belonging and support.

9. Self-Care: Taking time for self-care activities, such as practicing self-compassion, engaging in hobbies, pursuing interests, and engaging in activities that bring joy and relaxation.

10. Environmental Consciousness: Adopting eco-friendly habits, such as recycling, conserving energy, and making sustainable choices to contribute to a healthier planet.

These good habits contribute to personal well-being, happiness, and a fulfilling life. By incorporating these habits into their daily routines, individuals can create a positive and balanced lifestyle.

Career:

1. Goal Setting: Setting clear and achievable goals that provide direction and motivation in their professional endeavors.

2. Time Management: Effectively managing time by prioritizing tasks, avoiding procrastination, and maximizing productivity.

3. Continuous Learning: Cultivating a habit of lifelong learning and professional development to stay updated and enhance skills and knowledge.

4. Effective Communication: Practicing clear and concise communication with colleagues, superiors, and clients to foster collaboration and understanding.

5. Networking: Building and maintaining professional relationships, expanding connections, and leveraging opportunities for career growth and advancement.

6. Adaptability: Embracing change and being open to new ideas, technologies, and processes, enabling agility and staying ahead in dynamic work environments.

7. Accountability: Taking responsibility for one's actions, meeting deadlines, and delivering quality work to build trust and credibility.

8. Collaboration: Actively engaging in teamwork, respecting diverse perspectives, and contributing to collective success.

9. Work-Life Balance: Prioritizing personal well-being and maintaining a healthy balance between work and personal life to prevent burnout and promote overall happiness.

10. Self-care: Taking care of physical and mental well-being through regular exercise, adequate rest, mindfulness practices, and stress management techniques.

These good habits contribute to career success, personal growth, and overall satisfaction. By cultivating these habits, individuals can thrive in their professional lives and achieve their full potential.

Business:

1. Thorough Research: Conducting comprehensive research and analysis before making investment decisions, ensuring informed choices.

2. Risk Management: Implementing effective risk management strategies to protect the fund's capital and optimize returns.

3. Continuous Learning: Staying updated on market trends, economic indicators, and industry developments to make informed investment decisions.

4. Discipline and Patience: Adhering to investment strategies and staying patient during market fluctuations, avoiding impulsive and emotional decisions.

5. Long-Term Focus: Emphasizing long-term value creation and sustainable growth over short-term gains, aligning investments with long-term objectives.

6. Diversification: Spreading investments across different asset classes and strategies to mitigate risk and enhance portfolio performance.

7. Due Diligence: Conducting thorough due diligence on potential investments, analyzing financials, industry dynamics, and management teams.

8. Collaboration and Teamwork: Collaborating effectively with colleagues, sharing insights, and leveraging diverse expertise to make better investment decisions.

9. Compliance and Ethics: Upholding high ethical standards, following legal and regulatory requirements, and prioritizing transparency and accountability.

10. Investor Relations: Establishing strong relationships with investors, providing regular updates, and

maintaining open lines of communication to foster trust and confidence.

These good habits contribute to the success and reputation of hedge fund professionals. By cultivating these habits, individuals can navigate the complexities of the industry and strive for excellence in their work.

Addiction Resources[63]

Know the Signs of Addiction:
- Difficulties at school, disinterest in school-related activities, and declining grades
- Poor work performance, being chronically late to work, appearing tired and disinterested in work duties, and receiving poor performance reviews
- Changes in physical appearance, such as wearing inappropriate or dirty clothing and a lack of interest in grooming
- Altered behavior, such as an increased desire for privacy
- Drastic changes in relationships
- A noticeable lack of energy when performing daily activities
- Spending more money than usual or requesting to borrow money
- Issues with financial management, such as not paying bills on time
- Changes in appetite, such as a decreased appetite and associated weight loss
- Bloodshot eyes, poor skin tone, and appearing tired or run down
- Defensiveness when asked about substance use
- If you or someone you know has a mental health condition or a substance use disorder, there are

[63] DEA. "Recovery Resources." Drug Enforcement Agency, 5 January, 2022, https://www.dea.gov/es/node/204786. Accessed 9 June, 2023.

resources and services available to assist with screening, treatment, and recovery

Finding Help:
Step by Step Guides to Finding Treatment for Drug Use Disorders
American Society of Addiction Medicine - Patient Resources
Addiction Treatment Needs Assessment
American Addiction Centers
Find Treatment.gov
Opioid Treatment Program Directory
Take Action and Prevent Addiction
Narcotics Anonymous

SAMHSA's National Helpline
https://findtreatment.samhsa.gov
1-800-662-HELP (4357)
TTY: 1-800-487-4889
Website: www.samhsa.gov/find-help/national-helpline
https://www.findtreatment.gov
Also known as the Treatment Referral Routing Service, this Helpline provides 24-hour free and confidential treatment referral and information about mental health and substance use disorders, prevention, and recovery, in English and Spanish.

Drug-Free Workplace
1-800-WORKPLACE (967-5752)
Website: www.samhsa.gov/workplace/resources/drug-free-helpline
Assists employers and union representatives with policy development, drug testing, employee assistance, employee education, supervisor training, and program implementation.

Naloxone
Naloxone is a medicine that rapidly reverses an opioid overdose. It is an opioid antagonist. This means that it attaches to opioid receptors and reverses and blocks the effects of other opioids. Naloxone can quickly restore normal breathing to a person if their breathing has slowed or stopped because of an opioid overdose.

- Naloxone Drug Facts | National Institute on Drug Abuse (NIDA)
- Opioid Overdose Toolkit | SAMHSA
- Naloxone for Opioid Overdose: Life-Saving Science | National Institute on Drug Abuse (NIDA)
- Is naloxone accessible? | National Institute on Drug Abuse (NIDA)
- The Helping to End Addiction Long-term Initiative | NIH HEAL Initiative
- Medications to Treat Opioid Disorder | National Institute on Drug Abuse (NIDA)

Buprenorphine Practitioner & Treatment Program Locator
Find information on locating practitioners and treatment programs authorized to treat addiction and dependence on opioids, such as heroin or prescription pain relievers, at SAMSHA.gov.

Opioid Treatment Program Directory
Find treatment programs in your state that treat addiction and dependence on opioids, such as heroin or prescription pain relievers at Opioid Treatment Program Directory.

Learn More
Find out more about these treatment topics:

- SAMHSA Behavioral Health Treatment Services Locator: Confidential and anonymous source for individuals seeking treatment facilities for substance use disorder, addiction, and mental health concerns.
- Find a Health Center: Some health centers provide mental health and substance use disorder services.

Contact the health center directly to confirm availability of specific services and to make an appointment.

- Alcohol, Tobacco, and Other Drugs
- Behavioral Health Treatment and Services
- Implementing Behavioral Health Crisis Care
- Mental Health and Substance Use Disorders
- Substance Abuse and Mental Illness Prevention
- Suicide Prevention
- Principles of Drug Addiction Treatment
- Medication-Assisted Treatment

Recovery Resources:
Recovery is Possible
Life in Recovery
The Many Paths to Wellness
10 Guiding Principles of Recovery
Sober Apps: New Tools to Help Those in Recovery
What you need to Know About Treatment & Recovery
Self-Management And Recovery Training (SMART)
SMART Recovery Meetings
12 Steps to Recovery
Recovery Research Institute
Recovery and Recovery Support
StartYourRecovery.org (https://startyourrecovery.org)

Prevention & Resources:
Warning Signs of Drug Abuse
Stop Overdose
Resources for Families Coping with Mental and Substance Use Disorders
Growing Up Drug Free: A Parent's Guide to Substance Use Prevention (2021)
Raising Drug-Free Young People
Substance Use in Adolescence
National Institute on Drug Abuse - Teens
Opioids: Facts Parents Need to Know

Drugs, Brains, and Behavior: The Science of Addiction
Life Saving Naloxone
Good Samaritan Overdose Prevention Laws
Opioids
Drug Overdose

Quiz: Do You Have an Addictive Personality?

Read through the following questions. They are not meant to provide a true diagnosis but to get you started on determining if you may have a highly addictive personality and need help. We encourage you to answer honestly to yourself and then to seek out care from our team at FHE Health if you feel you are at risk.

1. Do you consider yourself to be a risk-taker?
   ○ True
   ○ False

2. Do you think that greater pleasure is tied to greater risk?
   ○ True
   ○ False

3. Do you commit to quitting an activity but find that you keep coming back to it?
   ○ True
   ○ False

4. Do you want to stop this behavior that you struggle to regulate? Do you see a problem with continuing?
   ○ True
   ○ False

5. Do you find that you self-medicate with certain activities to relieve stress?
   ○ True
   ○ False

6. Do you have strong feelings associated with completing certain activities, as if they are an itch that needs to be scratched?
   ○ True
   ○ False

7. Do you ever get in trouble at work or school because of the actions you've taken (or not taken) as a result of your engagement in this activity? Perhaps you failed to complete an assignment because you chose to drink, for example.
   ○ True
   ○ False

8. Have you gotten into legal trouble related to the activity? Perhaps this has happened more than once.
   ○ True
   ○ False

9. After a stressful day at work or school, do you find yourself thinking only about engaging in that activity, perhaps thinking it is the only way you are going to find relief from your anxiety, stress and fear?
   ○ True
   ○ False

10. Do you recognize how your life suffers because of your commitment to an activity? Even when you recognize this, do you still find it hard to stop engaging in that activity?
    ○ True
    ○ False

11. If you can't engage in a specific activity for a period of 24 hours, do you feel pain, anxiety, frustration or suffer a panic attack? Do you have physical complications resulting from not using it?
    ○ True
    ○ False

12. Has anyone ever expressed concern with you about your engagement in this activity, either the frequency or the activity itself?
    ○ True
    ○ False

13. If there is an activity you struggle to regulate, do you feel pleasure or a sense of relief when you engaging in using it?
    ○ True
    ○ False

14. Do you feel like you need to hide the people who you usually engage in this activity with you from your family and friends and keep your lives separate?
    ○ True
    ○ False

15. Do you find yourself thinking about an activity, be it an stress-relieving activity or any kind of substance use regularly? Do you think about this activity at least one or more times a day?
    ○ True
    ○ False

16. Have you ever become frustrated due to something interfering with your plan to partake in an activity you engage in often?
    ○ True
    ○ False

17. Have you developed a health problem that seems to stem at least in part from this activity?
    ○ True
    ○ False

18. Do you avoid openly admitting to how often you use this substance/participate in this activity with friends and family because you don't want people to know how much you do it?

○ True
○ False

19. Do you lie to other people about your activities or behaviors, which could indicate that you are ashamed of them?

○ True
○ False

20. If you're running out of a substance or won't have access to a particular activity or you know you cannot engage in that activity for a few hours or days, do you get angry and frustrated?

○ True
○ False

21. Do you have trouble sleeping because you are thinking about the activity or substance?

○ True
○ False

22. Are you not taking care of your health the way you would like to, such as eating healthy meals, getting exercise, maintaining personal hygiene and getting sleep?

○ True
○ False

23. Do you ever ask anyone else to supply a substance for you because you are worried that someone will think you are buying too much or, perhaps, you cannot get more?

○ True
○ False

24. Are you facing financial difficulties as a result (at least in part) of your engagement in this activity? It could be due to missing rent or mortgage payments to ensure you have enough of the substance or engaging in gambling away your food money.
○ True
○ False

25. Do you ever take risks to get the substance or participate in an activity, even when you know you should not? Perhaps that includes driving on a suspended license or ducking out of work to get the relief you need?
○ True
○ False

Reference: https://fherehab.com/learning/addictive-personality-quiz/?fbclid=IwAR1Wkh42Gb_ISlh8y-9fsfCvqPMcSp-9zt2qo9PcBIQfujFN0Pv9kNm08iA

Quiz: Do I Have a Gambling Addiction?
Are you concerned about the frequency of your gambling? Take this self-assessment to determine the likelihood that you have a gambling addiction.

1. Missed time from work or school due to gambling?
    ○ Yes
    ○ No

2. Felt remorse after gambling?
    ○ Yes
    ○ No

3. Gambled to make money to pay debts or solve financial difficulties?
    ○ Yes
    ○ No

4. Felt that you needed to gamble to win back money you lost during previous gambling sessions?
   - ◯ Yes
   - ◯ No

5. Gambled until you ran out of money?
   - ◯ Yes
   - ◯ No

6. Borrowed money to finance your gambling?
   - ◯ Yes
   - ◯ No

7. Sold personal or stolen property to finance your gambling?
   - ◯ Yes
   - ◯ No

8. Gambled for a longer period than you initially planned?
   - ◯ Yes
   - ◯ No

9. Gambled as a way to escape worry, boredom, loneliness or loss?
   - ◯ Yes
   - ◯ No

10. Engaged in illegal activities to finance your gambling?
    - ◯ Yes
    - ◯ No

11. Been emotionally distressed or lost sleep because of gambling?
    - ◯ Yes
    - ◯ No

12. Experienced intense urges to gamble after receiving good or bad news?

○ Yes
○ No

Reference: https://www.therecoveryvillage.com/process-addiction/compulsive-gambling/do-i-have-a-gambling-problem/

Quiz: Addiction Test

The Addiction Test is for people who are concerned about their use of alcohol or drugs. The questions focus on lifetime alcohol and drug use.

Please note: All fields are required. When thinking about drug use, include illegal drug use and the use of prescription drugs other than as prescribed.

1. Have you ever felt that you ought to cut down on your drinking or drug use?

○ Yes
○ No

2. Have people annoyed you by criticizing your drinking or drug use?

○ Yes
○ No

3. Have you ever felt bad or guilty about your drinking or drug use?

○ Yes
○ No

4. Have you ever had a drink or used drugs first thing
   in the morning to steady your nerves or to get rid
   of a hangover?
   ⭕ Alcohol
   ⭕ Marijuana
   ⭕ Cocaine/Crack
   ⭕ Heroin
   ⭕ Prescription Opioids
   ⭕ Stimulants (e.g. Speed, Meth, Prescription)
   ⭕ Benzodiazepines (e.g. Xanax, Valium)
   ⭕ Tobacco
   ⭕ Self-harm
   ⭕ Other (e.g. gambling, sex, shopping, food)

Reference:
https://screening.mhanational.org/screening-tools/ad
diction/

Made in the USA
Middletown, DE
22 October 2023

41124179R00195